Editorial Project Manager
Elizabeth Morris, Ph.D.

Editor-in-Chief
Sharon Coan, M.S. Ed.

Art Director
CJae Froshay

Art Coordinator Assistant
Kevin Barnes

Production Manager
Phil Garcia

Imaging
Alfred Lau

Publisher
Mary D. Smith, M.S. Ed.

Best Lesson Plan Web Sites for Educators

Author
Karla H. Spencer

Teacher Created Resources, Inc.
6421 Industry Way
Westminster, CA 92683
www.teachercreated.com

ISBN: 978-0-7439-3831-0

Reprinted, 2011
Made in U.S.A.

URL updates available at our Web site

Table of Contents

Introduction

Technology

Sadly, the very word often strikes fear in the heart of many teachers.

If it does for you, maybe you're thinking:

> "How am I going to teach technology to my students, when I don't even understand it myself?"
>
> "I've been teaching 20 years, and it's too late to learn all that stuff now. Let the new teachers do it."
>
> "It's overwhelming. Six trillion pages…how would I ever find anything?"
>
> "I already spend 50 hours a week teaching. When do I have time to get on the computer?"

If you've caught yourself thinking any of these thoughts, then maybe this book can help you.

The Truth About Technology

Actually, there are three truths you should know:

Technology is here to stay. To live and work successfully in an increasingly complex society, our kids must learn how to use technology effectively. And it's our job to model and teach it.

Technology can make your job as a teacher EASIER. Anyone can learn to use technology. It's your job as an educator, not only to teach, but to LEARN. No matter what age or level of education, anyone can use a computer and learn about the Internet. If an 8-year-old can learn to use computers, you can too!

One estimate says while there are over 100,000 educational sites on the Internet, less than 2/3 of teachers use the Internet in their lesson planning. Why not more? Because if you're not familiar with it, the Internet can be overwhelming and frustrating. It's time-consuming to wade through search results, trying to find the perfect lesson on Egyptian pyramids or introducing fractions.

What the Internet Offers Educators

No matter what subject you teach or whether you are a preservice teacher, a first-year intern, or a veteran with 20 years, this book will show you how the World Wide Web works and how to find EXACTLY what you are looking for.

Here are educational examples of what you can find on the Internet, at no cost:

- practice worksheets for math, spelling, vocabulary, more
- easy-to-use worksheet generators to make your own
- a skit based on the 1770 Boston Massacre (or any other historical event)
- follow-up activities based on *The Giver* (or any other book)
- online video tours of the human body
- an interactive clock that teaches kids to tell time
- teachers across the country who want to trade ideas with you
- what to say, or not say, in job interviews with principals
- first day of school activities
- creative ideas for your bulletin board
- organizing your classroom—what works, what doesn't
- strategies to survive your first day as a teacher
- strategies to survive your 20th year as a teacher

Why Use the Internet in Planning?

As the Internet and computer technology permeate the field of teaching more each year, many principals have begun to ask their teachers to use the Internet in their lesson planning. Thousands of public and private schools now expect teachers to use the Internet and computer technology for instructional purposes as well.

This intimidates some teachers while it excites others, and it all depends on where you stand. If you are not comfortable with computers in general, and you don't have much experience browsing the Internet, then you're not likely to be thrilled to be asked to use the Internet in lesson planning. If you've been using computers for a number of years and Amazon.com knows you on a first-name basis, then you're more likely to be excited to use the Internet for planning.

Either way, this book will save you time by describing the most popular and easy-to-navigate Web sites, no matter what subject or grade level you teach.

How Sites Were Selected

No formal research, rankings, or weighted criteria were used to select sites. The listings were generated by word-of-mouth from experienced teachers, links from education sites, and recommendations from educational organizations and foundations.

However, the sites selected for this book generally have these criteria in common:

- Information is targeted specifically to educators;
- Substantial lessons and detailed student activities—not just "fluff;"
- Contains a "decent" quantity of lessons/activities (worth your time to visit);
- Well organized, simple design, easy to find what you want;
- Don't have to register to use most of its features;
- Information contributed by experienced educators ("tried and true" ideas);
- Not too heavy on advertising or irrelevant clutter;
- Contains unique ideas not found on most other sites;
- Contains links to other related sites, so you can continue your search.

What is Technology?

To most people working in the field of education, "technology" is a catch-all name for all of the computer- and Internet-related developments over the past decade.

According to *Microsoft Encarta*, a popular online encyclopedia, the word more specifically means the "processes and systems by which human beings fashion tools and machines to increase their control and understanding of the physical environment."

As a result, technology becomes an essential component of advanced, industrial civilizations, encompassing a variety of tools, especially computerization.

There are numerous technology tools that you've probably heard about. These are the most popular that you're likely to encounter in today's schools:

- Personal computers and networks
- Internet and World Wide Web links
- Interactive DVDs and CD-ROMs
- Online textbooks and support materials
- E-mail and file transfer
- Word processing and spreadsheet software
- Web authoring and presentations

All of those things can be wonderful teaching tools, if used in the right way. You might be wondering though, how did education and technology get tied together? Why are education leaders and administrators making such a big deal about it?

Why Technology is Critical to the Future

The U.S. and most of the western world have experienced explosive growth in computer and information technology in the past decade. As a result, we have become a technological, information-based society. Much of the rest of the world is following suit.

Today there is virtually nothing in our society that is untouched by computer technology these days—health care, manufacturing, banking, shopping, communication, entertainment, and travel.

As a result of this technological growth in our society, the Internet is no longer a luxury or optional activity for our students. The Internet and computer technology has become an essential component of our daily lives, now and even more so in the future. Therefore, it has become an essential component of our children's formal education. Computer skills have become one of life's basic skills—just as important as reading, writing, and math.

Students must become proficient in using technology to find information and solve problems, so they are prepared to live and work in the 21st century. And it is the teacher's job to give them the skills to use technology effectively and efficiently. A child who grows up today without computer skills will be at a distinct disadvantage in their later school career, as well as the job market.

America's schools have made outstanding progress in the area of Internet access for students. The latest statistics from the U.S. Department of Education indicate that 98 percent of all public schools had Internet access as of Fall 2000. Australia's schools have made similar progress. Ninety percent of European schools have Internet access, and the European Commission has made it a priority to wire all schools. Although the percentage of Canadian schools with Internet access is slightly behind the U.S., the national ratio of students per connected computer is lower—8:1 in Canada compared to 9:1 in the U.S.

Factors Impacting Technology and Teaching

The national teacher shortage and new education standards that require technology proficiency are two factors impacting technology and teaching.

The field of teaching is undergoing a massive change because of the numbers of baby boom teachers who are retiring and the numbers of new teachers who are entering the field to replace them.

About a million U.S. teachers are within three years of retirement, which means they did not formally learn about computers while attending school, as new teachers do today. Many veteran teachers find that learning about technology is outside their comfort zone. For them, being required to demonstrate proficiency in an unfamiliar field often creates stress, frustration, or resistance to change.

The nation's colleges and universities are cranking out education graduates as fast as they can, but there is currently not enough supply of new teachers to satisfy demand. At the same time, many states are pushing for smaller class sizes, which means even more new teachers will be needed.

New teachers are generally overwhelmed during their first few years, learning the ropes, dealing with students, and adjusting to the demands of a new career. They're more likely to be experienced with technology, because they grew up with it or they learned it in school, but they're too busy to spend much time online.

According to a survey by NetDay, a California-based nonprofit organization that helps schools use technology, 78 percent of teachers cited lack of time as the number one reason for not using the Internet.

At the same time, education experts are calling for more accountability and higher standards in school, especially in the area of technology. More and more, teachers are being required to become proficient in technology. Many teachers have embraced it, while others are overwhelmed by or resistant to it.

National Education Plan for Technology

In response to the rapid technological developments in the early and mid-1990s, U.S. Secretary of Education Richard Riley released the nation's first education technology plan in 1996. As a result, the majority of public schools began to adopt new ways of using technology in curriculum so that students would learn how to use technology throughout their formative school years.

Given the continued advances in technology, as well as the progress made in integrating technology into schools, the government updated that plan in 1999. The new plan has five major goals for schools:

- All students and teachers will have access to information technology in their classrooms, schools, communities, and homes.
- All teachers will use technology effectively to help students achieve high academic standards.
- All students will have technology and information literacy skills.
- Research and evaluation will improve the next generation of technology applications for teaching and learning.
- Digital content and networked applications will transform teaching and learning.

The implementation of the technology plan now rests with the ISTE—the International Society for Technology in Education. ISTE is a nonprofit organization, funded by the federal government. It is providing the necessary leadership to develop the framework for curriculum standards and professional teacher development. The program that contains the framework and standards is called NETS—National Education Technology Standards.

See page 12 for a summary of national technology education standards for teachers.

There are technology standards for students too. Refer to page 13 for a summary.

Introducing Technology Into the Curriculum

If you are using little or no technology in your instruction, getting started is probably the hardest part. For teachers who are just beginning to introduce technology into the curriculum, here are a few suggestions to get started.

Computer Skills—Many schools have a specialized technology teacher who instructs students in basic computer skills, such as using a mouse, using a keyboard, opening and saving files, using word processing software, using Internet browsers, etc. For schools without such instructors, it may be up to the classroom teacher to teach these basic skills. Despite the time element, it is important to spend the time preteaching these basic skills, so that more important skills of using the Internet for information gathering can occur more effectively.

Research Skills—Teach students how to skim material and how to look for keywords. They must learn to quickly scan a large amount of information, searching for specific words or phrases, while screening out unimportant information. Practice with print material first, then assign Web pages to skim and find answers to preselected questions. Students also need to be familiar with search engines, which ones are the best for which kind of searches, and how to evaluate search results for relevance. See Chapter 2 for more information on search engines.

Research for Reports—When assigning projects and research papers, give students a list of preapproved sites they can use to find background information for their topic. See Chapter 9 Appendices for an example of a U.S. state report and also a sample of how to provide sites for general background research.

Web Quests—These are known by several names: Web quest, cyberhunt, and scavenger hunt. They are "designed to use learners' time well, to focus on using information rather than looking for it, and to support thinking at the levels of analysis, synthesis and evaluation" according to Bernie Dodge, who developed the Web quest model in 1995 at San Diego State University.

Web quests and scavenger hunts can be done two ways: print worksheets or online. Set up the Web quest centered around a certain theme or topic you're studying. There are plenty of scavenger hunt worksheets online you can print and use, or you can prepare one of your own. Students search for answers and write them on their sheet. Teachers should provide a list of sites students should use to find the information. See Chapter 2 Appendix for a sample of a cyberhunt about the sun.

The other way to use Web quests are online, using existing sites that host Web quests. Students sit down at the Web quest starting page, which has guiding questions, and they click on various links as they search for the answers. See Chapter 9 for sites featuring Web quests and scavenger hunts.

Summary: National Technology Education Standards (for Teachers)

- Demonstrate introductory knowledge, skills, and understanding, show continual growth in knowledge and skills, and stay abreast of current and new technologies;
- Design learning opportunities that use technology in instructional strategies, apply current research on teaching and learning, and identify technology resources and manage them within context of learning;
- Use technology to support learner-centered strategies, and apply technology to develop higher order skills and creativity;
- Apply technology in assessing student learning using a variety of techniques (collect/analyze data, interpret results, communicate findings);
- Use resources to engage in ongoing professional development, evaluate/reflect on professional practice to make informed decisions, use technology to increase productivity and communicate with peers/teachers/community;
- Model and teach legal and ethical practices, apply resources to empower learners, and promote safe/healthy use of resources.

Source: **http://cnets.iste.org/teachstand.html**

Summary: National Technology Education Standards (for Students)

The standards for what students should know are divided into six broad categories. Basically, students must become proficient information and technology users by learning how to:

- Locate and access information,
- Determine the information's relevance,
- Organize and communicate the information's results,
- Use information to solve problems,
- Evaluate the effectiveness/efficiency of the solution used.

Source: **http://cnets.iste.org/sfors.htm**

Chapter Sources:

Microsoft Encarta Online 2001 Encyclopedia, Microsoft Corporation, Inc.:

http://encarta.msn.com/

WebQuest Page by Bernie Dodge, Educational Technology Department, San Diego State University:

http://edweb.sdsu.edu/webquest/

Press Release, Internet Improves Quality of Education, NetDay, 3-29-01:

http://www.netday.org/news_survey.htm

National Technology Education Standards, International Society for Technology in Education Project:

http://cnets.iste.org/teachstand.html

Internet Access in U.S. Public Schools (1994–2000), National Center for Education Statistics, U.S. Department of Education:

http://nces.ed.gov/pubs2001/2001071.pdf

Executive Summary, 1999 National Educational Technology Plan, U.S. Department of Education:

http://www.ed.gov/technology/elearning/

General Internet How-to's—Explained in Plain English

Whether you are a beginning teacher or a 20-year veteran, the national technology standards developed by the U.S. Department of Education say all teachers are expected to have basic knowledge, skills, and understanding of technology.

Here are some of the Internet basics with which all educators should be familiar.

How Web Addresses Work

Every Web site in World Wide Web, anywhere in the world, has a specific address, similar to a street address for a house. You will find this address in the white box at the top of your browser (Internet Explorer or Netscape).

The address of a Web site, also called a URL (uniform resource locator), always begins with "http://". It is not necessary to type "http://" when entering an address in the URL box at the top of the browser. The browser will enter that part automatically. The "http" means it is a hypertext document. Hypertext means when you click a link, your browser automatically take you to another page or site.

After "http://", most Web addresses then begin with "www" (world wide web) but not always. When entering an address, it is important to type it exactly—with periods, hyphens, slashes (/), tildes (~), and so on. However, it does not matter about upper case or lower case letters. Often, Web addresses end with ".html" or ".htm", which is the code or language in which the document was created, and it's important to type that correctly also.

When you type an address in the URL box, then hit enter, your computer immediately sends a request for information to the server that hosts that address. The server will respond by sending the information back to your computer, in the form of a web page, assuming you have permission to access the information.

The two- or three-letter extension near the end of aWeb address usually gives you clues about what kind of site it is:

.com Commercial or company

.gov Government

.edu Education (usually a college or university)

.org Organization (usually nonprofit)

.mil Military

.net Network

.ca Canadian site (many countries have 2-digit codes, such as .au, .uk)

A site with a tilde (~) in the address usually indicates that the page is maintained or created by an individual, rather than an organization, business, or school. Additional three-letter extensions will be appearing in the future, as soon as there is general agreement in the industry as to what they should be.

About Plug-ins

As great as browsers (e.g., *Netscape Communicator*, *Internet Explorer*) are at presenting text, pictures, and sound files, there are often occasions where a browser needs help. Help often comes in the form of mini-programs, called plug-ins, that allow browsers to perform special functions, such as playing games, playing certain kinds of animation, allowing you to interact with a program, etc.

Some examples of common plug-ins that are widely used by Internet users: *Macromedia ShockWave*, *Adobe Acrobat Reader*, *Java*, *QuickTime*, and *RealPlayer*. Each one has a specific function and it works with your browser. They are all copyrighted programs, owned by the people or organizations that created them.

The great thing about plug-ins is that most of them are no cost and available to download from the Internet. Often, there are different versions, from basic (the free ones) to more elaborate versions with more features (that usually cost a few bucks).

The one referenced in this book most often is *Adobe Acrobat Reader*, which reads PDF files. A browser cannot read PDF files by itself—it must have a plug-in for this feature. PDF files look exactly like 8.5" x 11" printed pages from a book or magazine. When they print, they print exactly as they appear on your screen.

To download *Adobe Acrobat Reader*, go to their site and follow the steps:

http://www.adobe.com/products/acrobat/readstep2.html/

What is a Listserv?

A listserv (also known as a discussion list) is like the old-fashioned telephone party line, if you are old enough to remember those, where several households shared one phone number. If everyone on the party line picked up their phone at the same time, they could all talk to each other. That's kind of how listservs work.

There are literally tens of thousands of listservs around the world, from general topics to very fine subsets of subsets of topics (women under 30 who play tubas in Nepal). Lists tend to come and go, so there is no one definitive, up-to-date list.

A listserv is composed of members, all of whom have a common interest, who come together to share ideas, ask questions, suggest resources, and post problems and solutions. It's an excellent way to network with people who have similar interests as you. Listservs can be small, a few dozen people, or very large, with hundreds of people.

As with most associations or membership organizations, you will notice there is always a small core of members who are the most social and the most interested in discussions, and they usually very helpful to others. The majority of members are not very active—they rarely post messages or participate in discussions. They are called "lurkers" because they lurk in the background. There is nothing wrong with that—it's just the nature of the listserv beast. Spend your time getting to know the active folks—they are the ones who will share valuable tidbits with you.

To become a member of a listserv, you must first subscribe, just like subscribing to receive a magazine. When you subscribe to a listserv, you will receive all the messages for the list. You can also unsubscribe anytime you want.

Communicating in a Listserv

To communicate with other members of the list, simply send an e-mail to the e-mail address of the listserv. Everyone single person who subscribes to the list will receive your message as a regular e-mail message, and you'll usually get a copy of what you sent too. Then others can choose to respond to your message. When they do respond, everyone in the list will also see all the responses. Members can also talk to each other privately, through regular e-mail.

Remember that you will likely get a lot more e-mail when you're a listserv member. If it's too much, you can always unsubscribe. Keep the "welcome" e-mail that you receive when you first join, because it has instructions for unsubscribing as well as tips for using the listserv.

Netiquette is the social "do's" and "dont's" for being a member or user of a listserv. Here is a partial list of netiquette tips for sending listserv messages, provided by Loogootee Community Schools, Indiana (© Payton Educational Consulting):

- When responding to a listserv, keep your messages brief.
- Include a portion or a summary of the message you are responding to, but don't forward the entire message.
- Stick to the topics intended for discussion on the listserv. If you deviate from the intended discussion topics, someone may recommend a listserv more suited for your thread of discussion.
- Don't use all upper case letters when writing. This is considered shouting.
- Don't send meaningless messages with no content, such as "I agree" or "thank you."
- Identify yourself. This could be your first and last name and possibly your school or place of business.
- Avoid flaming (attacking or criticizing) individuals on the listserv. If you have a conflict with an individual, settle it by private e-mail messages.

More listserv user guidelines and netiquette (Florida Atlantic University):

http://www.fau.edu/netiquette/net/dis.html

Examples of Popular Education Listservs

ELED-L Elementary Education

For anyone interested in elementary education; discussion of general education and teaching issues. To subscribe, send an e-mail to listserv@ksuvm.ksu.edu. In the first line of the body of the message, type: "subscribe ELED-L firstname lastname" (without the quotation marks). Do not put anything else in the body.

FirstYears

The student teaching experience in the first few years is crucial to keeping teachers in the classroom. This list provides beginning teachers with a place for support, questions, advice, and general discussion.

The primary members of this list are student teachers, interns, and teachers with less than three years experience, with a small group of experienced teachers to provide guidance and support.

http://www.lsoft.com/ (Type "first years" in the search box)

Math Teachers

Sponsored by National Council of Teachers of Math, this listserv focuses on national standards and teaching practices. Instructions to subscribe are included in the link.

http://www.mste.uiuc.edu/listservs/NCTMlist.html

Middle-L

For anyone interested in middle school education. List has parents, teachers, representatives of professional associations and government agencies, faculty and researchers, students and teachers, librarians, and those interested in middle school. Instructions to subscribe are included in the link.

http://ericps.crc.uiuc.edu/eece/listserv/middle-l.html

List of Education Listservs

This site lists dozens of education listservs. It gives the name of the list and information how to subscribe. Follow the directions exactly to subscribe to the list:

http://www.siec.k12.in.us/~west/edu/list.htm

List of Education Listservs

Contains names of hundreds of listservs and e-mail to subscribe. Also has step-by-step instructions how to subscribe to any of these lists.

http://www.theteachersguide.com/listservs.html

List of Listservs

Instead of sending a command to subscribe, enter your e-mail address in the box of the list you want to join.

http://etsc.esd105.wednet.edu/edlistservs.htm?H=E

More pages with Listserv Links

http://www.theteacherspot.com/email_lists.html

http://www.ibiblio.org/edweb/lists.html

http://ericir.syr.edu/Virtual/Listserv_Archives/

Using Search Engines

It's nearly impossible to find anything in the billions of pages of the Internet without using search engines. When the Internet was first gaining popularity in the mid-1990s, there were only a half dozen search engines. Today, there are probably about a hundred to choose from, with a dozen or so being the most widely used by the majority of folks.

It pays to read the help section for using a particular search engine. Each search engine home page will have a link that gives hints and tips for more efficient and effective search results.

Each search engine works a little differently. Some find results that are based on the sites with the most hits, while others find results based on keywords on the first page. You have to experiment a little to find three or four that you like best.

Internet 101, a beginner's primer for Internet basics, explains about most of these search engines listed above, and it also provides a link so you can read the tips for searching with that engine.

http://www.internet101.org/search.html

Bookmarking your Favorite Sites

As you spend time surfing the Internet, you're going to find sites that you'll want to come back to in the future. Fortunately, your browser has a feature that makes it easy for you to save the names of those sites.

Internet Explorer calls it Favorites. *Netscape* calls it Bookmarks.

It works pretty much the same way in both browsers. Here's how:

Internet Explorer:

With the site open that you want to bookmark, go up to **Favorites**, click **Add to Favorites**. A new window will open.

Then you have a choice of either adding it to a general list of sites, or, if you like to be more organized about it, you can set up folders.

In the **Add Favorite** window, click **OK** to simply add it to a general list in no particular order. (*IE* 5.0 puts them in alpha order. Older versions put the most recent at the bottom.)

In the **Add Favorite** window, click **Create In <<** to put it into an existing named folder. Or click **New Folder**, to create a folder to put it in.

To rename folders later, delete or add new ones, click **Favorites**, then **Organize Favorites**.

To find your list of saved sites, click **Favorites** and there they are. Remember, if you put some inside folders, you'll have to click the folder to see them.

Netscape:

With the site open you want to bookmark, go up to **Bookmarks**, click **Add Bookmark**. No other window opens. *Netscape* adds the site to the bottom of the list.

If you want your bookmarks to be better organized, go up to **Bookmarks**, click **File Bookmark**. A new window will open.

In the **File Bookmark** window, you can click the folder's name (if you created one earlier) to put it in there. Then click **OK**. Or click **New Folder**, and it will open a small window for you to give that new folder a name. Then the saved site will go in there.

To rename folders later, delete or add new ones, click **Bookmarks**, **Manage Bookmarks**. Then you can click and drag sites to the folders. Click **OK** when you are done.

To find your list of saved sites, click **Favorites**, then scroll down to the folder(s) to see what's inside. Saved sites not in folders are at the bottom, with the most recent ones at the bottom of the list.

Setting up Favorites/Bookmarks for Classroom Use

If you set up favorites/bookmarks ahead of time, when you know students will be accessing certain sites, it will save a huge amount of time. Children are not generally known to be fast or accurate typists, so if they waste a lot of their computer time entering Web addresses, they won't have much time left to use the information or learn anything.

Follow the steps listed on the previous page, depending on which browsers your classroom computers have. It is highly recommended that you create folders for students, giving them subject names. For example, if your students are doing a Web quest on the sun and moon, put the five or six sites about the sun and moon in a folder called Solar System, rather than a folder called Science.

Popular Search Engines

Alta Vista—**http://altavista.digital.com**

Ask Jeeves—**http://www.askjeeves.com**

Ask Jeeves for Kids—**http://www.ajkids.com**

Dogpile—**http://www.dogpile.com**

Google—**http://www.google.com**

IxQuick—**http://www.ixquick.com**

Lycos—**http://www.lycos.com**

Northern Light—**http://www.northernlight.com**

Overture—**http://www.overture.com**

WebCrawler—**http://www.webcrawler.com**

Yahoo—**http://www.yahoo.com**

Yahooligans for Kids—**http://www.yahooligans.com**

Chapter Sources:

Listserv User Guidelines & Netiquette, Florida Atlantic University:

http://www.fau.edu/netiquette/net/dis.html

Ten Tips for Sending Messages to Listservs, Loogootee Community Schools, Indiana (© Payton Educational Consulting):

http://www.siec.k12.in.us/~west/edu/listman3.htm

Adobe Acrobat Reader Plug-in Download:

http://www.adobe.com/products/acrobat/readstep2.html/

Appendix: EXAMPLE OF A CYBER HUNT

The Sun (Gr. 2–4)

Introduction to the Sun:
http://www.enchantedlearning.com/subjects/astronomy/sun/

Our sun is a star located at the center of our ____________________.

The Greeks called the Sun ______________________.

Our sun is a ____________________________________ star.

NASA Kids (click on **Facts About The Sun**):
http://kids.msfc.nasa.gov/SolarSystem/Sun/

The sun is a ball of hot __________________.

The average distance from the Earth to the Sun is ______________ miles.

NASA Kids (click on **Depending on the Sun**):

http://kids.msfc.nasa.gov/SolarSystem/Sun/

The sun gives us heat. What other three things does it give us?

____

____

____

What is the sun's temperature at the surface? ________________ degrees

How long does it take light to travel from the sun to Earth? ________________ minutes

Without the sun, the Earth would be a ____________________ place.

Hot Sun Facts: **http://library.thinkquest.org/15215/Facts/**

The sun is so large that approximately ____________________ Earths would fit inside it.

The outermost layer of the sun is called ______________________, and it stretches millions of kilometers into space.

The center of the sun is made of ___________________.

The dark blotches on the sun's surface are called ______________________. Are they hotter or cooler areas of the sun? ______________________.

What Educators Should Know About Legal & Safety Issues

Anyone—individuals, companies, organizations, special interest groups, and governments—can publish something on the Internet. No one monitors or controls Internet content. Therefore, the Internet is a "free-for-all," which means you have to take the bad with the good.

It is up to parents, teachers, and other responsible adults to make sure that children are directed to "safe" sites and not exposed to inappropriate content.

As an education professional, it is important for you to be generally aware of some of the legal issues surrounding Internet use, especially since it involves the supervision of children and their computer use, as well as the use of public funds in many cases.

Keep in mind the following information is for general information only. It should not be considered legal advice, which can only be obtained from a licensed attorney who is familiar with a particular situation.

Should You Be Concerned About Copyright Laws?

A copyright is a set of legal rights an author (or owner) has over original work that he/she has created.

Examples of original works include written materials (books, stories, poetry, scripts, etc.), music, movies, art, photographs, software, etc. The author's copyright is usually for a limited time, and it begins at the time the work is created. These original works do not need to have a copyright notice (© 1994 by Bill Jones) to have legal protection, which used to be the case. The work does not have to be published or purchased to have protection either.

It is illegal for anyone to violate the rights provided by copyright law to the owner of the copyright, although these rights are not unlimited, according to the U.S. Copyright Office, Library of Congress. There are limits to copyrights, and one of the exceptions to those limits is the doctrine of "fair use." (See following page.)

Copyrights often expire after a certain period of time, usually between 50 and 75 years. According to Stanford University Library, "generally, for works created after 1978, thc copyright lasts for fifty years beyond the life of the author. For works created and first published between 1950 and 1978 the copyright lasts 75 years." There are other special rules that apply to works created prior to 1950.

Once a copyright expires, those original works can be placed in the "public domain," which means they are available for anyone to freely copy and use. For example, anything created prior to 1923 is now in the public domain, because those copyrights have expired.

Educators certainly need to be mindful of copyright notices, because it is no fun to receive an attorney's letter explaining that you might have violated someone's copyrights. However, there are instances when educators can use copyrighted information under "fair use" provisions of the law.

What is Fair Use?

Fair use describes the circumstances when an individual can copy, use, or distribute copyrighted information without the author's permission. Unfortunately, as there are no clear-cut guidelines as to what constitutes fair use, it's a rather gray legal area. Fortunately, educational use is usually given more leeway than other uses.

The University of Texas, Office of General Counsel, compiled some general guidelines for their faculty on copying materials for classroom use. Generally speaking, the UT office advises that multiple copies of materials (one copy per student) may be made by faculty for classroom use or discussion, provided that:

- copyright notices are included on each copy
- the amount of copyrighted text is not excessive
- and its use for "maximum teaching effectiveness" is greater than the time it takes to get permission.

Details on each of these provisions are available on the UT-OGC Web site:
http://www3.utsystem.edu/ogc/intellectualproperty/clasguid.htm

Fair Use and the Internet

Fair use pertaining to Internet usage is an even more gray area than for print materials. Again, educators are normally given quite a bit of leeway.

When problems arise, courts consider four areas when determining whether use of a certain item is fair use or copyright infringement. These areas are:

- purpose and character of the use,
- nature of the copyrighted work,
- amount of the work used, and
- effect the use will have on the marketability of the original work

If the purpose of the work is non-commercial and for educational purposes only, that weighs heavily toward fair use.

If the copyrighted work consists largely of facts, which are readily available in reference materials, rather than creative work that is the unique vision of its author, that also helps the fair use argument.

Normally, quoting small portions of a copyrighted work is preferable to copying the entire fabric of the work. This is especially true when it appears someone has copied the entire text of a readily available copyrighted work simply to avoid the expense of having to purchase multiple copies.

The final consideration is whether copying the work adversely affects the value of the original copyrighted material. This is especially important for materials collected from the Internet. If the author uses his unique content to draw visitors to his site or sells access and reprint rights to the material, it can be shown that distributing multiple copies of the work damages its value.

The best way to deal with questions of whether or not you are allowed to reproduce materials found on the Internet is simply to read any copyright notices the author may have placed on the site. If the author doesn't include information on whether or not the material may be reproduced, send a brief e-mail to the contact address for the site (usually found at the very bottom of the home page) and ask for clarification. The author's reply supplies written proof evidence that permission was given.

The last caveat—When you print and copy materials and worksheets from the Internet for your classroom, be sure to always leave the copyright notice intact.

What are Privacy Policies?

If you have spent any time at all surfing the Internet, you've seen the phrase "privacy policy." It has to do with an organization's or company's policy on how they will handle personal information that you provide to them or information they may request from you to be able to access their Web pages.

"The protection of privacy is one of the most important issues on the Internet today," according to a report by the Electronic Privacy Information Center (EPIC), based in Washington, D.C. EPIC reports that more and more Internet sites are collecting personal information from users through online registrations, surveys, and forms, as well as advertising and cookies (bits of data stored in your computer that alerts a company's Web site that you have visited there previously).

Most reputable companies doing business online have links on their sites that explain their privacy policy—something most consumers like. The majority of people whom regularly use the Internet favor having laws to protect their personal information and privacy. A June 2001 survey conducted by the Gallup Poll organization found that 66% of Internet users think that the government should pass laws protecting their privacy. Other similar surveys have found similar or higher percentages.

Keeping Kids Safe on the Internet

As a teacher, you need to be mindful about privacy policies in general. As you supervise student computer use, you should be sure that students are not sharing personal information or visiting unfamiliar sites that are requesting personal information. There are some sites where you and/or your students will need to register, in order to use some of the site's programs, and students should always get your permission first.

Here are some safety tips for parents and teachers to keep in mind when children use the Internet, compiled by the American Library Association's Guide to Cyberspace for Parents and Kids:

The best way to ensure your child's safety on the Internet is to be there. Just as adults teach children rules about dealing with strangers outside the home, teachers and parents must provide kids with rules for communicating online.

Remember, the vast majority of Internet sites are perfectly safe. But, like the real world, the virtual world contains a small number sites with sexual, violent, and other content that may not be appropriate for children.

Older children as well as younger children should be supervised, whether they are at home, at school, or at the library. In particular, young children should never be allowed to "surf the net" alone.

Tell students they should not respond to any messages they may receive that make them feel uncomfortable or uneasy.

Teach students to always ask a teacher's or parent's permission before using their name, age, address, phone number, or school name anywhere on the Internet.

In addition, the FBI's Parent Guide to Internet Safety advises parents to be aware of individuals who attempt to sexually exploit children through online services and the Internet, because they are out there looking for kids who aren't being supervised.

In general, the FBI says the most important factors in keeping your child safe on-line are the "utilization of appropriate blocking software and/or parental controls, along with open, honest discussions with your child, monitoring his/her online activity, and following the tips in the parent guide."

How Much of the Internet is Sex-Related?

The Electronic Privacy Information Center estimated in a 1997 Senate Legislative Hearing that sexually explicit content was less than one-tenth of one percent of all Web addresses. In a *USA Today* story (1999) about the popularity of pornographic sites, Internet marketing expert Donna Hoffman of Vanderbilt University said sex-related sites make up less than two or three percent of the Web's commercial sites. Whatever the number, the number of sex-related sites is still very small, compared with the tens of thousands of legitimate business and information sites.

Chapter Sources:

U.S. Copyright Office, Library of Congress, Copyright Basics:

http://www.loc.gov/copyright/circs/circ1.html

Stanford University Library, FAQ on Copyright and Fair Use:

http://fairuse.stanford.edu/library/faq.html

University of Texas, Office of General Counsel, Fair Use of Copyrighted Materials and Classroom Copying Guidelines (© Copyright Crash Course, Georgia Harper):

http://www3.utsystem.edu/ogc/intellectualproperty/copypol2.htm

http://www3.utsystem.edu/ogc/intellectualproperty/clasguid.htm

Electronic Privacy Information Center, Report on Personal Privacy and the Internet, June 1997:

http://www.epic.org/reports/surfer-beware.html

American Library Association, Guide to Cyberspace for Parents and Kids:

http://www.ala.org/parentspage/greatsites/guide.html

A Parent's Guide to Internet Safety, Federal Bureau of Investigation:

http://www.fbi.gov/publications/pguide/pguidee.htm

Donna Hoffman, Vanderbilt University quotes, Sex Sites Hot on the Web, *USA Today*, 1-26-99

http://www.usatoday.com/life/cyber/tech/ctb110.htm

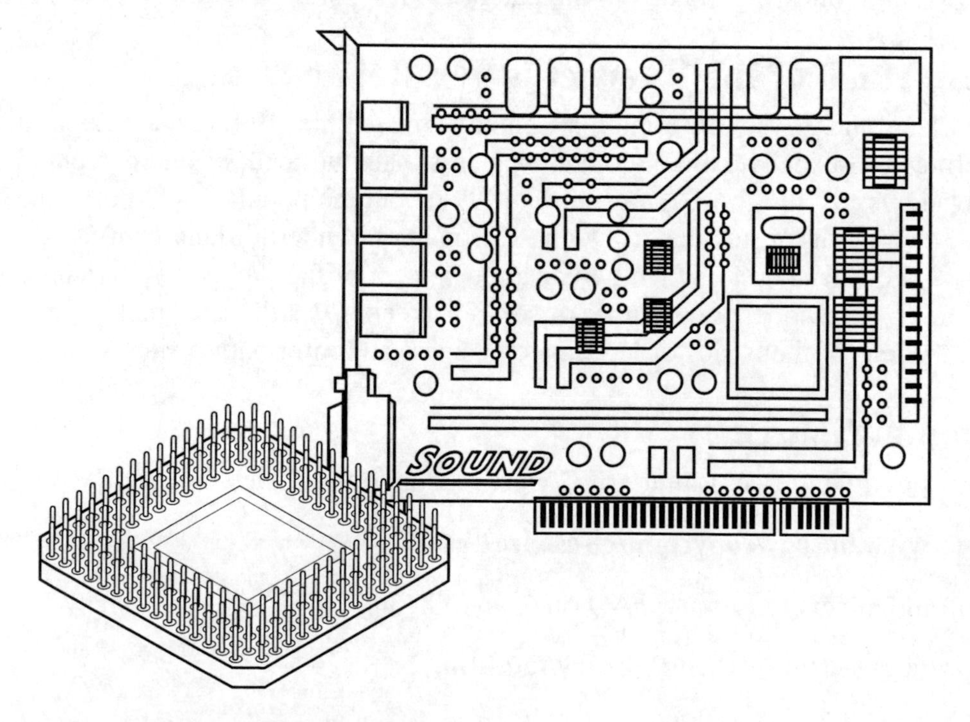

Top 16 Best General Sites for Educators

ABC Teach

http://abcteach.com/

You will find easy, online materials for use by kids, teachers, parents, and home schoolers on this award-winning site. They are organized into these categories: basics (ABCs, reading, writing, math, handwriting), research/reports, theme units (animals, habitats, holidays, sports, countries, and more), shape books, games and puzzles (connect the dots, mazes, coloring pages, etc). Teachers have permission to reproduce these pages for classroom use. Site developed by 24-year veteran Sandy. PreK–4.

Don't Miss: The shape books are popular and easy to use. They are grouped into themes such as animals, food, sports, money, school, nature, etc. Print and photocopy the pages you like. Then put a title and/or words you want on the page, then decorate or color. Your students can make booklets for math skills, poems, word families, science themes, etc.

Educator's Reference Desk

http://www.eduref.org/

Educator's Ref Desk took over the popular AskERIC site (Educational Resources Information Center at Syracuse University), which was a federally funded national information system for educators. You'll find most of the former AskERIC files still there, including the lesson plans and journal database. Educator's Ref Desk is divided into four tabs, one of which is the ERIC Database, with more than one million abstracts of documents and journal articles on education research and practice. The database is updated monthly with the latest citations available, providing access to document and journal citations from 1966 through early 2004. Another tab is a collection of more than 2,000 lesson plans which were written and submitted by teachers from all over the United States. Links to over 3,000 resources on a variety of educational issues. Another tab is called Resource Guides, a browsable collection that includes Internet sites, educational organizations, and electronic discussion groups. Site is maintained by the Information Institute of Syracuse. K–12.

Other Features: The Question Archive is a sample collection of responses to questions that were sent to the AskERIC service between 1992-2003.

BrainPop Movies

http://www.brainpop.com

A fresh, innovative site featuring hundreds of original animated movies (starring Tim and his robot friend Moby) in six major subject areas: health, science, technology, math, English/language arts, and social studies. Teachers can use BrainPop movies in a variety of ways: to introduce topics and give an overview, to review topics, as a break from text-based learning, as an integrated part of text-based learning, subject centers…the list goes on! The movies begin with an interactive quiz that can be repeated for reinforcement after the movie is played as well, or vice versa.

The health, science, and math sections are especially comprehensive, and they follow national math and science standards for grades 3 to 8. Each major subject area has from 20 to more than 100 topics. Each topic contains an entertaining animated movie (3 to 4 minutes), an interactive quiz, an experiment, a comic strip, a how-to hands on application, a timeline and a printable activity page. Students and/or teachers may watch up to two movies per day (per computer) at no cost, or schools may purchase an annual pass for unlimited access. Teachers who submit five lesson plans will receive a four-month pass. Macromedia Flash Plug-in (free to download) is needed to view movies. Created by BrainPop. Gr. 3-8.

The Educators Network

http://www.theeducatorsnetwork.com/

Although some sections of this site's sections are accessible only to members who register (which is free), there are tons of resources available to non-members. Look under Lessons, then Our Search Tools. Choose Level 4, which is what they call their Top 10 Search Tool. You will find a list of their recommended best sites by subject. Click on the subject of your choice, and you will be taken to the ten best sites for lessons, as well as resources for building lessons, in that subject area.

Don't Miss: Look under Posters, and you will find resources and sites for free posters for your classroom. Some require a written request to receive, and other small posters you can print on your color printer to laminate.

Other Features: You can make your own worksheets by clicking on Worksheets. You can also find a variety of useful tools such as rubrics and assessments.

Lesson Planz

http://www.lessonplanz.com/

Created by a teacher for teachers, LessonPlanz.com contains nearly 4,000 hand-selected lesson plans and resources. A searchable directory of free online lesson plans and resources for all grades and subjects. Enter the topic of study in the search box, or browse the index by choosing from the subject areas. There are direct links to lesson plans and resources in the search results. You can also browse among these subject categories: computers and technology, arts and crafts, language arts, math, health, P.E., science, social studies, thematic units, Web quests, songs and poetry, and worksheets and puzzles. PreK–12.

Other Features: To receive a free monthly newsletter, click on Newsletter at the top of the page. Sign up with your e-mail address. You'll receive info about new additions to the site, monthly theme ideas, and make suggestions about topics to be covered in the future. LessonPlanz does not give or sell its e-mail addresses to anyone else.

Columbia Education Center

http://www.col-ed.org/cur/

Based in Oregon, Columbia Education Center is a private, educational service organization established in 1972 to provide services and resources to schools and education agencies. CEC's Web site contains hundreds of lesson plans and mini-lessons contributed by a consortium of teachers from 14 states who came together at a 1995 summer workshop. Choose which subject: language arts, math, science, social studies, or miscellaneous, and which grade level: K–5, 6–8, or 9–12. When you click, your browser opens a new window, and you will see a list of lesson plan titles in simple text format. They are not in any particular order, so you may wish to use "find" feature in your browser, using a keyword. Each lesson has grade level, purpose and objectives, materials, procedures, outcomes, and author's name and school.

Other Features: At the top are two links with additional lessons and resources provided by CEC: Eisenhower National Clearinghouse and Internet-based Lesson Plans and Resources.

Discovery Channel School

http://school.discovery.com/teachers/

This popular cable television channel brings a wealth of education programs, activities, and lesson ideas to the Internet for educators, and it has sections for parents and students too. On TV describes commercial-free documentary series that free to videotape for classroom use. You can view a video clip and find lesson plans to accompany the series. In Lesson Plans you can view activities mostly in math, sciences, and technology. Search by grade level or subject. Teaching Tools features a variety of programs to create your own puzzles, worksheets, quizzes and activities. You can save all the work you created in a personal account in Custom Classroom (you'll have to register with an e-mail address). Conversations allows you to subscribe to an online weekly newsletter or participate on a discussion list with other users/teachers.

Don't Miss: Arguably, the most popular feature of this site is PuzzleMaker (under Teaching Tools) because of its ease of use. PuzzleMaker allows you to create and print customized word search, crossword puzzles and math puzzles using your word lists. Build your own maze or print one of their special hand-drawn mazes, based on special themes such as holidays or school. Eleven puzzle makers to choose from.

EdHelper

http://www.edhelper.com/

Nearly 11,000 lesson plans, organized by alphabetical category, more than 1,200 Web quests, 5,000 free worksheet generators, and 1,600 word and thinking problems. Create your own worksheets for math, spelling, vocabulary and more; you will need to supply an e-mail address to get answer sheets. The left column has 40 categories of lesson plans and activities, and each category has a number that tells how many lessons and/or Web quests you will find within that category. Site is not as neatly organized as it could be, so it can be difficult to find exactly what you want, but the sheer quantity of resources makes it worth visiting this site. Many worksheets are available only to paid subscribers. To receive a free monthly newsletter, enter your e-mail address in the boxat the bottom of the page. They do not collect personal information or share info with anyone else. K–12.

Other Features: The latest headlines in education from Canada and the U.S. can be found on the home page (near the bottom). Click the headline and it opens another window to show the full story.

Education World

http://www.education-world.com/

Updated daily, *Education World* is a complete online guide for educators. It features original content, including lesson plans, practical information for educators, information on how to integrate technology in the classroom, and articles written by education experts, site reviews, daily features and columns, teacher and principal profiles, Wire Side Chats with the important names in education, and career center and job listings, free e-mail newsletter, and much more.

The best part of Education World is the hundreds of education articles on all subjects, which are updated and added daily. No matter what topic, you will find an expert opinion on it by searching the articles.

Don't Miss: Be sure to check out Teacher Tools and Templates, which contains templates and forms you probably use on a regular basis. Templates include a seating chart, behavior documentation, too much talking essay, assignment sheet, book list, student grade tracker, homework excuse note, missing work notice, parent concern letter, and many more. If you have *Microsoft Office*, you can open, view, and print these forms.

Lesson Plans Page

http://www.lessonplanspage.com/

Site includes more than 1,000 lesson plans, primarily at the elementary level, that were developed by Kyle Yamnitz, students, and faculty at the University of Missouri. Additional lesson plans were submitted by the users of the Web site. Click on the subject you want (math, science, music, language arts, computers/Internet, social studies, art, P.E. and health, multidisciplinary, and other). Then click on grade level (PreK–1, 2–3, 4–5, 6–7, middle and high school). Click Most Recent Additions to see 50 lessons that other teachers recently contributed. It's easy to contribute a lesson to the site if you have one you'd like to share.

Other Features: On the left side column, look for Teacher Magazines for some discounts up to 80 percent. Magazines such as *Creative Instructor*, *Classroom*, *Teaching K–8*, *Teacher Magazine*, and many others are featured.

Lesson Plan Search

http://www.lessonplansearch.com/

A collection of 2,600+ lessons in all different subjects—all the major subjects plus secondary subjects like music, dance, drama, and health/P.E. When you click a lesson, your browser will take you to another site where that lesson is stored. If you need *Adobe Acrobat Reader* to view/print PDF files, there's a link at the top of the page to download it.

Don't Miss: Click Here for Penpals (left sidebar) will take you to page that shows a list of schools (alphabetically by U.S. state) that are seeking other classrooms for penpal exchange. International requests are included also. Send an e-mail to that teacher letting him/her know you are interested in corresponding with their class.

Other Features: The Thematic Units section is the second largest with 400+ lessons with themes such as Earth Day, amphibians and reptiles, ecosystems, environment, events, poetry, and more. Lots of great unit ideas.

New York Times Learning Network

http://www.nytimes.com/learning/teachers/lessons/archive.html

The NYT Learning Network keeps an archive of hundreds of free lesson plans geared for middle and high school. Topics include American history, civics, current events, economics, fine arts, geography, global history, journalism, media sciences, and technology. Each lesson plan has author's name, objectives, procedures, vocabulary, outcomes, extensions, cross-curricular ideas, and links to sites for reference and research. Developed by the *New York Times* in partnership with the Bank Street College of Education. Gr. 6–12.

Other Features: Student Connections (**http://www.nytimes.com/learning/students/**) is a great site to bookmark and use for daily discussion of current events.

ProTeacher

http://www.proteacher.com/

One of the most popular Internet education sites, ProTeacher is a comprehensive site for K–6 teachers—lesson plans in all subjects, education news, networking and support, teaching practices, classroom management, child development, leadership, technology. The search engine works well. Search results come back alphabetically with brief descriptions.

Don't Miss: Talk to other teachers who visit ProTeacher. BusyBoard is the place to read their messages, ask questions, and share advice. It has special sections for K–3 and 4–6 teachers, student teachers, substitutes, special education, and Canadian educators.

Other Features: Reference Desk is very helpful, with links to dictionaries, encyclopedias, news/weather, telephone/addresses, language translation, library references, weights and measures, and writing.

Sites for Teachers

http://www.sitesforteachers.com/

Summary: Sitesforteachers.com is a listing of education Web sites (with links) that are ranked by popularity. This means the more times users have viewed a particular site (known as "hits"), the higher the ranking. The home page lists the top 25 most popular sites. The bottom of the page has additional pages, each one containing the next 25 most popular sites, up to about 300 sites. Site statistics (hits) are updated hourly, and it starts over once a week to allow new sites a chance to rank higher during the next week. When you click a site, your browser will open a new window. The site was created by two education professors at California State University and is now hosted by Sites for Teachers.

Don't Miss: Check out the top 25 most popular sites on the main page, so see which education sites your fellow colleagues are using the most.

Other Features: In addition, in the left column, there are some links to specific subjects, such as math and language arts. The left column also features a "Web site of the week" that is usually worth a visit.

TeachNet

http://www.teachnet.com/

Started in 1995 by a husband/wife team in Wichita, Kansas, Teachnet.com is well organized and easy to navigate. The left column contains all the regular features such as lesson plans, teaching tools, and networking with other teachers. Click on **Lesson Plans** to view all the major subjects. When you click a subject, you will see subcategories. Search by subject. Some subjects don't have as many lessons as others do.

Don't Miss: Power Tools, in the left side column, has some excellent ideas in the areas of organization, classroom décor, grading and other routine tasks, back to school and end of year ideas, preparing for job interviews, and more.

Other Features: Sharing, in the left side column, has several ways to stay connected to other educators. You can choose to join a discussion list with other teachers, sign up for weekly news and announcements from TeachNet, or sign up to get a daily e-mail with tips and new site additions.

TeAch-nology

http://www.teach-nology.com/

Thousands of lesson plans and free printable worksheets, over 150,000 reviewed Web sites, rubrics, educational games, technology tips, advice from expert teachers, current education news, and Web quests are a few of the features of TeAch-nology.com. Based in New York, the site is maintained by a group of educators ranging from PreK to high school, professors of higher education, educational consultants, small business constituencies, and Web designers.

Don't Miss: Top Ten Areas (left side column) shows the top ten most popular features that visitors access. Lesson Plan Center is always in the top ten—a well-organized list of activities and lessons by subject. There are several thousand free worksheets, organized in a dozen themes such as language arts, critical thinking, and science.

Other Features: Make your own graphic organizers, rubrics, and language arts worksheets—look under Free Worksheets. You can also sign up for a weekly newsletter with teaching tips.

Best Sites for Teaching LANGUAGE ARTS

GENERAL

Educator's Reference Desk

http://www.eduref.org/cgi-bin/lessons.cgi/Language_Arts

Educator's Ref Desk took over the popular AskERIC site (Educational Resources Information Center at Syracuse University), which was a federally funded national information system for educators. You'll find most of the former AskERIC files still there, including the lesson plans (for all subjects) and journal database. The section on Language Arts is excellent because it is composed of practical lessons that work, contributed by classroom teachers across the United States. The major categories in Language Arts are alphabet, grammar, journalism, literature, speech, whole language, phonics, reading, spelling, story telling, vocabulary, writing, and others. Click on any of those categories to see an alphabetical list of lesson plans and activities, with grade level indicated. Site is maintained by the Information Institute of Syracuse. K–12.

Carol Hurst's Children's Literature

http://www.carolhurst.com/

Click on Table of Contents to see a more organized list of what this comprehensive site has to offer. It features hundreds of reviews for parents and teachers of children's books, using a star rating, listed by title, author, or grade level. In Curriculum Areas and Subject Themes you can find recommended books for any subject or unit you might be studying, from oceans and Appalachia to math and U.S. history. You'll find many ideas of ways to use them in the classroom. Created by Carol Otis Hurst, author and educational consultant. K–8.

Don't Miss: There is an archive of back issues of a monthly newsletter all about children's literature. You can also sign up to receive the newsletter by e-mail.

Other Features: Professional Topics contains articles by Hurst and recommended books on topics such as reading, writing, and whole language.

Integrating the Arts

http://www.op97.k12.il.us/instruct/IArts/

Developed by educators as part of an Illinois Comprehensive Arts Planning Grant, this is an excellent collection of lesson plans that integrate the arts (fine art, music, dance, theater, physical movement) into classroom curriculum. Some examples, organized by grade level, are earth-sun-moon, our community, reptiles, fairy tales, making connections, simple machines, prairie life, Civil War, and dance and drama. Lessons have objectives, materials needed, procedures, and outcomes. Created by Oak Park Elementary School District 97 (Illinois). K–6.

Don't Miss: A Celebration of Prairie Life for fourth grade is especially well done. It includes multidisciplinary activities (math, social studies, language arts, and science) involving prairie lifestyle plus music, dance, and visual arts activities.

LessonPlanz Language Arts

http://lessonplanz.com/Lesson_Plans/Language_Arts/

You can search for a specific lesson by typing a keyword in the search box at the top of the page, or you can click on the grade level below that to browse what is available. Over 700 lessons in the areas of book activities, reading, writing, literature, spelling, and more. Each of the sections also contains links to other Web sites about language arts lessons. Created by A to Z Teacher Stuff. K–12.

Other Features: LessonPlanz also has hundreds of lesson plans in all the major and secondary subjects. Look in the left sidebar for a complete list and click to go to that subject area. You can also subscribe to a free monthly e-mail newsletter, and your name will never be used for any other purpose. Click Free Newsletter, Find Out More link (left sidebar).

Mini-Lessons

K–5: http://yn.la.ca.us/cec/ceclang/ceclang-elem.html

6–8: http://yn.la.ca.us/cec/ceclang/ceclang-interm.html

9–12: http://yn.la.ca.us/cec/ceclang/ceclang-high.html

Over 90 language arts mini-lessons were developed and contributed by a consortium of experienced teachers. Teachers from all grade levels, who wrote these lessons, gathered from 14 states during 1995 summer workshop at Columbia Education Center. The lessons aren't in any particular order, but each has a descriptive title and grade level designation. When you click on a lesson, they are in text format, which makes them quick to print. It's an excellent place to browse if you're looking for general ideas. You can also find this same set of lessons on Columbia's site (**http://www.col-ed.org/cur/**). Created by Columbia Education Center. K–12.

Teachnet

http://www.teachnet.com/lesson/langarts/

About 50 language arts lessons divided by categories: general, reading, writing, spelling, speaking, terminology, and more. Started in 1995 by a husband/wife team in Kansas, Teachnet.com is well-organized and easy to navigate.

Don't Miss: If you like *Charlotte's Web*, click on this link to see more than 50 ideas and activities, such as design a birth announcement for Wilbur, create a billboard ad for the county fair, and write about what it means to be a friend.

Other Features: Under Writing, there is a link about Word Walls, where several teachers have contributed ideas from their own classrooms. Also check out the link for Writing Workshop, to get more ideas from other teachers. Created by Teachnet. K–12.

BrainPOP Movies

http://www.brainpop.com/english/seeall.weml

An innovative site featuring original animated movies (starring Tim and his robot friend Moby) on about 20 Language Arts topics. Each topic contains a 2 to 4 minute animated movie, an interactive quiz, an experiment, a comic strip, a how-to hands on application, a timeline and a printable activity page. Topics include: writing in sequence, business letter, various kinds of punctuation marks, similes and metaphors, run-on sentences, parts of speech, types of writing, and the writing process. . Students and/or teachers may watch up to two movies per day (per computer) at no cost, or schools may purchase an annual pass for unlimited access. Students can log in with a screen name and password to keep track of their points from completing activities. Points can be redeemed for prizes. Created by BrainPop. Gr. 3-9.

Treasure Chest of Web Resources (Secondary Teachers)

http://teachers.henrico.k12.va.us/Specialist/franceslively/

No need to search the Internet for the best sites to supplement your high school lesson plans and student activities…this site has already done the work for you! The purpose of the Treasure Chest site is to help secondary English, language arts, and reading teachers access information on the Internet to supplement their teaching. On the main page click New Treasures on the main page to see the sites they recommend for the current academic year. The main page also has "sites of the month" as well as a summer reading list.

Click on the tab called Resources to view links (organized by subject) that will lead you to outstanding sites that can be used as resources for teaching. Some of the sites are so helpful that you will want to go back all the time. These sites have been set up on the drop down menu called Quick Links. When you click on a link that takes you outside the Treasure Chest site, click the back button on your browser to return there. On the HCPS tab, most of the sites there are specifically for teachers in Henrico County. However, teachers in other states/districts may find the reading lists and software support sections quite helpful. Site compiled by Frances Lively, Joanne Spotts, and Linda MacCleave, Henrico County Public Schools, Virginia. Gr. 9-12.

READING

Educator's Reference Desk – Reading Lessons

http://www.eduref.org/cgi bin/lessons.cgi/Language_Arts/Reading

Educator's Ref Desk took over the popular AskERIC site (Educational Resources Information Center at Syracuse University), which was a federally funded national information system for educators. You'll find most of the former AskERIC files still there, including the lesson plans (for all subjects) and journal database. The section on Reading is excellent because it is composed of practical lessons that work. This link has about 50 lesson plans that focus on reading, contributed by classroom teachers across the United States Click the title of the lesson to see the author's name, email address, duration, description, objectives, materials, procedures, and outcomes. Many of them have Internet resources too. Some of the lessons feature specific authors and book titles. Sample lesson titles: Cemetery Path, Do the Opposite, Land of Sweet Candy, Learning About Prediction, Parts of a Plot, Phonics Fun, Propaganda Techniques, Rhyming Words, Reading Comprehension Techniques, and more. Site is maintained by the Information Institute of Syracuse. K–12.

Comprehension

http://www.rhlschool.com/reading.htm

This site offers free reading comprehension worksheets for teachers and parents, including original stories, sentences, poems, short essays, and articles. Worksheets are in web format, easy to print and photocopy. The format for most is a poem, story, or sentences, with questions at the bottom for students to write a short answer or circle a multiple-choice answer. They are grouped in volumes, in no particular order. You can read the title, then click on it to see the full text. Volumes 4–6 work best in *Internet Explorer*, while Volume 3 prints better with *Netscape*. Created by RHL School. Gr. 5–8.

Don't Miss: The Word Meanings From Context worksheets are excellent. There are short paragraphs to read that contain a bolded word. The student chooses the best meaning from the multiple choice answers. This would be a great dictionary activity if students cannot get the meaning from context.

ESL Lessons

http://humanities.byu.edu/linguistics/lp/home.html

Nearly 100 lesson plans for teaching English to speakers of other languages, provided by Linguistics student teachers. Sections include reading, writing, listening, speaking, grammar, culture, and literacy. Each lesson gives objectives, materials, procedures, and extensions. Created by Brigham Young University. K–12.

Don't Miss: There are some interesting lessons in the Literacy section especially appropriate for ESL students: tobacco advertising methods, reading a recipe, writing letters, greeting people, and scanning a bus schedule.

Literacy Web

http://www.literacy.uconn.edu/compre.htm

The Literacy Web is designed to promote the use of the Internet as a tool to assist classroom teachers in their search for best practices in literacy instruction, including the new "literacies" of Internet technologies. This site provides current research and theory that supports traditional and new literacy practices as well as guiding teachers towards particular classroom resources that can enhance literacy development for students at all grade levels. The complex processes involved in reading comprehension are divided into three categories on this site (much like the National Reading Panel Report). The categories include: Vocabulary Instruction, Text Comprehension Instruction, and Teacher Preparation and Comprehension Strategies Instruction. You'll also find useful web sites that students can visit to practice their use of comprehension strategies with fiction and non-fiction texts at a variety of reading levels. The section on Vocabulary Instruction is especially practical and useful, with strategies to help students retain word meanings beyond a test date. Created by the Literacy Web, University of Connecticut.

Primary Reading Games

http://www.primarygames.com/reading.htm

This colorful, award-winning site was initially created by a parent for her children, then it was expanded to students who are beginning readers. The site features online games that are easy to play and easy to read. After clicking on the game button, there is a brief description of what the game's purpose is, then the student clicks the green start arrow to begin playing. Samples include: color words (seek-and-find), treasure trove (matching contractions), see and spell (similar to moving around magnetic letters on a board), Squigly's apples (ordinal numbers), bookshelf (easy-to-read books, one page at a time), months of the year (seek-and-find), ABC game (matching objects with beginning letters), and more. Created by Susan S. Beasley, PrimaryGames. K-2.

Reading Comprehension Worksheets

http://abcteach.com/Reading/ReadingComp.htm

Organized by five grade levels (PreK–K, K–2, 2–4, 4–6, 7–12), these are excellent worksheets with short stories and paragraphs, with comprehension questions at the end. Files are in *Adobe Acrobat Reader* PDF format (a link is provided to download). The grade levels are approximate—Read before using with children to determine appropriateness of level. All the sheets are divided into Informational and Fictional categories. Click on the titles to view the worksheet. Topics range from seasons and animals (for younger children) to famous people and character stories (for older students). Some of the worksheets have a notation that it will also contain a writing component. Created by ABC Teach. K–12.

Reading Research

http://www.Toread.com/

If you want to find out the latest professional thinking concerning balanced literacy and reading research, this site features hundreds of journal articles and research findings. Topics covered include the reading process, teaching techniques, balanced literacy programs, reading cueing system, guided reading, read alouds, literature circles, book discussions, reading skills, reading of phonics, reading comprehension strategies, readers workshop, and more.

Janet Allen's Recommended Book List

http://www.schoolwide.com/janetallen.pdf

Dr. Janet Allen is a Milken Foundation National Educator Award recipient, and she has authored several books for teachers on literacy, shared reading, and vocabulary. She teamed with SchoolWide to compile this comprehensive list of books for middle and high school students. Categories include books to support writers workshop, critical thinking and problem solving, faculty meeting read-alouds, grammar study, independent reading, shared reading (novels), fiction, Latino, launching reading workshop, math and literacy trade books, science and literacy, short story, word study, Shakespeare and the arts, and more. Adobe Reader to view the file. Compiled by Schoolwide, Inc. Gr. 6–12.

Literature Circles

http://home.att.net/~teaching/litcircles.htm

Even if you've never done a lit circle before there's no need to buy any books on the subject when everything you need is online, created by experienced teacher Laura Candler, who is a Milken Foundation National Educator for 2000. Laura describes the basic model of a lit circle with various kinds of structure and group roles. You will also find all the forms you need to assemble your own packet, plus discussion questions, graphic organizers, assessment ideas, and reflection forms.

Reading Workshop

http://www.manatee.k12.fl.us/sites/elementary/palmasola/rcompindex.htm

Some of the same strategies used by remedial reading centers and tutors are right here. These activities are intended to be used online with students, with some assistance from an adult, rather than printing and photocopying. Sequential sections include: pre-reading strategies (phonological awareness), reading comprehension strategies (Gr. 1-2), online reading tutorial (Gr. 3–5), vocabulary builders (Gr. 3–5), comprehension worksheets and practice (Gr. 3–5), integrated online units (rainforest, space, ancient Egypt, deserts), and practice sheets on specific skills (by grade level). Created by Palma Sola Elementary School, Florida. Gr. 1-5.

Teacher's Corner

http://www.theteacherscorner.net/reading/

Teacher's Corner contains a lot more in the reading section than just reading, so you can get lots of great ideas that cross over to other language arts areas. Lessons and activities on reading activities, authors, genres, parts of speech, phonics, reading skills, spelling, vocabulary, Web sites, and worksheets. Created by theteacherscorner.net. K–12.

Don't Miss: Book Nook (left sidebar) has three sections for recommended children's books, teen and young adult books, and books and magazines for educators.

Other Features: The left sidebar also contains lesson plans, resources, and activities for all the other major subjects.

WRITING

Educator's Reference Desk—Writing Ideas

http://www.eduref.org/cgi-bin/lessons.cgi/Language_Arts/Writing

Educator's Ref Desk took over the popular AskERIC site (Educational Resources Information Center at Syracuse University), which was a federally funded national information system for educators. You'll find most of the former AskERIC files still there, including the lesson plans (for all subjects) and journal database. The section on Writing is excellent because it is composed of practical lessons that work. This link has about 100 lesson plans that focus on writing, contributed by classroom teachers across the United States. Click the title of the lesson to see the author's name, email address, duration, description, objectives, materials, procedures, and outcomes. Many of them have Internet resources too. Site is maintained by the Information Institute of Syracuse. K–12.

Assessment of Writing

http://www.nwrel.org/assessment/scoring.asp?odelay=3&d=1

It's often difficult to grade student writing because it seems like a subjective process. This analytical model of writing assessment, called 6+1 Traits Writing Scoring Guide, takes the guesswork out of your evaluation. It's based on seven key traits of what is considered strong writing, regardless of grade level. The scoring guide allows teachers to assign points in each of six areas of writing: ideas and content, organization, voice, word choice, sentence fluency, conventions (mechanical correctness), and presentation. Point rubric ranges from 1 (beginning writer) to 5 (strong writer: shows control and skill), with explanations of each. Pages are in *Adobe Acrobat Reader* PDF format. Created by Northwest Regional Educational Lab. K–12.

Don't Miss: Scoring Practice (bottom of page) allows teachers to practice scoring with the 6+1 model using real student papers from the practice page.

ProTeacher's Writing Ideas

http://www.proteacher.com/070037.shtml

ProTeacher has compiled hundreds of lesson plans, activities, and writing ideas for students. Lessons are divided into major categories of publishing, writing activities, writing ideas, the writing process, and writing skills. Writing Activities, the largest category, is divided into letters, folk and fairy tales, and poetry, plus lessons on persuasive writing, biographies, photo essay, advertising, and successful paragraphs. Writing ideas include story starters, young writer's club, and high-interest topics as starting points. The writing process includes peer editing checklist, steps of revision, and personal view. Created by ProTeacher. K–12.

Other Features: Message Boards (right sidebar) contain the subject topics for all kinds of current discussions taking place (more than writing topics). Click to go there and read what others have posted—you can jump in and join the discussion too.

Shape Books to Write/Color

http://www.abcteach.com/Shape%20books/SHAPEmenu.htm

This popular site allows students to create shape books, which are large pictures/graphics on which they write words, sentences, or stories. Pages can be used individually or combined to make shape books. Shape themes include: animals, buildings, flowers, fruit, holidays, insects, money, nature, people, transportation, and more. The front and back covers of the books can be laminated, then stapled or bound together with yarn to assemble the book. Created by ABC Teach. K–3.

Other Features: Click on Shape Book Instructions for details and ideas on creating and assembling the books. Also check out Color Pages for worksheets to color for youngsters.

Writing Video

http://www.bbc.co.uk/education/revisewise/english/writing/

Click Activity to see a colorful animated video with sound effects that shows various types of writing: story planning, beginning and ending of a story, factual writing, letter writing, and more. Also has online test and place to write and submit by e-mail. Plug-ins are needed to view video; click Help for more information. Created by BBC Schools. Gr. 3–6.

Other Features: The English section also has videos for reading and spelling.

Writing Lessons

http://www.teachnet.com/lesson/langarts/writing/

Here are a list of writing activities and ideas, contributed by teachers who know what works. Some of the suggestions are: writing workshop, nonlinear writing, hieroglyphic art project, newspaper activities, writing letters to the editor, resume writing, and Christmas activities. Created by Teachnet. K–12.

Other Features: This site has hundreds of lessons and activities on all different subjects, all grade levels. Click Lesson Plans in the left sidebar.

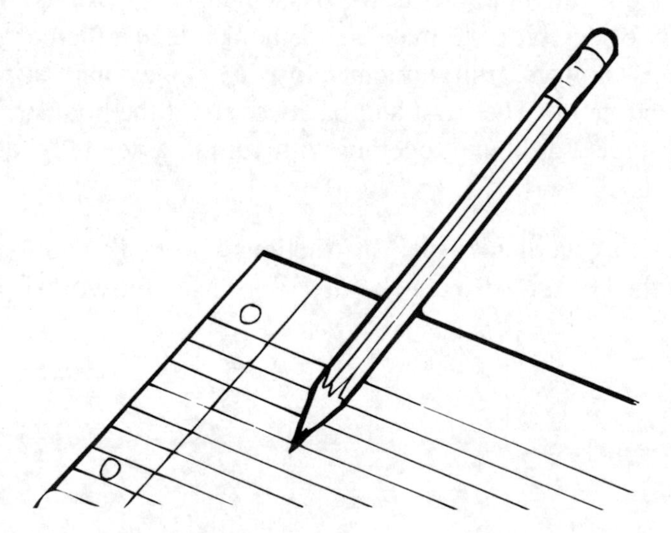

LITERATURE

---

100 Favorite Children's Books

http://www.nypl.org/branch/kids/100/todays.html

Compiled by children's librarians, this list of books (with brief descriptions) appeals to today's kids. Other popular book categories (click on sections at the top of the page) are animal stories, biographies, fantasy, historical fiction, humor, mystery, poetry, science fiction, and survival and adventure stories. Created by New York Public Library. Gr. 1–6.

Aesop's Fables

http://aesopfables.com/

Many of us grew up reading or hearing Aesop's Fables, so here is a site we can share with the youngsters and students in our lives. The fox and the sour grapes, the ant and grasshopper, and the flea and ox are all here. This comprehensive online collection includes more than 650 fables, indexed in alphabetical table format, with morals listed. There are many more to be added in the future. The site explains that most were translated into English by two writers from the 19th century, and the rest are from Jean De la Fontaine in French, which were also translated to English by volunteers. Created by John R. Long, Star Systems.

Other Features: Site also includes more than 120 fairy tales by Hans Christian Andersen. Several have sound files, so you can listen as a child's voice reads the story (look for the Real Audio icon). There are also suggested lesson plans (look at the top of each section).

Art of Storytelling

http://www.storyarts.org/lessonplans/lessonideas/

This collection of storytelling activities, developed by storyteller and author Heather Forest for her storytelling workshops with students, teachers, and librarians, can be expanded by teachers into language arts lesson plans to support speaking, listening, reading and writing skills. These are activities that can be springboards to developing formal lesson plans. Some sample titles include: storytellers on tour, story treasure hunt, old time radio show, collecting family stories, chain sentence, describing a stone, spontaneous poetry, autobiography of anything, creating personal fables, storytelling festival day, and a picture is worth a thousand words. Created by Heather Forest, Story Arts Online. Gr. 3-8.

Literature Circles

http://www.proteacher.com/070172.shtml

Literature circles can be a wonderful reading activity, when a small group of students come together temporarily, as they read the same story, book, or poem. The group meets once a week or so, to discuss what they've read, and they take turns leading discussions and sharing their reactions to the readings. ProTeacher has compiled dozens of links with ideas of how to introduce literature circles in your classroom, ways to organize them, guiding discussion questions, and ideas and theme units. Created by ProTeacher. K–12.

Literature Guides

http://www.nancypolette.com/litguides.asp

Why buy literature guides at the teacher supply store, when you could check here first and see if there's a guide for your book? These 30+ book guides are divided into picture books and novels. Some of the most popular listed here are *Horton Hatches the Egg*, *Annie and the Wild Animals*, *Black Pearl*, *Bridge to Terabithia*, *Holes*, *Stone Fox*, *Harry Potter*, and *Julie of the Wolves*. Each literature guide has a variety of cross-curricular activities, such as summarizing the readings, writing a poem, researching a locale, answering questions, listing characters by certain attributes, researching a Web site, completing sentences, critical thinking and analysis, and much more. Created by author, professor, and former teacher Nancy Polette. K–6.

Other Features: Click on **Handouts** (left sidebar) to view other articles and links such as books to build character, bringing history alive with literature, picture books with pizzazz for older students, and stretching minds without books.

Literature Library

http://school.discovery.com/lessonplans/lit.html

A nice collection of American literature lessons, mostly for middle and high school. Some of the titles are classics in American literature: *Pride and Prejudice*, *Moby Dick*, *Great Gatsby*, *Alice in Wonderland*, *Keiko*, *Lord of the Flies*, *Catch-22*, and many others. These lessons are quite extensive—In addition to objectives, materials, procedures, and outcomes, there are also discussion questions, extensions, suggested readings, vocabulary (with sound files for pronunciation), and links to other Web sites. Created by Discovery.com. Gr. 6–12.

Other Features: Discovery School features lesson plans on many other math and science subjects. Look at the left sidebar. Lessons are also organized by grade levels (K–5, 6–8, 9–12).

Newbery Books and the Net

http://www.eduscapes.com/newbery/new.html

Eduscapes has compiled a comprehensive collection of links—all based on the Newbery Medal winning books and the honorable mentions (Honor Books). Each listing has author information, lesson plans, activities, and other teacher resources. Many of the books have Web resources that can extend, expand, or enhance particular topics or themes from the book. Rather than discussion questions and chapter outlines, the focus is on real-world resources, interesting connections, and age-appropriate activities. Access the links by going about halfway down the page—you can find books listed by Award Year, By Title, By Author, or By Theme. Created by Annette Lamb. K–8.

Newbery Medal Home Page

http://www.ala.org/alsc/newbery.html

The Newbery Medal was named for eighteenth-century British bookseller John Newbery. It was the first children's book award in the world and is awarded annually by the American Library Association to quality children's literature published in the U.S., based on specific criteria. Previous years' winners include: *Sounder*, *Julie of the Wolves*, *Bridge to Terabithia*, *Shiloh*, *The Giver*, *Walk Two Moons*, *Holes*, and A *Year Down Yonder*. Created by the American Library Association. K–12.

Don't Miss: A printable list of all Newbery Medal winners (1922-present) and links to the Caldecott Medal Home Page are at the bottom.

ProTeacher

http://www.proteacher.com/070093.shtml

Great site for finding follow-up and comprehension activities to children's literature and story books. Here are hundreds of activities and lesson plans for popular children's books, alphabetical by title, compiled by ProTeacher. The page opens to show Intermediate Titles—click on Primary Titles to see those. Created by ProTeacher. K–6.

Other Features: Click Book Board to exchange ideas from others, ask questions, and get more ideas for a specific book. Post a book title as your subject line.

GRAPHIC ORGANIZERS

Descriptions and Use

http://www.sdcoe.k12.ca.us/score/actbank/torganiz.htm

Good site for introduction of graphic organizers, which are useful for helping students organize information and understand it, either prior to reading or afterward. The site features popular organizers, with descriptions and suggestions for use: chain of events, clustering, compare/contrast, continuum, cycle, family tree, fishbone, interaction outline, problem and solution, spider map, storyboard, Venn diagram, semantic mapping, KWHL, and more. Click **Graphic Organizers** to see an index of several organizers and their uses in describing, comparing/contrasting, classifying, sequencing, causal, or decision making. Created by SCORE (Schools of California, Online Resources for Educators), San Diego Co. Office of Education.

Four Blocks Graphic Organizers

http://www.k111.k12.il.us/lafayette/fourblocks/graphic_organizers.htm

This page contains dozens of graphic organizers, which are used to enhance pre- and post-reading experiences. These graphic organizers can be used with Four Blocks or independently. Some of the organizers you'll find are: K-W-L (several variations), chain of events, spider map, storyboard, Venn diagrams, story and character maps, response journal, question-prediction chart, plot map, circle map, and many more. Many of them offer a choice of viewing in PDF (*Adobe Acrobat Reader*) or *Microsoft Word*. Four Blocks is a popular multimethod, multilevel literacy framework developed by Pat Cunningham and Dottie Hall of Wake Forest University. Created by Kankakee School District (Illinois). K–4.

Other Features: In the left sidebar and at the bottom are links to other parts of the Four Blocks Literacy site, which are worth exploring if you're not familiar with this K–4 reading/writing program.

Houghton Mifflin's Graphic Organizers

http://www.eduplace.com/graphicorganizer/

About 30 graphic organizers, all vertical in design to make viewing easy. Directions included on each. Includes: clock, cluster and word webs, story maps, K-W-L, Venn diagram, flow chart, 5 Ws, ladder, sequence chart, sandwich, sense chart, tree chart, tic-tac-toe chart, time-order chart, and many more. The first link is to view organizers in web page format, and the second link shows them in PDF (*Adobe Acrobat Reader*) format. The PDF format prints larger than the web page format. Leave the Houghton Mifflin copyright notice in place when making photocopies. New organizers are being added in the future. K–8.

Houghton Mifflin's Graphic Organizers

http://www.eduplace.com/graphicorganizer/

Forty printable graphic organizers in all, divided into two sections. All Subject Organizers feature multi-column charts, cause and effect, K-W-L, various problem and solution charts, student homework checklist, Venn diagrams, and various web/concept maps. Language Arts Organizers include antonyms and synonyms, beginning-middle-end, conflict dissection chart, fact chart, herringbone and sequence maps, problem-climax-solution, and more. *Adobe Acrobat Reader* PDF format is easy to print and free to photocopy for classroom use (with copyright notices intact). Created by The Learning Network. K–8.

TeAch-nology's Organizers

http://worksheets.teach-nology.com/graphic/

You will find about a dozen creative graphic organizers here, even bingo cards! You can print and photocopy these for students, as long as you leave the copyright notice intact. Some of the organizers include: character analysis pyramid, concept web, story elements, K-W-L, multiple intelligence planning sheet, scope and sequence ladder, SQ3R chart, and triple circle Venn diagram. Created by Teachnology.com. K–12.

GRAMMAR

ABC Teach Grammar Basics

http://www.abcteach.com/grammar/grammartoc.htm

This site offers basic worksheets on nouns, verbs, pronouns, adjectives, and adverbs. You'll also find brainstorm activities and word search for each. Scroll further down to find worksheets on other aspects of grammar, like homonyms, opposites, contractions, suffixes, plurals, and more. More lessons and activities are being added in the future. Created by ABC Teach. K–5.

Adjectives/Adverbs Video

http://www.bbc.co.uk/education/revisewise/english/spelling/

Click Activity to see a colorful animated video with sound effects that explains about adjectives and adverbs, plus guidelines of when and how to use them in writing. Also has an online test and a place to write samples to submit by email. Plug-ins are needed to view video; click Help for more information. Created by BBC Schools. Gr. 3–6.

Other Features: The English section also has videos for reading, writing, and spelling.

BrainPop English & Grammar

http://www.brainpop.com/english/grammar/

Allow Tim and his robot friend Moby, who are animated characters, to bring new life and humor to English topics. Teachers can use movies (3 min. each) to introduce topics, give an overview, or review concepts. The movies conclude with an interactive quiz. Topics included here are Parts of Speech, Types of Sentences, Nouns, Subject and Predicate, Interjections, Diagramming Sentences, Adjectives and Adverbs, Pronouns, Punctuation, Contractions, Verbs, and more. Teachers/students may view two movies per day per computer at no cost. *Macromedia Flash* Plug-in is needed (free to download). Gr. 3–8.

English Worksheets

http://www.tut-world.com/

Free colorful worksheets from Tutorial World that you can print and use with students. Look for the chart at the top. Choose your grade level, then click on the color dot under the column for English. Depending on which level, you will many worksheet samples in: vocabulary, grammar, sentence structure, comprehension, and cloze passage (fill in the blanks with vocabulary words). Besides the dozens of free worksheets, if you register with the site, you will have access to even more. If you have struggling Kindergartners, the Pre-K section contains sheets for basics of writing, counting, spelling, and coloring. Created by Strategic Thinking Business P/L Singapore. PreK–6.

Other Features: On the main page, you will also see worksheets for math with the same grade levels.

Grammar Gorillas Game

http://www.funbrain.com/grammar/

This interactive game makes it fun for students to practice nouns, verbs, and other parts of speech. Two levels: beginner and advanced. When the student clicks on the correct noun or verb, the gorilla gets another banana. A help feature pops up when the incorrect answer is given. A scorecard at the top shows correct/incorrect answers, or you can click Start Over. Created by The Learning Network. Gr. 2–6.

Grammar Worksheets

http://www.rhlschool.com/english.htm

Useful for teaching, reinforcement, and review, RHL School offers a variety of grammar worksheets. They are not in any particular order (except by date posted). Subjects covered are analogies (using holiday and other themes), sentence completion, homonyms, noun and verb searches, suffixes (vowels and consonants), rhyming words, proofreading, contractions, irregular verbs, plural nouns, and much more. For answer keys, go to the bottom of the page and click Answer Keys. They will be e-mailed to you. Created by RHL.

Other Features: RHL offers worksheets in other subject areas, including math and reading. Click on links at the top of the page.

Lesson Tutor

http://www.lessontutor.com/ltlist.html

Practical lesson plans using topics that interest students (sports, music, movies), while teaching grammar at the same time. Scroll down about halfway until you see Language Arts, and there is a section for Grammar that contains lessons for Gr. 5–11. Click the checkmarks to see the lesson. Created by Lesson Tutor. Gr. 5–11.

Other Features: There are lots of other subject lesson plans on this site besides Grammar. The more checkmarks you see in a section, the more lessons there are.

Parts of Speech

http://www.lessonplanspage.com/LA.htm

Here are hundreds of grammar lesson plans contributed by experienced teachers, hosted by Lesson Plans Page. Click which grade level you want, then you'll see dozens of lesson plans in all different areas of Language Arts. Scroll down until you see Parts of Speech. You'll see a list of descriptive lesson titles (click on it to view), and each one contains objectives, materials, procedures, and outcomes. Created by EdScope, LLC. K–12.

Other Features: This general site also has lesson plans for all major and secondary subjects. Look at the left sidebar and click Lesson Plans. You can also search the site with a keyword—Go the bottom of the left sidebar to Search This Site.

TeAch-nology's Grammar

http://www.teach-nology.com/teachers/lesson_plans/language_arts/grammar/

Nearly 50 creative lesson plans, all different grade levels, with a brief description for each. Some of the samples include: adverbily, colorful parts of speech, football-based punctuation, grammar journals, grammar war, historical grammar bites, horrid homonyms, punctuation penguins, subject and predicate puzzle, and many more. Each lesson includes objectives, materials, procedures and exercises, outcomes, and author's name. Created by Teachnology.com. K–12.

Other Features: This site is jammed full of lessons for every subject you can think of. Go to the top of the page and click Lesson Plans. The entire Language Arts section is excellent, with lessons covering topics like reading, spelling, vocabulary, writing, literary analysis, phonics, and much more.

SPELLING & VOCABULARY

TeAch-nology's Spelling

http://www.teach-nology.com/teachers/lesson_plans/language_arts/spell/

Nearly 40 creative lesson plans, all different grade levels, with a brief description for each. Sample lesson titles include: spelling stories, spelling song, pipe cleaner spelling, rhyming games, sparkle and many other spelling games, memory cues, and more. Each lesson includes objectives, materials, procedures and exercises, outcomes, and author's name. Created by Teachnology.com. K–8.

Other Features: This site is jammed full of lessons for every subject you can think of. Go to the top of the page and click **Lesson Plans**. The entire Language Arts section is excellent, with lessons covering topics like reading, spelling, vocabulary, writing, literary analysis, phonics, and much more.

Spelling Tricks and Activities

http://www.teachnet.com/lesson/langarts/spellingwds040299.html

When memorizing spelling words just isn't working, here's a list of over three dozen tricks and activities that make learning more enjoyable for students. Some of the activities listed here are: writing words backwards and forwards, making silly sentences, scrambling the words for a peer, using them in a short story, making a word search and trading with a friend, using pasta or magnetic letters to spell, and more. Created by Teachnet. K–8.

Spelling Worksheets

http://www.edhelper.com/spelling.htm

Each lesson includes word lists and practice worksheets, listed by grade level. Some of the practice worksheets are: finding words, filling in the missing letter, respelling, unscrambling words, circling correctly spelled words, and missing vowels. There are some worksheets for subscribers only. You can also use the worksheet generator, which means you can build a new worksheet using your spelling list and it will create ten worksheets automatically. Every time you click to create a worksheet, a new one is generated. You'll need to be a subscriber to use some of the worksheet generators but not all. Created by EdHelper. Gr. 1–12.

Don't Miss: The crossword puzzle creator is available to anyone without a subscription. It's a great way to reinforce spelling or vocabulary words.

Other Features: Near the top of the page is Read our Printing Worksheets Tip Section, which explains how the site works and how to get worksheets printed.

Vocabulary Builders

http://www.superkids.com/aweb/tools/words/

Super Kids offers several online, interactive games and puzzles for students to help build vocabulary skills. Word of the Day has sections for upper elementary, junior high, and college admission prep tests. Hangman is played online by clicking the letters—each wrong click results in another piece of the hangman's noose. There is also a Word Search Puzzle creator—enter your words and specify the grid size. Word Scrambler is a great way for students to practice spelling or vocabulary words. Enter the words you want scrambled, click Make My Worksheet, and there you go. Print and photocopy all the worksheets as needed for each student. Created by Knowledge Share LLC. Gr. 3–8.

Other Features: Super Kids also has a section to make math drill worksheets for addition, subtraction, multiplication, division, fractions, and more, plus answer sheets. Look under Educational Tools.

Vocabulary Lessons & Activities

http://www.proteacher.com/070169.shtml

This site offers about a dozen lesson plans, games, and activities that focus on building vocabulary, contributed by teachers around the United States. The lesson plan titles are descriptive; just click to view it. Many have Internet resources too. Some of the titles are Einstein Club, Synonyms and Antonyms, Learning Tips, Vocab Games, Word of the Day, weekly vocab activities, daily buzzword, and more. Hosted by ProTeacher Web Directory. ProTeacher is an excellent source of lessons, worksheets, activities, games, and more for all subject areas. Gr. K–6.

Notes:

BASICS

Alphabet & Handwriting Basics

http://www.abcteach.com/contents/basicstoc.htm

Click on **ABC Activities**, which is loaded with basics for primary students: alphabets, coloring pages, word cards, tracing pages, alphabet and number flash cards, easy worksheets, easy word searches and puzzles, game ideas, and recommended books. Click on **Colors and Shapes** to find activities to help teach basic shape patterns, colors, and everyday objects. Click **Handwriting** to practice letter and number worksheets and desktop alphabet lines. Created by ABC Teach. PreK–3.

Alphabet Books

http://curry.edschool.virginia.edu/go/wil/

Click **Alphabet Books** when you get to this page, to jump down to that section. Research has shown that repeated readings of alphabet books help children learn and recognize letters. Education faculty at University of Virginia, who compiled these activities, do not believe in directly teaching the alphabet but rather, providing opportunities to encounter letters and their names/sounds. The site is set up to offer a new alphabet book each month. Student use them first at school, then take them home for families to read together. Must have *Adobe Acrobat Reader* to open these files (a link is available here to download the program). The alphabet books are organized by month, beginning with September and ending with April. Created by Curry School of Education, University of Virginia.

Colors and Shapes

http://www.abcteach.com/color/colorshapestoc.htm

For primary students, learning colors and shapes is an important foundation skill. ABC Teach offers worksheets, games, and coloring pages to practice. Click on **Colors** to see coloring pages you can print and copy for students. Flashcards will be added to the site in the future. Under Patterns, there are a couple of sections that contain pages with large shapes (circle, square, rectangle, trapezoid, etc.) on them for students to practice naming, coloring, comparing, and cutting out. Created by ABC Teach. K–3.

Handwriting Worksheets

http://www.teach-nology.com/teachers/lesson_plans/language_arts/handwriting/

TeAch-Nology has compiled a handful of links to sites with handwriting worksheets, practice, activities, and games. Each one has a title and description; click to go to that link. Some sample titles include: a day of popcorn, beginning handwriting, color code writing, handwriting math, D'Nealian sheets, and manuscript writing. Created by Teachnology. Gr. 1-4.

Language Arts Basics

http://lessonplanz.com/Lesson_Plans/Language_Arts/_Grades_K–2/

Lesson Planz has over 100 lesson plans for primary students, categorized by alphabet/phonics, centers, handwriting, phonemic awareness, words, and writing. The writing section is the most comprehension, and you will get all kinds of theme ideas and practical lessons to help your primary students achieve success in written expression. The bottom of the page contains links with even more ideas for this age group: author study, book boxes, class big book ideas, design a book jacket, farm sounds, Japanese folktales, memory box, pet training, and more. Created by A to Z Teacher Stuff. K–2.

Other Features: This is a comprehensive site for all subjects and grade levels. Look the left sidebar and click on whatever grade or subject interests you.

Sight Words

http://www.createdbyteachers.com/sightfreemain.html

Created By Teachers has a great page that features Dolch sight words. The 200+ sight word list is coded (with dots) for grade level. The phrases page has 140+ of the most common phrases children will run across in their readings. The page also contains a noun list, 3x5 cards (that can be printed, enlarged, and used as flash cards), checklists, sight boards, take-home cards, and about a dozen word search puzzles. Created by Teacher2Teacher. K–3.

Notes:

Best Sites for Teaching MATH

GENERAL

ABC Teach

http://www.abcteach.com/Math/mathTOC.htm

From green frog counters to 100th math activities, ABC Teach has done an excellent job of offering basic math worksheets and fun activities for elementary students. Worksheets, grids, charts, number lines (one has ladybugs), and manipulatives, place value, multiplication, division, fractions, measurement, time, graphing. A section for 100th day of school activities includes chart fill-in, booklet cover, graphing jelly beans, bookmarks, poems, attendance certificate, and more. Created by ABC Teach. K–6.

Don't Miss: Literature-Math Connections, a suggested reading list of books with math concepts (PDF format).

Math Computation & Problem Solving Worksheets

http://www.rhlschool.com/mathematics.htm

Practice makes perfect! Teachers who want to drill their students will find plenty of worksheets for all four operations plus rounding. There are links under each operation that tell what the worksheet focuses on, such as 2-digit addition, 2-digit subtraction (with and without regrouping), 2 digit x 3 digit, etc. The great thing about this web site is every time you visit or refresh the page, you get all new worksheets. The link for Problem Solving has more than 50 word problem and puzzle sheets. Some are holiday themes; others are games, patterns, or codes. All pages printable, ready to photocopy for classroom use. Users can register free to receive email answer sheets. Created by RHL School. Gr. 3-6.

Educator's Reference Desk—Math

http://www.eduref.org/cgi-bin/lessons.cgi/Mathematics

Educator's Ref Desk took over the popular AskERIC site (Educational Resources Information Center at Syracuse University), which was a federally funded national information system for educators. The section on Math is excellent because it is composed of practical lessons that work. This link has hundreds of lesson plans, contributed by classroom teachers across the U.S. The major categories are algebra, arithmetic, applied math, careers, functions, geometry, measurement, number sense, patterns, probability, probability, statistics, and more. Site is maintained by the Information Institute of Syracuse. K–12.

Don't Miss: Arithmetic contains a nice collection of about 50 lessons, games, and activities, including the 21 Game, Fraction Fun, m&m Math, Marble Game, Number Munchers, Snake, and Subtraction Rhyme.

Other Features: Educator's Reference Desk has lessons on all the major teaching subjects. Click on the Lesson Plans tab at the top to view subject areas.

Ask Dr. Math

http://mathforum.org/dr.math/

Dr. Math is a question and answer service for math students and their teachers. Students can search the archives for previously asked questions, and if it's not there, they can send a question to Dr. Math. Questions must be in English and can be about homework, puzzles, or math contest problems. Answers are sent back by e mail. The best questions and answers are entered into a searchable archive organized by grade level (elementary, middle school, high school) and topic (exponents, infinity, polynomials, etc.). Over 300 volunteer math teachers and professors are involved in this project. Created by The Math Forum at Drexel University (Pennsylvania).

A to Z Teacher Stuff

http://lessonplanz.com/Lesson_Plans/Mathematics/

Over 300 lesson plans grouped by grade level (K–2, 3–5, 6–8, 9–12). Easy to follow plans, posted by experienced math teachers across the U.S. The K–2 section is especially large, with lessons and activities for 100th day of school, basic operations, centers, fraction, sorting, estimation, money, math games, and problem solving. Each page you view also has links at the bottom that will take you to other sites for even more math fun. Created by A to Z Teacher Stuff. K–12.

National Council of Teachers of Math

K-5: http://www.nctm.org/elementary/

6-8: http://www.nctm.org/middle/

9-12: http://www.nctm.org/high/

What better place to find the perfect math lesson than from the largest nonprofit association of math educators, the National Council of Teachers of Mathematics! And of course, all the lessons on this site meet national NCTM standards. Math teachers will find hundreds of real-world, Internet-based lesson plans with real student appeal. Most are individual lessons with hands-on student activities, and there are many units too. Lesson plans are organized by grade level. Click on the bolded lesson title to view the lesson.

Internet-based lesson plans are examples of how the Internet can be used to help create effective standards-based math lessons. For example, many web sites can provide real-world data that can be analyzed or used to develop mathematical concepts. Other sites may provide detailed information about areas in which math is applied or contain tools that can be used to graph, visualize, or compute.

Most of the site's features, including the lesson plans, are free. Any items that are for NCTM members only are marked with a red "M." Even if you are not a NCTM member, be sure to look at the activities sections, because there are "free previews" for non-members that are quite comprehensive.

Don't Miss: Teachers can find a Problem of the Week on the main page of this site, plus all the other problems (and solutions) from past weeks.

Illuminations

http://illuminations.nctm.org/lessonplans/

The top association of math teachers created this site to make math fun and relevant for students. These Internet-based lesson plans are examples of how the Internet can be used to help create effective, standards-based math lessons. The key shows which lessons are multi-day, sequenced activities or single-day learning concepts. To view lessons, go to the top or bottom and click the grade level (PreK–2, 3–5, 6–8, 9–12). Excellent selection of detailed activities and math games that appeal to kids. Created by National Council of Teachers of Mathematics. K–12.

Lesson Plan Index

http://mathstar.nmsu.edu/teacher/math_lesson_index.html

Math Star is a comprehensive listing of math lesson plan and activity Web sites. There are over 100 links organized by category: algebra, applied math, arithmetic, calculus, circumference and area of circles, factoring, fractions, fractals, functions, general math, geometry, graphing, history of math, integers, percent, measurement, number and operations, number theory, patterns, probability, problem solving, process skills, reasoning and proofs, spreadsheets, statistics, and trigonometry. Created by Math Star, New Mexico State University.

Other Features: Click on **Mathematical Resources** to view a list of video and more lesson plan Web sites.

Lesson Plans Page

http://www.lessonplanspage.com/Math.htm

Hundreds of math lesson plans, grouped by grade level, were contributed by teachers from all over. Plenty of cross-curricular lessons and activities can be found in each section. You can also Search This Site to find lessons with keywords or topic titles. Created by EdScope, LLC. K–12.

Other Features: Lesson Plans Page has hundreds of lesson plans and activities on all the other subjects, also grouped by grade level.

Math Central

http://mathcentral.uregina.ca/RR/

A Canadian-based site for math educators to share resources: ideas, lesson plans or any other resource having to do with the teaching of math. Lessons are stored in a database. Scroll to Browse Our Database and click—you will see three grade levels (K–5, 6–9, 10–12). After choosing a grade level, you will see a dozen or so math topics from which to choose lessons. Some lessons are in PDF format (it is noted which ones). You can also search for a specific lesson by typing a keyword—look for Search By Keyword or Author on the main page. Created by SchoolNet and the Canadian Mathematical Society. K–12.

Other Features: At the bottom are additional math resources, such as a math glossary and a link for mostly Canadian education-related sites.

Math Forum @ Drexel

Elementary: http://mathforum.org/teachers/elem/

Middle: http://mathforum.org/teachers/middle/

High: http://mathforum.org/teachers/high/

Hosted by Drexel University (Pennsylvania), this site is not only for math teachers but was built in part by math teachers. To find lessons, click **Individual Lesson Plans** in each of the grade level sections. Each lesson shows the author's name and has a detailed description of the concept. There are also many links to other math education sites in all the areas. The elementary section is divided into two sections for primary and intermediate students. Created by The Math Forum, Drexel University (Pennsylvania). K–12.

Math Readiness Exercises

http://math.usask.ca/emr/menu.html

Mental Arithmetic can be used for assessment of speed in basic skill operations. Contains about a dozen quizzes with ten problems each. Each quiz is timed with sound effects. (That section works better with IBM compatible computers than with Macintosh.) Other topics covered are algebra I and II, geometry, trigonometry, exponential and logarithmic functions, set theory, theory components. Each section has introductory, moderate, and advanced explanations and practice problems. Site created by the Canadian Mathematical Society and hosted by University of Saskatchewan. Gr. 3–12.

Houghton Mifflin Textbook Support

http://www.eduplace.com/math/mhm/

If your math textbooks are published by Houghton Mifflin, then this site is perfect for you, because it complements K–6 math series. Choose your grade level, then the chapter, then click Support Topic. You'll get a summary of the chapter, which is suited for sending home with students if your school does not allow textbooks to go home. Also on that page, you will see lesson plan suggestions for introducing and/or developing the concepts in that chapter. Created by Houghton Mifflin Co. K–12.

Don't Miss: Tips and Tricks has lots of ideas for teachers, such as having students use graph paper to align numbers when adding/subtracting. Also check When Students Ask, because it has answers/explanations to questions that kids commonly ask about math.

Math Fact Café

http://www.mathfactcafe.com/

Easy-to-use site for elementary students to reinforce basic math skills. It contains a worksheet generator, to print and copy for students—you choose the operation (10 different problem types), number of problems, number of digits, font size, etc. The site also provides an answer sheet. Math Fact Cafe also offers preprinted practice worksheets (Fact Sheets by Grade), with the four basic operations. You can choose regular problem solving, missing number, and answer sheet. Students will like the Flashcard section, which is done online. You choose the skill that needs practice. Student types the answer, clicks Enter, then gets immediate feedback if it's correct or wrong. Created by Math Fact Café. Gr. 1-4.

Don't Miss: Relax and Play A Game, which can be used by students or teachers. It's like Chinese checkers, where you click pegs to make them jump over holes.

Math Teaching Ideas

http://www.teachingideas.co.uk/maths/contents.htm

More than 75 math lessons, teaching ideas, games, and worksheets for elementary students, divided into three main categories: general math, number, and shape-space-measurement. Lessons are organized by title, age group, and brief description. Click on the titles to view lessons, which were all contributed by UK classroom teachers. Most pages are printable from your browser, but a few will need *Adobe Acrobat* to view and print. Although the site was developed with UK teachers in mind, all ideas can be used by teachers around the world. Created by Mark Warner, Teaching Ideas, United Kingdom. K–5.

Other Features: Click on the main link for Teaching Ideas and you will see lessons for a variety of subjects.

Mega-Mathematics

http://www.cs.uidaho.edu/~casey931/mega-math/

Numerous conundrums and interactive puzzles involving high-level concepts such as algorithms, finite-abstract, graphs, knot theory, and more. . Some of the titles are: the most colorful math of all (map coloring), degree/diameter problem, building block knots, braids and links, proving you found the minimum, ice cream stands problem, and many more. When you reach a page, click on Activities at the bottom to see games and activities. Created by Nancy Casey, Los Alamos National Laboratory and hosted by University of Idaho. Gr. 10–12 and advanced math students.

Mini-Lessons

K–5: http://yn.la.ca.us/cec/cecmath/math-elem.html

6–8: http://yn.la.ca.us/cec/cecmath/math-interm.html

9–12: http://yn.la.ca.us/cec/cecmath/math-high.html

Over 50 math mini-lessons were developed and contributed by a consortium of experienced teachers. Teachers from all grade levels, who wrote these lessons, gathered from 14 states during 1995 summer workshop at Columbia Education Center. The lessons aren't in any particular order, but each has a descriptive title and grade level designation. When you click on a lesson, they are in text format, which makes them quick to print. It's an excellent place to browse if you're looking for general ideas. You can also find this same set of lessons on Columbia's site: **http://www.col-ed.org/cur/**. Created by Columbia Education Center. K–12.

Mrs. Glosser's Math Goodies

http://www.mathgoodies.com/lessons/

Self-directed, interactive activities on these topics: introduction to statistics, pre-algebra, probability, integers, percentage, number theory, circumstances and area of circles, and perimeter and area of polygons. Click the "x" under Shortcut to view the lesson. Student reads the information on the screen, then enters answers in the boxes. Pages are filled with colorful illustrations as well as "moveable" images: dice that roll, spinners that spin, etc. To print, follow instructions at the top of the puzzle page. Created by Mrs. Glosser's Math Goodies. Gr. 5–8.

Don't Miss: Click **Puzzles** to view crossword puzzles and word search puzzles in all the same math topics as above. Teachers can print these and copy for students. There is also a solution page for each.

N.Y. Times Learning Network

http://www.nytimes.com/learning/teachers/lessons/mathematics.html

Features dozens of math lessons for middle and high school. Each lesson plan has author's name, objectives, procedures, vocabulary, outcomes, extensions, cross-curricular ideas, and links to sites for reference and research. Created by the New York Times in partnership with the Bank Street College of Education. Gr. 6–12.

Other Features: The main site (**http://www.nytimes.com/learning/teachers/lessons/archive.html**) has hundreds of lesson plans on all different subjects, such as American history, civics, current events, economics, fine arts, geography, global history, journalism, media sciences, and technology.

Online Math Activities

http://www.k111.k12.il.us/king/math.htm

Hundreds of links to some of the top interactive math Web sites on the Internet. You could spend hours checking out all the links! Sections are: beginning math, basic facts, factors, fractions, geometry, graphing, integers, logic puzzles, mean/median/mode, metric, measurement, place value, probability, rounding, money, vocabulary and mind bender puzzles. Click the topic you're interested in, and it jumps to that section. Many of the sites need *Macromedia Shockwave* to view (link to download on their site). Created by King Middle Grade School (Illinois). K–12.

Science & Math Initiative (SMILE)

http://www.iit.edu/~smile/mathinde.html

Hundreds of math and science single concept lessons. These lessons may be freely copied and used in a classroom but they remain the copyright property of the author. The mathematics lessons are divided into the following categories: geometry and measurement, patterns and logic, probability and statistics, recreational and creative math, practical and applied math, graphs and visuals, and algebra and trigonometry. SMILE (Science and Mathematics Initiative for Learning Enhancement) is designed enhance the learning of science and math through the use of the phenomenological approach. Created by the Illinois Institute of Technology. K–12.

Scholastic Lesson Plans: Math

http://teacher.scholastic.com/ilp/index.asp?SubjectID=3

Hundreds of lesson plans, activities, reproducibles, games, and Internet hunts for math for all grade levels, organized by two dozen categories including: addition and subtraction, algebraic expressions, area and volume, charts and graphs, consumer math, data analysis, decimals and percents, estimation, fractions, geometry, logical reasoning, measurement, patterns, place value, probability, problem solving, ratio and proportion, symmetry, and time. Once you click a subject, lessons are grouped by K-2, 3-5, and 6-8. Some of the resources are in PDF format. To open these files, you will need Adobe Acrobat Reader software, which is free and can be downloaded by clicking on the Adobe PDF link on the main page. Created by Scholastic Inc. K-8.

Notes:

FRACTIONS & DECIMALS

WebMath

http://www.webmath.com/index2.html

Whether students need help with converting decimals to fractions (and vice versa) or calculating fractions, this is an excellent problem-solving site because it is interactive. A student enters the problem, then clicks the "solve" button to get the answer. First, click on the category: Numbers, Decimals, Number Crunching, Fractions, or Scientific Notation. You will see a quick explanation of what the category means and how to do it, then you will see blank boxes in which you can enter digits to solve the problem. Not only does the solution give the answer, but there is also an explanation of how the answer was derived, just like having a teacher there!

Other Features: There is a pull-down menu at the bottom for about two dozen other interactive problem solvers, from Calculus to Geometry. At the top WebMath offers help in other areas of math: Math for Everyone (finances, unit conversion), K–8 Math (basics, fractions, ratios), Algebra, Plots and Geometry, Trig and Calculus, and Miscellaneous (polynomials, statistics).

Fraction Worksheets

http://www.edhelper.com/fractions.htm

EdHelper has hundreds of fraction worksheets, and every time you click to create a worksheet, you get a new one. Categories are basics of fractions (decimals and fractions), lowest common terms, mixed fractions, basic operations, prime factorization, simplifying algebraic fractions (varying levels of difficulty), fraction puzzles, and more. You must supply an email address to view sheets or get answers. EdHelper does not share your address with anyone else. See Printing Tips if you have trouble printing the worksheets. Created by EdHelper. Gr. 3–12.

Homework Help—Decimals

http://www.math.com/homeworkhelp/HotSubjects_decimals.html

Math.com offers this excellent site to help upper elementary and middle school students with all aspects of decimals: place value, decimal numbers, estimating and rounding, and the four basic operations. Each section shows first glance introduction, in-depth explanation, practice examples, and interactive workout that keeps track of student's answers. Created by Math.com LLC. Gr. 4–8.

Don't Miss: Need a calculator? Click Calculators and Tools to use an online calculators that are as fast as hand-held models. Basic calculator, scientific calculator, and trigonometry calculators—they are all here.

Other Features: Go to the main site (**http://www.math.com**) to view homework help for other math areas: fractions, integers, exponents, inequalities, percents, and square roots.

Homework Help—Fractions

http://www.math.com/homeworkhelp/HotSubjects_fractions.html

Math.com offers this excellent site to help upper elementary and middle school students with all aspects of fractions: basic operations, factors and multiples, least common factor, and least common multiple. Each section shows first glance introduction, in-depth explanation, practice examples, and interactive workout that keeps track of student's answers. Created by Math.com LLC. Gr. 4–8.

Don't Miss: Need a calculator? Click Calculators and Tools to use an online calculators that are as fast as hand-held models. Basic calculator, scientific calculator, and trigonometry calculators—they're all here.

Other Features: Go to the main site (**http://www.math.com**) to view homework help for other math areas: decimals, integers, exponents, inequalities, percents, and square roots.

GEOMETRY & MEASUREMENT

Animal Weigh-In

http://www.bbc.co.uk/education/mathsfile/shockwave/games/animal.html

Students practice converting standard to metric and vice-versa, as they drag weights to a scale that weighs animals. Sounds effects add to the fun. Three levels of difficulty. Requires *Macromedia Shockwave* plug-in. Created by BBC Schools. Gr. 3–6.

Geometry Worksheets

http://www.edhelper.com/geometry.htm

EdHelper has hundreds of geometry worksheets, and every time you click to create a worksheet, you get a new one. Categories are: basics of line segments, polygons, perimeter and area of figures, measuring circles, volume of solid figures, angles, Pythagorean Theorem, trigonometric functions, and more. You must supply an e-mail address to view sheets or get answers. EdHelper does not share your address with anyone else. See Printing Tips if you have trouble printing the worksheets. Created by EdHelper. Gr. 3–12.

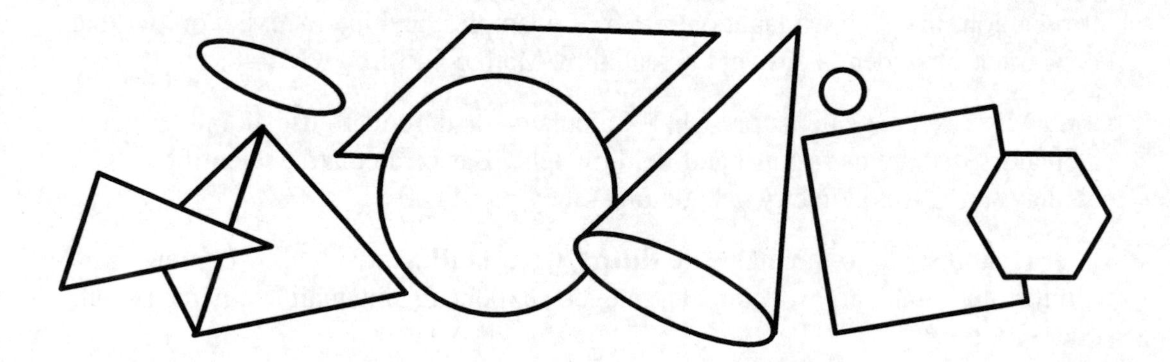

Homework Help—Geometry

http://www.math.com/homeworkhelp/Geometry.html

Geometry students will be happy to find a site that is perfect for explaining all the basic, intermediate, and advanced concepts. Geometry Building Blocks has sections on: vocabulary, coordinates, pairs of lines, and classifying angles. Relations and Sizes has congruence, similar, squares and roots, and Pythagorean Theorem. Polygons features triangles, quadrilaterals, and circles, and there's also a section for three-dimensional figures. Each section has detailed explanations and illustrations, examples, and problems for students to work online, plus a unit quiz at the end. Created by Math.com LLC. Gr. 5–10.

Other Features: The page also includes tables, formulas, and a circle calculator.

Pi Mathematics

http://archive.ncsa.uiuc.edu/edu/RSE/RSEorange/buttons.html

One of few sites devoted to the concept of pi, an irrational number that has been calculated and explored throughout history from biblical times to the present. Click Teacher Resources for classroom implementation ideas, concept map, national education goals, and to see projects from other classrooms. Some of the fun things (look under Information Video) are: memorizing pi to 20 places to the tune of a famous musical drama, calculate your birthday in pi, and try a challenging trivia game. To see formulas and illustrations of how pi works, click on Application. Created by National Center for Supercomputing Applications, University of Illinois-Urbana-Champaign. Gr. 5–12.

ProTeacher Geometry & Measurement

http://www.proteacher.com/100021.shtml

Nearly one hundred links to math lesson plans, worksheets, puzzles and games, and hands-on activities to introduce or reinforce concepts in geometry, measurement, and shapes. The main page has these links: angles, circles, congruency, fractals, lines and rays, pi necklace and songs, tessellation tutorials, pythageorean puzzle, and more. Click Shapes (at the top) to see links for pyramids, plate geometry, platonic solids, polygons, shape mobiles, and tangrams. Click Measurement (at the top) to see links for clock puzzles and worksheets, estimations, money, and the metric system. Created by ProTeacher. K-8.

BASIC SKILLS & COMPUTATION

Basic Worksheets

http://www.edhelper.com/math.htm

EdHelper provides hundreds of worksheets and puzzles for every grade level, every subject: operations, sequences, decimals, integers, fractions, percents, ratios, measurement, geometry, probability algebra, statistics, trigonometry, word problems, and more. You must supply an e-mail address to view or get answer sheets. EdHelper does not share your address with anyone else. Created by EdHelper. K–12.

Computation Worksheets

http://www.rhlschool.com/computation/

RHL School has hundreds of basic skill worksheets, and every time you click to create a worksheet, you get a new one. Categories are addition, subtraction, multiplication, and rounding (nearest ten and hundred). Choice of two- and three-digit problems, with regrouping and without. You must supply an email address to view sheets or get answers. RHL does not share your address with anyone else. Easy to print and photocopy. Created by RHL. Gr. 3–6.

Multiplication

http://www.multiplication.com/

The award-winning teacher who created this site believes that rote memory is the least effective way of teaching multiplication. This system is based on the latest research on how the brain remembers and how students learn—using pictures, rhymes, stories, and activities using the three different teaching modalities. The website contains hundreds of tips, tricks, teaching strategies, classroom games, and interactive websites that are excerpts from a book that can be purchased on this site. Created by Krimsten Publishing. Gr. 2–6.

Math Worksheets

http://www.tut-world.com/

Free colorful worksheets from Tutorial World that you can print and use with students. Look for the chart at the top. Choose your grade level, then click on the color dot under the column for Math. Depending on which level, you will see many worksheet samples for all the operations, measurement, money, ratio, fractions, angles, etc. Besides the dozens of free worksheets, if you register with the site, you will have access to even more. Created by Strategic Thinking Business P/L Singapore. PreK–6.

Other Features: On the main page, you will also see worksheets for English and Science.

Place Value Video

http://www.bbc.co.uk/education/revisewise/maths/number/

(Click on Number System Activity)

Great site for introducing or reinforcing the concept of place value to primary/elementary students. Colorful animated video with sound effects explains practical uses of our numbering system and how place value works. Also has a fact sheet and an online test. Plug-ins are needed to view video; click **Help** for more information. Created by BBC Schools. Gr. K–3.

Other Features: The main page also features fractions, percentages, basic operations, using a calculator, problem solving, and number patterns.

Worksheet Creator

http://www.superkids.com/aweb/tools/math/index.shtml

Many teachers are big believers in daily or weekly math drills for practice of basic skills. You can make your own math drill worksheets for addition, subtraction, multiplication, division, fractions, greater than/less than, and rounding, plus answer sheets. You set the level of difficulty, number of digits, and number of problems on a sheet. Created by Knowledge Share LLC. Gr. 2–8.

Other Features: Super Kids has several online, interactive games, including hangman and logic games. Look under Educational Tools (left sidebar). Vocabulary Builders also has some puzzles and online games.

Notes:

TIME AND MONEY

Money Math

http://www.aaamath.com/mny.html

This site is for anyone, child or adult, who needs extra practice with counting money, making change, converting small coins to larger ones, and adding and subtracting money. Consumer math sections include: calculating tax, discounts and markups, sales commissions, tips, simple interest, shipping costs, etc. Each page has practice areas, where student can enter numbers and click to see the answer. Created by J.C. Banfill, New Mexico. Gr. K–8.

Don't Miss: You can click on a grade level (K–8) and see concepts usually taught at that level. Includes explanations and interactive problem solving.

Other Features: AAA Math's main site (**www.aaamath.com**) offers help on all kinds of math topics, such as basic operations, algebra, equations, exponents, ratios, properties, statistics, and more.

Teaching Time

http://www.teachingtime.co.uk/

The perfect site for teaching time to elementary students! A "whole class clock" (analog and digital) which is large enough for group viewing—teacher or students can click by incremental minutes to move the hands forward or backward. Five interactive games where students must click-and-drag the digital displays to the matching analog clock—these are timed games with five grade levels. With a few clicks, teachers can create millions of different clock face worksheets—students read each clock and write the time underneath. There are also digital-to-analog worksheets, a section to create clock flashcards, blank clock worksheets, and much more. Beautiful Web site, well-organized. No downloading or PDF file reader needed. Created by Mark Cogan, N.B. Primary Games. Gr. 1-5.

ALGEBRA, STATISTICS, CALCULUS

Algebra Worksheets

http://www.edhelper.com/algebra.htm

Basics of equations, inverse operations, solving, word problems, rules of equality, and more. You must supply an e-mail address to view sheets or get answers. EdHelper does not share your address with anyone else. Created by EdHelper LLC.

Eisenhower Clearinghouse

http://www.enc.org/weblinks/lessonplans/math/

Hundreds of math lesson plans are featured in these categories: number and operations (computation, counting, fractions, money), algebra (word problems, equations, graphing, functions), measurement, reasoning and proof, problem solving, patterns, history, geometry (figures, Pythagorean Theorem, pi, ratio and proportion), data analysis and probability, applied math, and advanced math topics (calculus, trigonometry, functions). Each lesson shows the date posted, grade, and a synopsis. Most of the links will redirect your browser to another site that contains that lesson. Created by the Eisenhower National Clearinghouse for Math and Science Education, U.S. Department of Education. K–12.

Other Features: Site also contains hundreds of lessons in the sciences. Click ENC Home to view other sections.

Mrs. Lindquist, Algebra Tutor

http://www.algebratutor.org/

This is a patent-pending, intelligent tutoring system for helping middle and high school students write expressions for algebra word problems. It's a progressive sequence with five levels, beginning with Level One: "one operator problems" up to Level Five: "Three and four operator problems." The student's work is saved at the end of each session. You can also download the software to avoid network delays. The program is free, partially funded by the National Science Foundation. Created by Neil Heffernan, Carnegie Mellon University.

Don't Miss: Click on **What Is Here for Teachers** to see how it works, view some example problems, and ideas for using it in the classroom.

Mean-Median-Mode

http://www.manatee.k12.fl.us/sites/elementary/palmasola/mathlabtutstat1.htm

This colorful tutorial led by Dr. Ufigure shows students, step by step, how to find the range, mean, median, and mode of a set of numbers. Students practice by following the steps online, typing or choosing their answers at each step. Does not require much help from teacher, because text and steps are self-explanatory. Created by Palma Sola Elementary School (Florida). Gr. 4–6.

Statistics Help

http://www.aaamath.com/sta.html

This site covers basic concepts of mean, median, and range, with choice of one-, two- or three-digit numbers. Each page has practice areas, where student can enter numbers and click to see the answer. Created by J.C. Banfill, New Mexico. Gr. 4–8.

Other Features: AAA Math's main site (**www.aaamath.com**) offers help on all kinds of math topics, such as basic operations, algebra, equations, exponents, ratios, properties, and more.

INDIVIDUAL LESSONS

Coloring A Map

http://www.cs.uidaho.edu/~casey931/mega-math/workbk/map/mpbkgd.html

It used to be a puzzle for mathematicians, but now we know that four colors is enough to color any map, without the same colors touching. This colorful site has maps you can print for students—have them try it! Click on the graphics to enlarge and print. There is also plenty of theory and narrative for older students to read and analyze. Created by Nancy Casey. Mega-Mathematics, Los Alamos National Lab. Gr. 3–12.

Roman Numerals

http://www.romannumerals.co.uk/

Roman Numerals were used in ancient Rome, and they still have a specialized use today: in lists, book chapters, watches, and copyright dates, to name a few, so the concept still needs to be taught. This is an excellent site that helps students understand and practice the concept of Roman numerals. The home page shows charts with a basic explanation of which Arabic base number equals which Roman numeral. Click Chart to view the general principles—writing left to right with largest numerals first, etc. Click History to see why they have a long history and also why they're here to stay. List shows a lengthy list of Roman numbers from 1 to 2016. Converter allows online practice, where students type in an Arabic number or Roman numeral, and it gives the corresponding answer. Teaching gives resources and links for educators and parents, and Pictures shows colorful examples of how Roman numerals are used in everyday life. Created by Mark Cullen, United Kingdom. Gr. 3–8.

Notes:

____

____

____

BRAIN TEASERS & FUN STUFF

(Also see Chapter 12, Sites for Student Use)

Brain Benders & Puzzles

http://www.coolmath4kids.com/puzzles.html

As soon as you open this page, you'll be entertained by the bouncy number string that follows the cursor all over the page. Kids will have fun taking the genius quizzes that are packed with trick questions ("Does England have a fourth of July?"). There are about a dozen math puzzles, riddles, and games, beginning with easier ones and ending with harder ones near the bottom. Samples: alphabet soup (riddle), number fun, several triangle puzzles, Karen's age (prime numbers), and corner riddle. Created by Coolmath4Kids. Gr. 1–12.

Brain Binders

http://www.teachnet.com/brainbinders/

Sounds easy until you try it! There are nearly 50 colorful puzzles that you print, cut out, and fold to match the finished picture. The goal is to fold the puzzle into a flat shape with a solid color on each side. The level of difficult increases as you work through the four levels, from two to five folds. Printing the PDF file (*Adobe Acrobat Reader*) works much better than print from the Web page, because you'll have more control over the finished size. TeachNet is temporarily sponsoring this site. The URL may change in the future, but there will most likely be a link to redirect you if/when that happens. Created by TeachNet.com. Gr. 2–8.

Cool Math 4 Kids Games

http://www.coolmath4kids.com/games/

As soon as you open this page, you'll be entertained by the bouncy number string that follows the cursor all over the page. Dozens of online, interactive games are divided into two sections: Thinking Games (that need a math mind) and Mindless Games (get teacher's permission). Some of the thinking games are: memory, lemonade stand, lunar landing, 3D maze, crab race, marbles, word search, concentrate, and lights out. No plug-ins are needed to play these games, but you need to make sure Java is enabled on your browser (look under Tools, Internet Options). A few of the games indicate that one browser (*Netscape* or *Internet Explorer*) works better than the other. Created by Coolmath4Kids. Gr. 2–12.

Fun Math Activities

http://math.rice.edu/~lanius/Lessons/

These online games and activities show students how much fun math can be. If you go to the bottom, there is a list of the games (in text)—run your cursor over the name to see a description and grade level. Some of the lessons are online (using Java) and others are traditional (print and photocopy for students). Title samples: Let's Graph, Who Wants Pizza? (fractions), Let's Count (English and Spanish versions), Cartography, Dueling Pinwheels, Polyamines, Stressed Out (slope as rate of change), The Hot Tub (slope and function). Created by Math Professor Cynthia Lanius, Rice University (Texas). K–12.

Fun Brain Numbers

http://www.funbrain.com/numbers.html

This is a great site to use as a home page for math class, because even older-model computers can handle most of the games. Soccer shootout, math car racing, what's the point, operation order, number cracker, power football, line jumper, and change maker are a few of the titles. Most of the games have varying levels of difficulty—from easy to super brain. Created by The Learning Network Inc. Gr. 2–8.

Don't Miss: Quiz Lab is a free, online database of assessment quizzes in ten subjects. Teachers select quizzes for students to use in the classroom, library, or at home, or you can also create your own. Quizzes are graded by Fun Brain and sent to you by e-mail. The database keeps track of most frequently missed questions, score averages, and other assessment data. You must register to use Quiz Lab.

Other Features: Fun Brain also has games in other subject areas, like Words, Universe, and Culture.

Notes:

Best Sites for Teaching SOCIAL STUDIES

GENERAL

Educator's Reference Desk—Social Studies

http://www.eduref.org/cgi-bin/lessons.cgi/Social_Studies

Educator's Reference Desk took over the popular AskERIC site (Educational Resources Information Center at Syracuse University), which was a federally funded national information system for educators. The section on Social Studies contains nearly 400 lesson plans contributed by classroom teachers across the United States. The major categories are Civics, Current Events, Economics, Geography, History, Holidays, Process Skills, Psychology, Sociology, State and U.S. History, U.S. Government, World History, and others. Site is maintained by the Information Institute of Syracuse. K–12.

Other Features: Educator's Reference Desk has lessons on all the major teaching subjects. Click on the Lesson Plans tab at the top to view subject areas.

A to Z Teacher Stuff

http://www.lessonplanz.com/Lesson_Plans/Social_Studies/

This site offers about 400 lesson plans grouped by grade level. The easy to follow plans are posted by experienced social studies teachers across the United States. The 3–5 and 9–12 sections are the largest, with lessons and activities for Canada, economics, geography, government, and history. Each page you view also has links at the bottom that will take you to other sites for even more social studies fun. Created by A to Z Teacher Stuff. K–12.

Don't Miss: There's a link for a dozen worksheets and printable pages: coloring pages for maps and famous historical figures, geography theme pages, and puzzles and word searches. Some files are *Adobe Acrobat* PDF.

Scholastic Lesson Plans: Social Studies

http://teacher.scholastic.com/ilp/index.asp?SubjectID=2

Hundreds of social studies thematic units, lesson plans, activities, reproducibles, games, and Internet hunts for all grade levels, organized in five major categories: civics and government, early learning (communities and families), geography and time lines, United States, and world, each with a dozen or so subcategories. Civics and government subcategories: citizenship, civil rights, U.S. Constitution and Bill of Rights, current events, elections, and government. U.S. subcategories: African-American history, cities, Civil War, colonial America, heroes and leaders, wars, westward expansion, and women's history. World subcategories: Africa, Asia, customs and cultures, holidays, Holocaust, middle ages, technology and invention, and more. Once you click a subcategory, lessons are grouped by K-2, 3-5, and 6-8. Some of the resources are in PDF format. Created by Scholastic Inc. K-8.

Gateway

http://www.thegateway.org/SubjectBrowse.htm

A huge site with more than 10,000 social studies lessons for all grade levels. On the main page, click Social Studies to jump down to that section to see about two dozen categories: anthropology, criminology, human relations, economics, sociology, U.S. and world history, political systems, and many more. When you click a category, you'll get about a dozen on each page; click next page at the bottom to see more. You will see a title, detailed description, and grade level for each lesson—click on the title to view it. When you click, you will see a database entry for that lesson, so you'll need to click the title once again to see the actual content. Lessons are linked to a variety of sites, and they feature a variety of photos, illustrations, sound files, reference materials, maps, and more. Created by the U.S. Department of Education and the ERIC Clearinghouse. K–12.

Harcourt Textbook Support

http://www.harcourtschool.com/menus/harcourt_brace_social_studies.html

If your classroom uses Harcourt textbooks for social studies, check out this site. Click on the title of your textbook to see additional activities that coincide with the book's themes and chapters. Students can reinforce their learning, play games, study cities and cultures, see museum pieces, use maps, and test their knowledge. Created by Harcourt School Publishers.

Other Features: To see textbook support in other subjects, go to the main site (**www.harcourtschool.com**) and choose from reading, language arts, spelling, math, science, health, and art.

Houghton-Mifflin Resources

http://www.eduplace.com/ss/

Social studies-related resources that include textbook support, an interactive geography game, outline maps, a discussion forum, history update, and current events. You can use this site even if you don't use their textbooks. Current Events features Word Game (puzzles), Online News Quiz, Express Yourself (vote on an issue), and For Teachers, which has lesson plans, teacher guides, and activities on all kinds of topics (by grade level), and Kids Place, which has online games, puzzles, and web word finds, reading scene, and more. History Update has news features on the latest discoveries around the world. Outline Maps has more than 50 high-quality, printable maps from regions all over the world: historical, political, and physical (some are PDF). Created by Houghton Mifflin Co. K–12.

Don't Miss: Project Center has dozens of activities and projects posted by teachers. Sample titles: Great State Mystery, I Have a Dream, Math Risk Game, USA Quilt Project, The Day I Was Born, Memories to Wear, Museum Mania Treasure Hunt, and more.

Lesson Plans

http://www.csun.edu/~hcedu013/eslsp.html

Thousands of lesson plans can be found in this very long list of links to social studies sites. Lessons are in no particular order (except alphabetical) so it's best to use the Find On This Page feature in your browser to locate a specific lesson by keyword. Some links may not be active, but overall, the site is worth a look because of the comprehensive collection covering all social studies subject areas. Some of the topics featured: African folktales, Age of Imperialism, American Revolutionary War, ancient and modern China, Anne Frank, civics jeopardy game, CNN lessons, Constitution, economics, geography's five themes, immigration, and so much more. K–12. Created by Dr. Marty Levine, California State University Northridge.

Lesson Plans Page

http://www.lessonplanspage.com/SS.htm

You choose which grade level, each of which features lessons in the categories of: community and sociology, culture, rain forests, environment, family, geography, government, morals and life skills, plus cross-curricular connections to art, PE, health, and science. Examples of the lesson plans: Amish communities, bartering and trade, Earth Day, Mexican literature, making a state cookie, mountains of the world, recycling, building the continents, making a paper quilt, national park brochure, and hundreds more. You can search for specific lessons with a keyword. Created by EdScope LLC. K–12.

Other Features: Lesson Plans Page has hundreds of lesson plans and activities on all the other subjects, also grouped by grade level.

Mini-Lessons

K–5: http://yn.la.ca.us/cec/cecsst/sst-elem.html

6–8: http://yn.la.ca.us/cec/cecsst/sst-interm.html

9-12: http://yn.la.ca.us/cec/cecsst/sst-high.html

Over 200 social studies mini-lessons were developed and contributed by a consortium of experienced teachers. Teachers from all grade levels, who wrote these lessons, gathered from 14 states during 1995 summer workshop at Columbia Education Center. The lessons aren't in any particular order, but each has a descriptive title and grade level designation. When you click on a lesson, they are in text format, which makes them quick to print. It's an excellent place to browse if you're looking for general ideas. You can also find this same set of lessons on Columbia's site: **http://www.col-ed.org/cur/**.

NCSS's Lessons

http://www.ncss.org/resources/lessons/

About a dozen lessons as they appeared in Social Education, a publication of National Council of the Social Studies. Titles include: using fiction to support history reading, Great Depression and the New Deal, crisis in Bosnia, the new South Africa, Holocaust, women's suffrage, and more. You will need *Adobe Acrobat Reader* to view PDF files. Lessons include maps, photos, illustrations, and references. Created by National Council for the Social Studies. Gr. 9–12.

Nystrom Hands-on Geography

http://www.nystromnet.com/lessonsandtips.html

Scroll down to see three grade-level sections of lessons featuring lots of geographic references. Primary level has basic geography activities, such as locating and coloring states, distinguishing continents from countries, naming the seven continents, and more. Intermediate level has the four key ideas of geography, tracing a route, and discovering America. High school level has the world in spatial terms, regions and landscapes, human systems and language families, and more. Created by Nystrom, publisher of maps, globes, and innovative social studies and geography programs in schools. K–12.

Don't Miss: Be sure to check out the games where students have fun while learning geography: Atlas ABCs, GeoPictionary, Where Am I, and Globe Probe.

N.Y. Times

http://www.nytimes.com/learning/teachers/lessons/socialstudies.html

Features more than 50 social studies lessons for middle and high school. Each lesson plan has author's name, objectives, procedures, vocabulary, outcomes, extensions, cross-curricular ideas, and links to sites for reference and research. Developed by the New York Times Learning Network in partnership with the Bank Street College of Education. Gr. 6–12.

Other Features: The main site (**http://www.nytimes.com/learning/teachers/lessons/archive.html**) has hundreds of lesson plans on all different subjects, such as American history, civics, current events, economics, geography, global history, journalism, media sciences, and technology.

ProTeacher's Social Studies

http://www.proteacher.com/090000.shtml

ProTeacher's popular site features hundreds of games, activities, and lesson plans in these categories: culture (holidays, ancient civilizations, art history, Native Americans, around the world), citizenship (elections, presidents, American government, U.S. Constitution), current events, economics, family and community (homes, farm, neighborhoods), religion and ethics, geography (50 states, map skills), teaching practices (lesson plan collections and materials, standards), and history (measuring time, museums, people, world and U.S. history). Created by ProTeacher. K–12.

Other Features: Message Boards (right sidebar) contain the subject topics for all kinds of current discussions taking place (more than writing topics). Click to go there and read what others have posted—you can jump in and join the discussion too.

Webquests and Worksheets

http://www.edhelper.com/cat263.htm

Almost 400 Web quests and more than 1,700 lesson plans pertain to social studies. Web quests are a fun way for students to learn and answer questions while visiting preselected social studies sites. Categories are by grade level and by subject (anthropology, archaeology, civics, current events, government, history, psychology, state and U.S. history, and world history). An alphabetical list of lesson plan categories indicates how many lessons are found in each—same categories as above. Created by EdHelper. K–12.

Other Features: EdHelper contains thousands of lesson plans and Web quests on all the major and minor teaching subjects.

HISTORY

American History and Culture

http://memory.loc.gov/ammem/ndlpedu/lessons/theme.html

Dozens of quality lessons grouped in themes and units: civics and government (Constitution, Congress, American Indian reservations), literature/poetry (Great Depression, Twain), a new nation (George Washington), expansion and reform (women's rights), Civil War, industrial America (child labor, Great Depression), World War II (immigration, *To Kill a Mockingbird*), and more. Created by Library of Congress. Gr. 4–12.

Other Features: Go to the main site (**http://memory.loc.gov/ammem/ndlpedu/**) and click **Activities** to see several hands-on activities and web puzzles that can be used with the themes or used independently. Port of Entry uses detective skills to uncover the stories of U.S. immigrants.

British & American History

http://www.libraries.rutgers.edu/rul/rr_gateway/research_guides/history/texts_by_subject.shtml

Rutgers University Libraries has an excellent collection of reference and research material, featuring all periods of British and American history. Main subject headings: African-American culture, Civil War, Colonial America and revolution, early modern England, geographical, Holocaust, law/crime/police, medicine/science/technology, medieval, Native American, Victorian era, popular culture, presidents, religion, urban history, women's history, and more. The resources you will find include government documents and records, journal articles and indexes, Internet Web links, writings of famous authors, searchable databases and bibliographies, photographs, maps, and more. Gr. 9–12.

CNN Student News

http://cnnstudentnews.cnn.com/fyi/

This site offers lesson plans and activities in several subject areas, including current world events, geography, government, U.S. history, politics and more. There are plenty of resources and lesson ideas for social studies teachers here. Each lesson includes background information, photos, transcript, discussion questions, Internet resources, and more. The highlight of the main page is Weekly Rewind, which has highlights of the top two or three news stories from the current week. If you subscribe, you and your students can watch the show. Teach from the Show has follow-up lessons and activities. Scrolling down the page, you will find Curriculum Specials. Those are special one-hour, commercial-free programs that are broadcast on CNN (late at night) that can be recorded onto videotape or DVD, then shown in the classroom. Along with each of these programs, there is a full lesson plan with an overview, lesson objectives, national standards, procedures, and student activities and discussion. Excellent site that is updated on a regular basis. Created by Cable News Network. Gr. 6–12.

History Channel

http://www.historychannel.com/classroom/

A&E's History Channel has compiled a nice collection of U.S. and world history lessons and activity guides, mostly for middle and high school. Many of the lessons compliment the television programs, which are provided as a service to teachers. Programs may be videotaped and used in the classroom for up to one year from airdate. Click on Study Guide, and titles are listed alphabetically. Samples include 20th century first ladies, the Alamo, Ancient Rome, Spanish-American War, history of automobiles, biographies of famous leaders, slavery and the Civil War, Great Depression, Salem witch trials, immigration and Ellis Island, and hundreds more. Created by A&E Television Networks. Gr. 6–12.

Don't Miss: Classroom Calendar features a monthly programming calendar for several months in advance, so you can set your video recorder for the commercial-free, hour-long programs.

Lesson Tutor

http://www.lessontutor.com/ltlist.html

Practical lesson plans using topics that interest students (sports, music, movies), while teaching history at the same time. Scroll down about halfway until you see History. Click the checkmarks to see the lesson, which are organized by grade level and by theme: American, Canadian, European, ancient civilizations, and general study. Samples: A first grade theme is "go eat your homework" and features cultural recipes from around the U.S. Fifth grade features several lessons from a Marco Polo unit on exploration. Ninth grade has a unit on Martin Luther King, Jr. Created by Lesson Tutor. Gr. 1-9.

Other Features: There are lots of other subject lesson plans on this site besides History. The more checkmarks you see in a section, the more lessons there are.

Middle Ages

http://www.learner.org/exhibits/middleages/

What was it really like to live in the medieval or Middle Ages? Most people think of knights in shining armor, banquets with wandering minstrels, kings and queens, bishops and monks, and glorious pageantry. Good background information for students as they study this period in history. Sections to click: feudal life, religion, medieval homes, clothing of the various classes, health and hygiene, arts and entertainment, town life and commerce, and links to other Internet resources. Each section contains narrative, with a link at the bottom to read even more on that topic. Site is a partnership between the Annenberg Foundation and Corporation for Public Broadcasting. Gr. 6–12.

Odyssey Online

http://carlos.emory.edu/ODYSSEY/MidElem_Home.html

A beautifully designed site with plenty of graphics and photographs (with small chunks of text) to keep students interested. Odyssey Online is a virtual journey that explores the ancient Near East, Egypt, Greece, Rome, and 19th and 20th century sub-Saharan Africa (separate links for each). When you see a picture of a museum object, click on it to learn more. Site created by three museums (Michael C. Carlos Museum at Emory University, Memorial Art Gallery of the University of Rochester, and Dallas Museum of Art) all contributed photos and information. Also has games and puzzles. Gr. 4–8.

Don't Miss: Scroll down to Teacher Resources and click to get more ideas for elementary and middle school. You'll find ways to integrate art into the social studies curriculum while exploring world culture.

Time Machine

http://www.usmint.gov/kids/

(Click on **Time Machine**)

The U.S. Mint has created an interactive time machine for kids to learn about the people, places, and events that are honored on U.S. coins. Through games, stories, characters, and other activities, the site brings to life both the historical figures that appear on coins and the generations of citizens who used them. About a dozen time periods are featured, including: colonization of America, Lewis and Clark expedition, California gold rush, Civil War, World War I, and the Cold War. After student clicks on a time period, a time machine appears, the doors open, and the student gets to choose era clothing, before beginning the journey. *Macromedia Flash* Player plug-in is needed. Gr. 4–8.

U.S. Congress

http://www.congresslink.org/classroomresources.htm

CongressLink provides information about the U.S. Congress: how it works, its members and leaders, and the public policies it produces. The site hosts lesson plans on several topics (congressional history, its powers and processes, members of Congress, U.S. Constitution). Historical Materials contains documents, photos, and descriptions to supplement lesson plans (various congressional acts, a case history, leadership statements, and state of the union message). Classroom Aids contains tools and reference materials, such as a glossary, historical notes, lesson plan template, scavenger hunt, and Bloom's Taxonomy. Created by Dirksen Congressional Center, a nonprofit, nonpartisan research and educational organization as a service for American history and civics teachers.

Notes:

GEOGRAPHY & MAPS

Blank Outline Maps

http://geography.about.com/cs/blankoutlinemaps/

Extensive collection of links to find blank and outline maps to print out for educational or personal use at home or classroom. Examples of links: outline maps of each country, 50 U.S. states and counties, the entire U.S., continents and world maps, Canadian provinces, and more. Click on the next page at the bottom to see more. When you click most of these links, you'll see an alphabetical list of states/countries/continents. Created and compiled by About.com. K–12.

Other Features: The left sidebar has related links, such as cartography, census/population, country facts, cultural geography, historic maps, time zones, and much more.

---

50 States

http://www.50states.com/

This site is a must for any student needing research for a U.S. state report. Click on a state or U.S. territory and get all the facts: admission to statehood, area codes, famous people, live web cams, climate, current events and news, economy, fast facts, flag, historical landmarks, license plate, motto, nickname, population, and much more. Each factoid has a link (many are local to that state) for more information. Easy site to navigate. Created by Weber Publications (California).

Don't Miss: Fast Facts and Trivia, for quick reference to interesting facts and trivia for each state. Older students could compile these into a trivia game.

GeoBee

http://www.nationalgeographic.com/geobee/

Created by National Geographic, the GeoBee Challenge is an online game to test geography knowledge in a fun way. Each day five new questions are posted. Students can click on a link to see previous days' questions, or click Play The Game to play that day's challenge. Each year thousands of U.S. schools participate in the National Geographic Bee, hosted by Jeopardy's Alex Trebek. Students in grades four through eight are eligible to participate in the national competition, but anyone can play this online game! Gr. 2–6.

Geography

http://school.discovery.com/lessonplans/geog.html

About two dozen quality lessons on Africa, China and Asia, Galapagos, foreign cultures, Atlantis, Australia, U.S. cities, archeology, equator countries, rain forests, floods, and more. Each lesson includes materials needed, procedures, evaluation, vocabulary, adaptations, discussion questions, suggested readings, extensions, and links to other sites. Divided into three grade levels: K–5, 6–8, and 9–12. Created by Discovery.com.

Other Features: Discovery School features lesson plans on many other subjects, mostly math and science.

Geography Ideas

http://www.teachingideas.co.uk/geography/contents.htm

Ten practical lessons and activities pertaining to geography, mostly for elementary. Learning With Postcards has seven activities you can try while building a collection of postcards from around the world. Inflatable Globes is a fun game that teaches names of countries. Beaufort Scale has information and resources pertaining to the scale we use to measure wind speed. Global Pumpkins is a great October activity to teach about latitude and longitude. Click on the titles to view lessons, which were all contributed by UK classroom teachers. Although the site was developed with UK teachers in mind, teachers around the world can use all ideas. Created by Mark Warner, Teaching Ideas, United Kingdom. K–5.

Label the Diagram

http://www.EnchantedLearning.com/label/

About 100 black-and-white diagrams and maps for students to read and label. Each diagram has definitions, vocabulary, student instructions, plus a separate link for the answer sheet. The main page has all the diagrams in alphabetical order or you can click on social studies categories: geography (continent and country maps, compass rose), geology (Earth diagram, soil layers, volcano), and USA (state maps, capital maps, 13 colonies, regions, and a few individual state maps). Created by Enchanted Learning. K–6.

Other Features: Diagrams and maps pertaining to science are also available: biology, solar system, animals, human anatomy, plants, and more.

Latin America

http://ladb.unm.edu/retanet/plans/soc/

Lessons created by secondary teachers, includes a searchable archive of over 70 lesson plans (in English) about Latin America. Categories include: introductory lessons to Latin America, building communities, human rights, Mexico (Aztec conquest, border art, economy and exchange rates, stereotypes), indigenous issues (cultural identity, Indian Wars, Mayan culture, urbanization), African-American issues (Haiti/Jamaica/Brazil, slave women), immigration and migration (borders, ethnic groups in Ecuador/Panama/Argentina), and geography. Created by Latin America Database (online publisher) and University of Mexico. Gr. 9–12.

Map Collection

http://www.lib.utexas.edu/maps/index.html

The collection contains outlined and detailed JPEG and GIF files of outline maps of the entire world. Categories are: Africa, the Americas, Asia, Australia and Pacific, Europe, Middle East, polar regions and oceans, Russia and the former Soviet republics, United States, Asia, and Middle East. Most maps were originally produced by the CIA and available here for easy access. Most files are 200 to 300 K; a few are larger. Some users may have trouble viewing the larger images. FAQ has directions how to save to your hard drive and to print (open *Microsoft Word* and insert as an image). Maps are not copyrighted—they are in the public domain. Created by Perry-Castaneda Library, University of Texas at Austin.

Other Features: The Perry-Castenada Library also has links to other references in their collection, such as databases and indexes to articles, journals and books, news and newspapers, government information, patents, statistics, and research by subject.

National Geographic Maps

http://www.nationalgeographic.com/xpeditions/atlas/

Site features sharp black and white GIF files for printing. Good quality illustrations. Select location from pull-down menu first: world, Africa, Antarctica, Asia, Europe, North America, South America, Oceania, Canada, U.S., and Mexico. Then specify basic or detailed, country borderlines or none. If you want to print the map for classroom use, you'll most likely want a larger "clean" copy, without menus and title information. Underneath the map image, you can choose whether to enlarge it (by clicking Enlarge-GIF), or view it as a PDF file (which fills the size of the paper). You will need *Adobe Acrobat Reader* to view PDF files (link to download is provided). Maps provided by National Geographic.

World CIA Factbook

http://www.cia.gov/cia/publications/mapspub/index.shtml

All the countries of the world with maps, flags, data, and facts for each. At the top where it says Select A Country, click on the arrow to see an alphabetical menu to choose the country you want. Each country profile contains a color detailed map, an introduction summary, geography (map, area, land climate, terrain, elevation, environmental issues), people (population, age, ratios and vital statistics, literacy), government (capital, legal system, constitution), economy (GDP, poverty statistics, unemployment, labor, industries, currency), communication (phone, broadcasting), transporation (land, sea, air), military, and miscellaneous issues (illicit drug use, international disputes). Information was used in the preparation of the CIA World Factbook 2002.

Other Features: On the main page are: a link for Flags of the World, as well as a link to download the entire World Factbook in zip format.

Reference At Your Desk

http://www.archives.gov/research_room/alic/reference_desk/geographical_links.htm l

Reference at Your Desk is a library service of the National Archives and Records Administration, the official library of the U.S. government. It is designed to provide quick access to the type of ready-reference tools needed by archivists, records managers, researchers, students, and educators. The geography room contains links to cartography, flags of the world, fact books, historical maps, geographical maps, trip routers, time information, and famous U.S. explorers. Created by the U.S. National Archives and Records Administration, Wash., D.C. Gr. 9-12.

Notes:

CULTURE & SOCIETY

Australian Studies Network

http://www.austudies.org/info/aushist.html

Australia's unique geographic characteristics and history serve as a useful case study of key global concepts. This site contains a comprehensive list of jumping-off points to explore Australia through other Internet resources, written especially for K–12 teachers and students. Major categories are government, Aboriginal, military, mining, music, science, geography, and a few others. A few of the links are outdated, but overall, this site is worth looking at. Supported by Australian Education Office. K–12.

Holidays Around the World

http://www.theteacherscorner.net/thematicunits/holiday.htm

A comprehensive collection of web links, lesson plan links, and recommended teacher resources and books for teaching about customs, traditions, and holidays around the world. When you click any of the links, a new window opens with that page. Most of the web site links are about Christmas. Scroll down to Lesson Plans & Activities to find lesson ideas, activities, crafts, and projects. The last section is Books, which has links to book sellers so you can purchase various resources to teach about cultural holidays, again mostly focusing on Christmas. Created by The Teachers Corner. K–5.

Global Cultures

http://www.worldtrek.org/odyssey/teachers/lessons.html

The Odyssey provides two kinds of lesson plans—to be used with the Trek (virtual tour of a country or region) or used independently. Egypt, Mali, Zimbabwe, Peru, Guatemala, and Mexico are the featured countries so far—others to be added in the future. Each country's themes and lessons are extremely detailed and would take a month or more to study. Each section contains objectives, suggested readings, activities, discussion guides, maps and illustrations, and assessment tools for each country theme. Sponsored by The Odyssey: World Trek for Science and Education. Gr. 6–12.

Other Features: Past countries and lessons/activities featured by The Odyssey: (**www.worldtrek.org/odyssey/teachers/**).

Native American Links

http://www.ameritech.net/users/macler/nativeamericans.html

Marilee has assembled several hundred links to sites celebrating Native Americans, organized by these topics: clip art, clothing, craft projects, folk art, games and legends, recipes, songs and dances, teaching aids and class projects, and miscellaneous tribe info. Click on the pawprint, not the words, to see the link. There are over 100 links for each tribe category: Algonquin, Apache, Cherokee, Comanche, Haida, Hopi, Iroquois, Navajo, Plains, Pomo, and Sioux. Information is perfect for elementary and middle school age. Created by Marilee Macler. K–8.

Native American Lesson Plans & Activities

http://www.carolhurst.com/subjects/nativeamericans.html

The study of Native American people and their cultures is a challenge because of the stereotypes that exist, not only in the literature, but in our own minds and in those of the children we teach. Carol Hurst created this site because of the stereotypes of Native Americans that persist. She says many studies of Indians leave students convinced that all Indians lived in tepees then, and still do, or that they were all wiped out when white men came to America. You will find suggestions including; a display that children can contribute to, picture book starters (with lots of links and suggestions), the term "Native American," how to begin dispelling stereotypes, suggestions for quality informational books, famous Native Americans, Indian mythology, poetry and prose, novels, and plenty of links to related sites. Created by Carol Hurst's Children's Literature Site. K-8.

OTHER

Distinguished Women of Past and Present

http://www.distinguishedwomen.com/

Comprehensive site contains thousands of biographies of women who contributed to our culture in many different ways—writers, educators, scientists, politicians, civil rights crusaders, artists, and entertainers. Some lived hundreds of years ago and some are living today. Search by Subject has more than 50 subject areas: archaeology, art, biology, broadcasting, education, health and medicine, human rights, invention, law, military, music, photography, and much more. Search by Name allows you to find women alphabetically. Separate section for Black History Month, to search for African-American women by subject area, plus additional links. Created by Danuta Bois. Gr. 4–12.

Other Features: Books About Women has a suggested reading list of biography collections and general books about women in history.

EconEdLink

http://www.econedlink.org/lessons/

About 100 lessons based on economics. Some of the topics featured: Federal Reserve System, monetary policy, gross domestic product, inflation rate, unemployment, international trade, government and fiscal policy, school voucher issue, Napster, car shopping, buying versus renting, income, cash versus credit, many case studies, and other real-world study of economic theory and application. Each lesson also shows the grade level. Created by the National Council on Economic Education. K–12.

Economics Lesson Plans

http://ecedweb.unomaha.edu/ecedweek/lessons.htm

Although these lessons are tied to Nebraska's education standards, they are applicable to any school. Most of these use stories and real-world activities to convey economic concepts. Sample lesson titles: Why We Save Money, The Goat in the Rug (producers and consumers), If You Give a Mouse a Cookie (goods and services), Homer Price's Donut Machine (supply and demand), The Real McCoy (inventions), Why Nations Trade, and many more. K–12. Created by Economics Education Web, University of Nebraska, Omaha.

Explorers

http://www.lessonplansearch.com/Thematic_Units/Social_Studies/Explorers/

More than 30 lessons all about explorers and those who blazed trails of discovery, all grade levels. Lessons are not in any particular order, except alphabetical, and each has a detailed description and link. Sample titles: A Study of the Portola Expedition (1769), Adventure to the New World, Christopher's (Columbus) Crossing, Explorer Go Fish Game, Explorer Interviews, Follow an Explorer Worksheet, Marco Polo Word Search, Mini-Poster for New World Explorers, Parts of a Ship, Printable Spanish Galleon Ship, and What Would You Take to Sea. Created by Lesson Plan Search.

FBI's Ten Most Wanted

http://www.fbi.gov/mostwant/topten/tenlist.htm

Started in 1950 by the (U.S.) Federal Bureau of Investigation in partnership with the news media, the Ten Most Wanted List features individuals who have a lengthy record of serious crimes, are considered to be a particularly dangerous menace to society, and likely to be apprehended with nationwide publicity. There are usually around 500 names on the entire list at any given time, and fewer than ten names have been women. Osama Bin Laden is/was on the list for terrorist attacks against America. The list would be a good reference material for a social studies theme on criminal justice. Gr. 9–12.

History of Money Museum

http://www.moneymuseum.com/

An online museum devoted to the use of money in civilization, from antiquity to the present. Unless your native language is German, click English Version on the main page before entering the virtual museum. (You may run across a few rooms in German only anyway.) As you run the cursor across the museum's foyer, you'll see 27 rooms you can visit on three floors. Each room you visit has virtual tours, slide shows, stories, articles, games and activities, and beautiful illustrations. Unusual, well-designed Web site.

Notes:

Best Sites for Teaching SCIENCE

GENERAL

BrainPOP Science Movies

http://www.brainpop.com/science/seeall.weml

An innovative site featuring original animated movies (starring Tim and his robot friend Moby) on nearly 100 science topics. Each topic contains a 2 to 4 minute animated movie, an interactive quiz, an experiment, a comic strip, a how-to hands on application, a timeline, and a printable activity page. Sample topics include: acids and bases, atomic model, atoms, batteries, buoyancy, compounds and mixtures, crystals, electricity, energy sources, magnetism, mass volume and density, measurement, moon, scientific method, six kingdoms, states of matter, temperature, and many more. Students and/or teachers may watch up to two movies per day (per computer) at no cost, or schools may purchase an annual pass for unlimited access. Students can log in with a screen name and password to keep track of their points from completing activities. Points can be redeemed for prizes. Created by BrainPop. Gr. 3-9.

CNN

http://fyi.cnn.com/fyi/teachers/

Lesson plans in several subject areas including science and technology, from the respected CNN. Click on Science/Technology, and a small window will open showing nearly 100 lesson plans by title; click the one you want and your browser will open to that lesson. Each lesson plan gives an overview, applicable national science standard, materials, time, procedures, assessment, challenge, and extension, with links throughout for additional background. Sample titles: Evolution of Space Exploration, Calculate Wind Chill, Science of Diamonds, Ozone Holes, Mars Exploration, Perseid Meteor Showers, Drilling in Alaska, Viking Mission Revisited, and many more. Created by CNN (Cable News Network). Gr. 9–12.

Don't Miss: Numerous news links on the CNN home page, such as daily news transcripts, upcoming and current TV news specials, and education news stories.

How Stuff Works

http://science.howstuffworks.com/

A fresh, innovative site that explains how everyday things work! Students will find clear, reliable explanations of how everything around us actually works, which they can use in their science research. Browse by category, such as earth science, life science, physical science, engineering, military science, space, and a few others. There are hundreds of featured topics, with easy-to-understand explanations, illustrations, and links to learn more. Sample topics include: quicksand, skyscrapers, aerosol cans, space suits, hurricanes, space shuttles, rip currents, magnetism, cloning, animal camouflage, MRIs, body systems, night vision goggles, wiretapping, gyroscopes, lasers, semiconductors, and many more. To see an alphabetical list of all topics in the science section, click Browse the Science Library (left column). Featured in *Time Magazine's* 50 Best Web Sites of 2002 and 2003.

Other Features: How Stuff Works has a whole lot more than science topics! You can also find explanations for computers, automobiles, money, people, electronics, entertainment, and travel. How Stuff Works is also a popular series of books, an acclaimed children's magazine, and a syndicated newspaper column.

Gateway

http://www.thegateway.org/SubjectBrowse.htm

A huge site with more than 10,000 science lessons for all grade levels. On the main page, click Science to jump down to that section to see about two dozen categories: agriculture, biology, chemistry, metallurgy, oceanography, space, botany, physics, pharmacology, and more. When you click a category, you'll get about a dozen on each page; click next page at the bottom to see more. You will see a title, detailed description, and grade level for each lesson—click on the title to view it. When you click, you will see a database entry for that lesson, so you'll need to click the title once again to see the actual content. Lessons are linked to a variety of sites, and they feature a variety of photos, illustrations, sound files, reference materials, diagrams, and more. Created by the U.S. Department of Education and the ERIC Clearinghouse. K–12.

K-12 Science Topics

http://www.sciquest.com/k12/

Alphabetical science categories, each of which has dozens of lessons, activities, and links. Categories include: agriculture, animals, astronomy, biology, birds, caves, chemistry, dinosaurs, earth science, frogs and bugs, gems and minerals, genetics, human body, inventors, oceans and water, physics, plants, senses, weights and measures, and more. Also includes info on science fairs, experiments, and "ask a scientist." Created by SciQuest, Inc. K–12.

Label the Diagram

http://www.EnchantedLearning.com/label/

About 100 black-and-white diagrams and maps for students to read and label. Each diagram has definitions, vocabulary, student instructions, plus a separate link for answer sheet. The main page has all the diagrams in alphabetical order or you can click on the categories: biology (animals, human anatomy, insects, plant life cycle), animals (mostly anatomy diagrams), planetary (Earth and solar system, moon phases, water cycle, volcano), human anatomy (heart, brain, eye, skin, skeleton), plant anatomy and life cycle, geography (continent and country maps, compass rose). Created by Enchanted Learning. K–6.

Lesson Plans Page

http://www.lessonplanspage.com/Science.htm

You choose which grade level, each of which features hundreds of lessons plus cross-curricular connections to art, language arts, PE, health, and computers. Topic categories for all grades: astronomy, animal biology, atmosphere and weather, human body, insects and spiders, chemistry, ecology, geology and earth science, and physics. You can search for specific lessons with a keyword. Created by EdScope LLC. K–12.

Other Features: Lesson Plans Page has hundreds of lesson plans and activities on all the other subjects, also grouped by grade level.

Lesson Tutor

http://www.lessontutor.com/ltlist.html

Practical lesson plans using topics that interest students (sports, music, movies), while teaching science at the same time. Scroll down about halfway until you see Science. Click the checkmarks to see the lesson, which are organized by grade level and by two themes: biology and general study. Some examples: The first grade theme is bees, featuring worksheets, games, dance, and activities. Third grade biology is the plant life cycle. Fifth grade biology features anatomy lessons on lungs, eyes, and skin, featuring worksheets, diagrams, discussion questions, and links. Created by Lesson Tutor. Gr. 1-6.

Other Features: There are lots of other subject lesson plans on this site besides History. The more checkmarks you see in a section, the more lessons there are.

Magic School Bus

http://www.scholastic.com/magicschoolbus/theme/

This site complements the animated TV science-adventure series (PBS) and the best-selling books by Joanna Cole and Bruce Degen. Titles are keyed so you know if it is a lesson plan, book, video, CD-ROM, or link. Science themes include: animals (ants, bats, butterflies, insects, bees, whales and dolphins, spiders), motion and forces (electricity, floating, gravity, flight, energy, air pressure), physical science (heat, light, sound, volcanoes, water), solar system, life science (cells, circulation, digestion, food chain, germs), and machines (computers, engines). Created by Scholastic, Inc. Gr. 2–4.

Other Features: Click on Teachers (top of page) to see all kinds of resources and special services, such as Teacher Toolkit (world maps, international weather, Web page builder) and online activities and lessons from Scholastic.

Marco Polo

http://marcopolo.worldcom.com/

Many science teachers are crazy about Marco Polo, a program that provides no-cost, standards-based Internet content for the K–12 teacher and classroom, developed by science experts. Online resources include panel-reviewed links to top sites in many disciplines, professionally developed lesson plans, classroom activities, materials to help with daily classroom planning, and search engines. Download the free kit, which has step-by-step directions for implementing the program, an overview of its units, presentation notes for each unit, and reproducible handouts for distribution to students. Created by a partnership between MCI WorldCom and seven educational organizations. K–12.

Mini-Lessons

K–5: http://yn.la.ca.us/cec/cecsci/sci-elem.html

6–8: http://yn.la.ca.us/cec/cecsci/sci-interm.html

9-12: http://yn.la.ca.us/cec/cecsci/sci-high.html

Over 200 science mini-lessons and experiments/activities were developed and contributed by a consortium of experienced teachers. Teachers from all grade levels, who wrote these lessons, gathered from 14 states during 1995 summer workshop at Columbia Education Center. The lessons aren't in any particular order, but each has a descriptive title and grade level designation. When you click on a lesson, they are in text format, which makes them quick to print. It's an excellent place to browse if you're looking for general ideas. Kids will love all the hands-on activities which are vital to making science enjoyable. You can also find this same set of lessons on Columbia's site: **http://www.col-ed.org/cur/**.

National Science Resources Center

http://www.si.edu/nsrc/pubs/stc/lessons/overv.htm

Science and Technology for Children is an innovative hands-on science program for children that develops their critical-thinking and problem-solving skills. Although the full program of 24 units is available for purchase, the site features an excellent sample selection of 20 detailed lesson plans and hands-on activities in life, earth, and physical sciences. Sample titles: Life Cycle of Butterflies, Microworlds, Soils, Rocks and Minerals, Ecosystems, Measuring Time, Change, Electric Circuits, Magnets and Motors, Motion and Design, Solids and Liquids, and Weather. From the National Science Resources Center. Gr. 1-6.

National Science Standards

http://www.nap.edu/books/0309053269/html/

The National Science Education Standards provide criteria toward a vision of a unified science education for U.S. school-age children. The criteria describe what teachers of science at all grade levels should understand and be able to do. At the heart of the standards is that science teachers must plan an inquiry-based science program for students, which means that students are discovering concepts and understandings for themselves, rather than the teacher "handing it" to them. The standards are available for review in HTML (Web browser) format or *Adobe Acrobat* PDF format. Text copyrighted by National Academy Press.

National Wildlife Federation

http://www.nwf.org/education/

Offers workshops and resources for educators. Some are fee-based, but there are many free resources and ideas too. Two sections: school programs (school yard habitat, educator workshops and resources, ecology, and National Wildlife Week activities) and community programs (backyard habitat program, environment kids club, teen adventure, and leadership program) are the main categories. Created by National Wildlife Federation. K–12.

Don't Miss: Kids Zone has games (riddles, quizzes, mix and match), cool tours, kids survey, outdoor stuff, and reader's corner. Gr. K–3.

Requires *Macromedia ShockWave* plug-in (link to download). K–12.

NOVA

http://www.pbs.org/wgbh/nova/teachers/

This award-winning, science television program from the Public Broadcasting System has a section especially for teachers. Classroom resources include: program contents, printable activities, online activities, teacher's ideas, and Web site overviews. You can also search the database, by keyword or program title, for program information, lessons, and online activities. When you click **Program Title**, you'll see an alphabetical list of topics. Samples include: The Best of Loch Ness, Mad Cow Disease, Cracking the Code of Life, Jet Streams, Electric Heart, Faster Than Sound, Hitler, Ice Mummies, Lightning, The Five Senses, and dozens more. Created by WGBH/Boston.

Don't Miss: Click **Teachers Guide** to subscribe to the semiannual NOVA Teacher's Guide (print version). Complete the online order form and submit.

N.Y. Times

http://www.nytimes.com/learning/teachers/lessons/science.html

Features about 50 science lessons for middle and high school. Each lesson plan has author's name, objectives, procedures, vocabulary, outcomes, extensions, cross-curricular ideas, and links to sites for reference and research. Sample titles: Weathering the Odds, Surrounded by Radiation, Mummies Unwrapped, Whale of a Problem, On the Attack (overfishing and shark behavior), Is All Fair in Germs and War?, and Spacing Out. Created by the New York Times Learning Network in partnership with the Bank Street College of Education. Gr. 6–12.

Other Features: The main site (**http://www.nytimes.com/learning/teachers/lessons/archive.html**) has hundreds of lesson plans on all different subjects, such as American history, economics, fine arts, geography, global history, journalism, media sciences, and technology.

ProTeacher's Science

http://www.proteacher.com/110000.shtml

ProTeacher's popular site features hundreds of games, activities, and lesson plans in these categories: doing science (experiments, scientists, museums, and links to other hands-on sites), earth science (dinosaurs, geology, water, weather, geography, space), physical science (chemistry, electricity, simple machines, light, magnets, space), health and medicine (heredity, health, bones and skeletal, brain and nervous, heart and circulatory), invention and technology (flight, computer science, architecture, transportation), science news, and teaching practices. Created by ProTeacher. K–12.

Other Features: Message Boards (right sidebar) contain the subject topics for all kinds of current discussions taking place (more than writing topics). Click to go there and read what others have posted—you can jump in and join the discussion too.

Science NetLinks (Marco Polo)

http://www.sciencenetlinks.com/matrix.cfm

This is one site all science educators will want to bookmark! At the heart of Science NetLinks are hundreds of lesson plans that incorporate reviewed Internet resources, and can be selected according to specific benchmarks and grade ranges. Each lesson is tied to at least one learning goal and uses research-based instructional strategies that support student learning. The lessons are written for the teacher, but include student-ready materials (reproducibles) or e-sheets (online interactive worksheets). Lessons are sorted according to grade level by default. To sort the lessons by lesson title or benchmark, click on the corresponding header. Science NetLinks is part of the MarcoPolo Education Foundation.

Science Videos

http://www.bbc.co.uk/education/revisewise/science/

Colorful animated videos with sound effects explain several basic science concepts. Click **Activity** in each section. Living Things section features life processes, food chain, animal teeth, animal bones, and plants. Materials section has grouping and classifying, thermal and electrical conduction, states of matter, and changing materials. Physical Processes has videos on electricity, magnetism, gravity, light, and sound. Each section also has a fact sheet and online test. Plug-ins are needed to view video; click Help for more information. Created by BBC Schools. Gr. K–4.

Scholastic Lesson Plans

http://teacher.scholastic.com/ilp/index.asp?SubjectID=4

This Scholastic site offers hundreds of lesson plans, activities, reproducibles, games, and thematic units, divided into four categories: earth and space science, life science, physical science, and the scientific process. After you click the category you want, you will see more details that tell what grade level for which it is appropriate. Sample subcategories include force and motion, electricity, energy, heat and light, magnetism, atmosphere, erosion, seasons, solar system, weather, water cycle, cells, evolution, fossils and dinosaurs, human body, insects, marine life, classifying, experiments, and careers in science. Created by Scholastic Inc. K–8.

Teachnet Science

http://www.teachnet.com/lesson/science/

Teachnet contains about 40 science lessons divided by categories: general, biology, Earth, physics, technology, dinosaurs, scientific method, space and time, and weather. Some sections have more lessons than others. Started in 1995 by a husband/wife team in Kansas, Teachnet is well-organized and easy to navigate.

Other Features: Teachnet features lessons for all subjects, all grades. Check the sidebar under Lesson Plans.

Virtual Field Trips

http://www.surfaquarium.com/it/vft.htm

Virtual Field Trips include over 100 famous places, cities, and historic sites for students to visit without ever leaving the classroom! Select a place to visit that has a clear connection to something you are studying. The site reminds teachers that since you are taking your class outside the four walls of your classroom, albeit via cyberspace, you must provide just as much supervision and structure as you would on a traditional field trip. Other guidelines: Teach a preparatory lesson before the trip, preview the site and know the content, provide step-by-step tasks for students to accomplish, make sure the trip is in your lesson plan, place a time limit, have a follow-up lesson after the trip, and assess the student task that was completed. Examples of sites: Acropolis, biomes, Civil War, Iceland, Grand Canyon, Great Depression, human heart, solar system, frog dissection, Normandy 1944, Oregon Trail, World War I or II, Estruscans, microbes, White House, and many more. Created by Innovative Teaching. Gr. 4–12.

Other Features: Click Theory Community (top) to view comprehensive information and resources for multiple intelligence as well as see about a dozen unit-based lessons designed for multiple intelligences. In addition, the pull-down menu (top left) has many other resources for all subject areas.

EARTH SCIENCE

Desert USA

http://www.desertusa.com/

One of the most comprehensive desert sites on the Internet with lots of photos and facts. Desert Life features the environment of deserts around the world, minerals and geology, wildlife, plants and flowers, people and culture. Click **Index** to see deserts and state parks, animals, plants, rocks, cultures, and Southwestern states listed in separate indexes for easy location. Maps contains visitor guides and maps for the most popular desert parks. QuickTime VR (virtual reality) shows photos in 360 degrees of the nation's most beautiful desert parks (click and drag photo). Excellent for classroom use. Created by Digital West Media, Inc. Gr. 1-8.

Other Features: Each month there is an animal, plant, and culture is featured for that month. Subscribe to a monthly newsletter with info on hiking and camping, reviews on state parks, and upcoming events in the Southwest.

Earth Science Theme Units

http://www.edhelper.com/Science.htm

A nice collection of theme units pertaining to earth science (and a few physical science topics too) in these categories: Animals and Biomes, Earth's Crust, Earth's Land, Matter, Plants, Rocks and Minerals, Solar System, Volcanoes, and Weather. Click on a category and you'll find dozens of reading comprehension activities, math problems and activities, vocabulary, puzzles and mazes, and printable worksheets. Created by EdHelper. Gr. 2-6.

Fun Science Resources for Students

http://www.reachoutmichigan.org/resources.html

A colorful, student-friendly collection of links to other sites on all kinds of earth science topics. Links are organized by these categories: Animal Kingdom, Creepy Crawlies, Extinct Animals, Flying Friends, Fungus Among Us, Inside Your Body, Lost In Space, Seriously Science, Today's Forecast, The World Around Us, And Wolves/Tigers/Bears. This excellent collection includes lots of pictures, sound files, activities, and background information—everything a student needs to research or reading just for fun. Site also includes quick links to NASA for Kids and Teens. Compiled by Reach Out! Michigan, a nonprofit community outreach and education program hosted by University of Michigan. Gr. 3-8.

JASON Project

http://www.jasonproject.org/

Founded by Dr. Robert Ballard, who discovered the submerged Titanic wreckage, this award-winning program offers students and teachers a comprehensive, multimedia approach in earth science that covers all other subjects. Content is delivered through a print curriculum, videos, fully interactive Internet programming, and live satellite broadcasts. Past topics included rain forests, oceans, polar regions, and volcanoes. Program is available for individual or school purchase. Created by JASON Foundation for Education. Gr. 4–9.

NASA Education Center

http://spacescience.nasa.gov/education/educators/

The folks at NASA firmly believe mathematics, science, and technology education is critical to the future of our nation. Teacher resources include an annotated list of lesson plans and activities from university and government sites. Nice photo images of planets and space missions, past and present, are all here. Created by National Aeronautic Space Administration. K–12.

Don't Miss: SpaceKids activities include sending student names on the next Mars mission, sun's peak of an 11-year cycle, amateur astronomy, and education page with contests, games, and quizzes.

NASA Coloring Pages

http://kids.msfc.nasa.gov/puzzles/coloring/

Forty coloring pages: space shuttles, satellites, aircraft, space station, rockets and blast off stages, astronauts, and the solar system. Easy-to-print line drawings, no plug-in needed. Created by National Aeronautic Space Administration. K–4.

The Nine Planets: A Multimedia Tour

http://seds.lpl.arizona.edu/nineplanets/nineplanets/nineplanets.html

Beautiful photo images, facts, glossary, and links to additional resources are the strengths of this well-organized site. Many pages have sound or movie files. Click on a small photo to see it expand and fill the screen. Contents: intro, what's new, express tour, overview of solar system (planet and their moons), sun, other solar systems, seeing the solar system, space craft, how you can help, glossary, and additional links. Excellent site for any classroom studying space. Created by William A. Arnett, University of Arizona. K–12.

Paper Models and Animations

http://interactive2.usgs.gov/learningweb/teachers/paper_models.htm

Three-dimensional, cut-and-paste paper models (mostly black and white) and computer animations illustrating geologic processes and other geologic phenomena. Topics available: Antarctic ice sheet, sand dunes, Karst topography model (limestone cave), Chicxulub (dinosaur extinction process), crinoids, ocean trenches, Arctic Delta, sea floor animation and model, paper fossils, tectonic globe (glued onto a tennis ball), landslide effects, earthquake effects animation and model, map projections, volcano, types of Earth faults, and others. Although a few are PDF files or Web versions, most are for Macintosh as hypercard documents. They are also available for purchase (disk or paper) for small fee. Created by U.S. Geological Survey. Gr. 9–12.

3D Planetary Orbits

http://liftoff.msfc.nasa.gov/academy/space/solarsystem/solarsystemjava.html

Click and drag your mouse around on the photo to view three-dimensional orbits and positions of all the planets. You can also zoom in and out using certain keys. Need to have adequate RAM (memory) to view this site. Created by National Aeronautic Space Administration, Marshall Space Flight Center.

Other Features: More links (sidebar) to other solar system sites, some by NASA.

Solar System Introduction

http://www.abcteach.com/SolarSystem/SolarSystemTOC.htm

Over a dozen links to various charts, graphs, report forms, and activities for primary students. Solar system distances chart, solar system graph, moon phase chart, astronomer report, planet report form, did you know cards, word scramble, poetry form, story planner, booklet covers, crossword puzzle, shape book pages, constellation project, KWL chart, and more. Created by ABC Teach. K–3.

Earth Science Gems

http://www.sciencegems.com/earth.html

Over 11,000 Internet resources. A comprehensive site full of links to other sites on nearly every earth science subject imaginable created by a university professor. Some links have lesson plans; others are for background and research. Part I: measurement, science investigation, earth in space, solar system, astronomy. Part II: atmosphere and weather, land and geology, oceans, water, and resources. Developed by physics Prof. Frank Potter, Univ. of California-Irvine. K–12+.

Other Features: A short list of recommended links: virtual observatory, views of the solar system, clickable world maps, satellite passes, and others.

Notes:

LIFE SCIENCE

Back Porch Activities

http://www.agr.state.nc.us/markets/kidstuff/backporch/book.htm

Learn about North Carolina commodities with puzzles, word searches, mazes and coloring pages. The Back Porch was the name of an exhibit at a North Carolina State Fair, and the pages were part of an activity book. Sample page titles: Cattlemen Color-by-Numbers, Pork Pyramid, Honeybee Crossword, Hidden Peanuts, Potato Plant Parts, Pine Needle Fill-in-the-Blanks, Pecan Maze, Christmas Tree Code, Scrambled Vegetables, Chef Tomato, and lots of coloring pages. Created by the North Carolina Department of Agriculture. K–4.

Life Science Lessons

http://www.middleschoolscience.com/life.htm

Aimed at middle school science teachers, this is a top notch site compiled by a retired educator. It's a very easy site to peruse; topic categories are listed on the left, and the name of the lesson or worksheet is on the right. Click the name to view it. Categories included are Scientific Method, Lab Notebook, Cells, Genetics, Microscope, Classification, Viruses, Bacteria, Protists, Fungus, Animals, Sponges, Cnidarians, Worms, Mollusks, Arthropods, Insects, Other Invertebrates, Biomes, Evolution, and Plants. Some links are other sites (which open in a new window), and others are worksheets or activities. Compiled by E. S. Belasic. Gr. 6–8.

Don't Miss: At the top, click Lab Notebook to see a comprehensive list of the author's lab observation sheets for all kinds of experiments, games, and activities—enough to fill a school year. You will need *Adobe Reader* to view the PDF files; some are HTML pages. The author recommends teachers plan out the entire year and have all the needed lab sheets in a binder that stays in the classroom.

Eisenhower Clearinghouse

http://www.enc.org/weblinks/lessonplans/science/

Hundreds of physical science lesson plans are featured here, along with all the other branches of science. Click on **Life Science** to see categories: chemistry, atomic theory, chemical properties and reactions, electricity, energy, forces, gravity, heat, light, magnetism, matter, motion, Newton's Laws, nuclear chemistry, optics, organic chemistry, periodic table, physical properties, simple machines, and sound. Each lesson shows the date posted, grade, and a synopsis. Most of the links will redirect your browser to another site that contains that lesson. Created by the Eisenhower National Clearinghouse for Math and Science Education, U.S. Department of Education. K–12.

Other Features: Process Skills contains lessons that emphasize critical thinking, problem solving, observation, measurement, data collection, and classification.

Insect Resources

http://www.uky.edu/Agriculture/Entomology/ythfacts/resourc/resourc.htm

Created by Department of Entomology, University of Kentucky

Life Science Gems

http://www.sciencegems.com/life.html

Over 11,000 Internet resources. A comprehensive site full of links to other sites on nearly every life science subject imaginable created by a university professor. Some links have lesson plans; others are for background and research. Part I: measurement, science investigation, origins and molecules, cells, molecular genetics, evolution, ecology. Part II: viruses, plants, animals, and human biology. Created by physics Prof. Frank Potter, University of California–Irvine. K–12+.

Other Features: A short list of recommended links: sheep cloning, dinosaur exhibit, whales, interactive frog dissection, endangered species, and molecular genetics.

Virtual Frog Dissection

http://www-itg.lbl.gov/vfrog/

No more queasy students or formaldehyde smell—now you can dissect a virtual frog named Fluffy in this award-winning site from Berkeley. Before using the program with students, teachers will want to spend time with the tutorial to become familiar with how to rotate the frog, remove and replace organs, see the organ's name and function, and make a movie (digital recording) of the dissection. The program is available in multiple languages, but the tutorial is in English only. Created by Lawrence Berkeley National Laboratory, University of California and U.S. Department of Energy. Gr. 6–9.

Don't Miss: Virtual Frog Builder Game tests your knowledge of the 3D spatial relationships between the organs in the frog. It's harder than it sounds!

Notes:

PHYSICAL SCIENCE

Discovery School

http://school.discovery.com/lessonplans/physci.html

Mostly for middle and high school, Discovery School offers some high-quality lessons in the physical sciences. Middle school samples: Antarctica, constructing earthquake proof buildings, electromagnetic spectrum, gravity, forces and motion, famous bridges, rocket science, sight and light, stormy weather, time, stable and unstable structures, and reading satellite images. Gr. 9–12 samples: animating motion, electricity, flight, magnetism, metals and nonmetals, savage sun, stargazers, chaos game, color spectrum, and understanding uncertainty. Each lesson includes materials needed, procedures, evaluation, vocabulary, adaptations, discussion questions, suggested readings, extensions, and links to other sites. Created by Discovery.com. Gr. 6–12.

Eisenhower Clearinghouse

http://www.enc.org/weblinks/lessonplans/science/

Hundreds of physical science lesson plans are featured here, along with all the other branches of science. Click on Physical Science to see categories: adaptations, anatomy, animals, behavior, biochemistry, cells, conservation, ecosystems, energy cycle, environment, evolution, genetics, health, human biology, insects, life cycle, plants, population, and reproduction. Each lesson shows the date posted, grade, and a synopsis. Most of the links will redirect your browser to another site that contains that lesson. Created by the Eisenhower National Clearinghouse for Math and Science Education, U.S. Department of Education. K–12.

Other Features: Process Skills contains lessons that emphasize critical thinking, problem solving, observation, measurement, data collection, and classification.

GLOBE Program

http://www.globe.gov/

This hands-on, international environmental program links students, teachers, and the scientific research community, involving student data collection and observation of our environment. Teachers must be trained and certified to participate, so that student data collection follows scientific protocol (click **Teacher's Workshops**). Water, air, and soil are just a few of the environmental measures that are investigated. Students submit their data on the Internet, to be used by scientists to see how the planet's resources are changing. Site text is available in multiple languages. Created by National Oceanic & Atmospheric Administration (NOAA) and three other government agencies. K–12.

Don't Miss: The online GLOBE Teacher's Guide is available in its entirety in *Adobe Acrobat* PDF format. Click **Teacher's Guide**.

Hands On Activities

http://www.reachoutmichigan.org/funexperiments/agesubject/physicalsciences.html

Students learn scientific concepts best when they can touch, investigate, and experiment. Over 200 experiments, divided by grade level (early elementary, later elementary, middle, high). Sample titles for elementary: Gliders, How Does Soap Work?, Shoebox Guitar, Paper Clip Sailing, Pizza Box Solar Oven, Musical Sounds, Balloons, Dancing Penny, Fish Tank Optics, Engineering Toothpaste, Nickel Karate, and Peanut Power. Sample titles for middle/high: Bernouilli Cans, Dew and Frost, Balloon Vacuum, How Do Clocks Keep Time, Liquid Bottle Rocket, Locks and Dams, Making a Wind Sock, Wet Compass Experiment, Optical Illusions, Hollywood Stunts, and Frisbee Physics. Created by the Southeastern Michigan Math-Science Learning Coalition. K–12.

Periodic Table of Elements

http://www.webelements.com/

Colorful site featuring the periodic table. Click on any element to see all its attributes: name, symbol, atomic number and weight, group name, color, and description. You will also find numerous links for each element containing its properties (electronic, physical, nuclear), its structure, and where it's found.

Created by Mark Winter, University of Sheffield. Gr. 9–12.

Physical Science Gems

http://www.sciencegems.com/physical.html

Over 11,000 Internet resources. A comprehensive site full of links to other sites on nearly every physical science subject imaginable created by a university professor. Some links have lesson plans; others are for background and research. Part I: measurement, science investigation, mathematical methods, energy, linear momentum, motion, solids and fluids, vibrations. Part II: electricity and magnetism, light, relativity, atomic physics. Part III: chemistry, chemical reactions, organic chemistry, biochemistry, biosphere. Created by physics Prof. Frank Potter, Univ. of California—Irvine. K–12+.

Notes:

Best Sites for Teaching TECHNOLOGY

GENERAL

Building a Web Site

http://teachers.teach-nology.com/themes/comp/sitebuild/

Great site for experienced Internet teachers who want to assist students with Web page development. This site contains more than 50 links, organized by categories: animated GIFs (images), resource sites, backgrounds, rubrics for evaluation, interactive sites for students, Web designer beginner's tutorials, lesson plans, Web graphic tutorials, places to make free Web pages, and Web quests. Unfortunately, many of these links have annoying pop-up ads and blinking ads, which help pay for the site's free resources. Created by Teachnology, Inc. K–12.

Busy Teachers' Website

http://www.ceismc.gatech.edu/busyt/homepg.html

Site is designed to provide teachers with direct source materials, lesson plans, and classroom activities with a minimum of site-to-site linking, especially for teachers who are learning to use the Internet. Hundreds of high-quality sites organized by 20+ subjects: archaeology, art, astronomy, biology, chemistry, computer technology, English, geology, history, interactive web projects, math, physics, social studies, and more. Also a separate section for Elementary School, with sites that are geared to K–5 teachers and students. Created by C. Cole and A. Kerr, Georgia Institute of Technology. K–12.

Computer and Internet Lessons

http://lessonplancentral.com/lessons/Computers_and_Internet/Computer_Science/

This site offers hundreds of wonderful lesson plans and activities—covering all subject areas and all grade levels—that involve computer use and Internet resources. First, choose a category: Clipart, Collaborative Projects, Computer Science, Data Sets, Internet Safety, Lesson Plans, Multimedia, Online Projects, Scavenger Hunts, Shareware, Technology Integration, Tutorials, Webquests, and more. The Lesson Plans section has about 70 lessons, from Missing Tooth Mystery to Fictional Genres, and there are a dozen lessons just on *Excel.* Scavenger Hunt has about 20 hunts on topics such as animals, Anne Frank, Egypt, holidays, and dinosaurs. Clipart has thousands of images…it would take hours to see every page.

Other Features: There are thousands of lessons plans on other subject areas besides Computers and Internet. Choose from Art, Science, Geography, Social Studies, and Math. Look for the links at the top.

BrainPOP Technology Movies

http://www.brainpop.com/tech/seeall.weml

An innovative site featuring original animated movies (starring Tim and his robot friend Moby) on more than 30 tech topics. Each topic contains a 2 to 4 minute animated movie, an interactive quiz, an experiment, a comic strip, a how-to hands-on application, a timeline, and a printable activity page. Sample topics include mp3 files, airbags, binary code, cell phones, CDs, parts of computers, fax machines, fireworks, flight, fuel cells, GPS, inclined plane, laser, radio, robots, submarines, television, and more. Students and/or teachers may watch up to two movies per day (per computer) at no cost, or schools may purchase an annual pass for unlimited access. Students can log in with a screen name and password to keep track of their points from completing activities. Points can be redeemed for prizes. Created by BrainPop. Gr. 3–9.

Discovery

http://school.discovery.com/lessonplans/tech.html

Over two dozen lessons, all age levels, of technology and computer-based lesson plans. K–5 sample titles: All About Computers, Inventors and Inventions, and Technology at Work. Gr. 6–8 samples (the largest section): Bridges, Clone Age, Extraterrestials, Origins, Robots, Stable and Unstable Structures, and Understanding Computing. Gr. 9–12 samples: Cyberspace, The Real Bionic Man, Space Travel, Television, and War of the Worlds. Each lesson includes materials needed, procedures, evaluation, vocabulary, adaptations, discussion questions, suggested readings, extensions, and links to other sites. Created by Discovery.com. K–12.

Other Features: Discovery School features lesson plans on many other subjects, mostly math and science. Look at the left sidebar to navigate other sections of the site. Be sure to check out Teacher Tools, which has an excellent puzzle maker.

EdHelper on Technology

http://www.edhelper.com/cat295.htm

More than 50 lesson plan links (mostly from Microsoft Encarta Schoolhouse) for all grade levels, plus over a dozen web quests. Samples of lesson titles: A World of Biodiversity, Global Understanding Through E-mail Exchange, Create a Colonial Newspaper, How We Communicate, Design a Theme Park, How Disasters Occur, UFOs and Mystery Beasts, State Travel Brochure, and The Limits of Free Speech. Each lesson title gives a description, and you click on it to see the full lesson plus grade level. Created by EdHelper. Gr. 3–12.

Other Features: EdHelper (**www.edhelper.com**) has thousands of worksheets for math, spelling, vocabulary, algebra, plus worksheet generators. Quick and easy to print and reproduce for student use.

Technology Lesson Plans

http://www.kent.k12.wa.us/curriculum/tech/lessons/

More than 65 lessons that use technology to conduct research, gather information on a topic, create web pages, create pictures and documents, write stories, and learn about famous people. Developed by experienced elementary teachers in Washington, these are "tried and true" lessons that have been successfully used in the classroom. Click on the lesson to view details such as purpose, materials needed, step-by-step procedures, web links, and assessment. Lessons are divided by grade level. Sample lesson titles for K-3: let it snow, zoo search, I went walking, are you eating right, pet survey, tall tale slide show, and online book report. Sample lesson titles for 4-8: region reports, totems, digital camera poetry, letters home from Oregon Trail, simple machine animation, body systems, and elevator art project. Created by teachers in the Kent School District, Washington. K-6.

Five Easy Technology Lessons

http://www.education-world.com/a_lesson/lesson285.shtml

If you been hesitating to introduce technology into your classroom because you think your students know more than you do, then here's a helpful article from *Education World.* Today's the day to conquer that fear with some easy lessons that even a newbie (someone who is not comfortable with technology) can teach and learn from. These are lessons for teaching—and learning—about using technology in the classroom. The five lessons are titled: What's Inside my Computer (drawing activity), Mousing Around (scavenger hunt using a mouse), Word Processing can be Lots of Font (a fun poem activity), Finding Your Way in the World Wide Web (grouping activity about databases), and There's a Monster in my Email (collaborative email project). Click on the title of the lesson to see details.

Don't Miss: Scroll down below the article to see an excellent list of resources for teaching technology. Some of the topics listed here (click to see the link) are: creating classroom *PowerPoint* presentations, middle school math lessons, using digital cameras in the classroom, computer skills lesson plans, K-12 technology lessons, best practices of technology integration, and collaborative projects.

Internet-Based Lesson Links (Math & Science)

http://www.col-ed.org/smcnws/msres/curriculum.html

Often teachers don't have specific lessons in mind when searching the Internet. Sometimes they are open to new ideas they see, which lends itself to perusing this site. There are more than 40 links to Internet-based sites with hundreds of lesson plans and activities in math and science. Both subjects are divided into elementary and secondary links. Some of the concepts you will find include: applying math to real world situations, experimenting with math ideas, interactive geometry, simulations like Internet pizza server, balance the national budget, interactive science games and quizzes, virtual earthquake lab, online frog dissection, and many more. Created by Columbia Education Center.

Lesson Plans Page

http://www.lessonplanspage.com/CI.htm

Hundreds of computer and Internet lesson plans. Each plan has the author's name, grade level, objectives, materials needed, preparation and introduction, procedures and activities, evaluation, and extensions. You choose which grade level, each of which features dozens of lesson plans in the categories of: applications (software), general e-mail, Internet, technical, typing, plus cross-curricular connections in art, language arts, math, science, and social studies. Created by EdScope LLC. K–12.

Other Features: Lesson Plans Page has hundreds of lesson plans and activities on all the other subjects, also grouped by grade level. You can also join a mailing list and receive an online newsletter with lots of teaching tips, new lesson plans added to the site, and networking ideas from other teachers.

LessonPlanz Technology

http://LessonPlanz.com/Lesson_Plans/Computers___Technology/

More than 1,100 unique lesson plans. You can search for a specific lesson by typing a keyword in the search box at the top of the page, or you can click on grade level below that to browse what is available. Each of the sections also contains links to other Web sites about language arts lessons. Created by A to Z Teacher Stuff. K–12.

Other Features: LessonPlanz also has hundreds of lesson plans in all the major and secondary subjects. Look in the left sidebar for a complete list and click to go to that subject area. You can also subscribe to a free monthly e-mail newsletter, and your name will never be used for any other purpose. Click **Free Newsletter, Find Out More** link (left sidebar).

MidLink Magazine

http://www.ncsu.edu/midlink/

Online magazine, established in 1995, that highlights exemplary work from classrooms around the globe where technology is the vehicle or enhancement, but academics are the focus. Teacher Resource Room has sections for critical thinking skills (graphic organizers and hundreds of links to resources), rubrics and handouts (including a Web page evaluation form), Web publishing (copyright guidelines, author resources, and Web toolbox), and Web tricks and tips (bookmarks, etc.). You will need *Adobe Acrobat Reader* to view PDF files. MedLink Archives, dating to 1995, contains hundreds of teaching themes, unit ideas, lesson plans, and hands-on projects on all subjects, all grade levels. You could easily spend hours on this site. Created by MidLink Magazine, a nonprofit educational project sponsored by SAS inSchool, North Carolina State University, and University of Central Florida.

NASA Education Center

http://education.nasa.gov/

NASA believes it is important to work with educators, providing expertise and facilities to help them access and utilize science, math, and technology materials aligned with national standards and NASA's unique mission. The "meat" of this site can be found by clicking on any of the 12 NASA space and flight centers. They each contain K–12 resources for teachers, virtual tours, experiments, science investigations, multimedia projects, classroom materials and printables, and much more. A Guide to Educator Resources has short descriptions of NASA education programs with contact points and content areas. You can click on **K–12** to see the links, or go to the bottom of the page and search for programs by NASA center, subject matter, type of program, or grade level. It's easy to spend hours looking at all NASA has to offer. Created by Education Division, NASA Headquarters.

NASA Space Education

http://spacescience.nasa.gov/education/educators/

The folks at NASA firmly believe mathematics, science, and technology education is critical to the future of our nation. Teacher resources include an annotated list of lesson plans and activities from university and government sites. Nice photo images of planets and space missions, past and present, are all here. Created by National Aeronautic Space Administration. K–12.

Don't Miss: SpaceKids activities include sending student names on the next Mars mission, sun's peak of an 11-year cycle, amateur astronomy, and education page with contests, games, and quizzes. Support Organizations (top) has dozens of links to science institutes, observatories, laboratories, and flight centers with even more educational resources.

NETS Technology Lessons

http://cnets.iste.org/search/t_search.html

Searchable database for English, language arts, foreign language, math, science, and social studies lessons that use technology. You can search for lessons and/or units by lesson plan title, grade level, subject, or key word. Lessons have Web links and other resources. You can choose to view the document using your Web browser or *Adobe Acrobat Reader*. Funded by the U.S. government, NETS (National Education Technology Standards) is the primary organization setting the standards and overseeing the integration of technology in American school curriculum. Created by International Society for Technology in Education. K–12.

N.Y. Times Technology Lessons

http://www.nytimes.com/learning/teachers/lessons/technology.html

Features more than 50 technology lessons for middle and high school. Each lesson plan has author's name, objectives, procedures, vocabulary, outcomes, extensions, cross-curricular ideas, and links to sites for reference and research. Sample lesson titles: Good Inventions, Critically Surfing the Web, Spacing Out, Business Plans to Sell Products, Can We Talk? (communication), Playing with History (computer games), Music to Your Ears (sound with everyday objects), and many more. Created by New York Times Learning Network in partnership with the Bank Street College of Education. Gr. 6–12.

Other Features: The main site (**http://www.nytimes.com/learning/teachers/lessons/archive.html**) has hundreds of lesson plans on all different subjects, such as American history, civics, current events, economics, geography, global history, journalism, media sciences, and technology.

Online Lesson Plans

http://education.otago.ac.nz/NZLNet/technology/lesson_plans.html

Has technology lesson plans in these categories: atmosphere and space technologies (flight, states of matter, buoyancy, space stations), technologies relating to water (online museum exhibits), simple machines (experiments using the six simple machines, inventors toolbox, inventions, rockets), energy, problem solving using technology (design a house for three little pigs, power boat design), and section for secondary teachers (science of hockey, chemistry polymer project, hands on plastics), graphic design (advertising and labels), and biotechnology (enzymes, antibiotics, fermentation). Created by New Zealand Learning Network. Gr. 3–12.

Other Features: Technology lessons are available in other subjects, including English, math, science, social studies, music/art, and health.

Photo Image Library

http://www.pics4learning.com/

Thousands of free photographic images that have been donated by students, teachers, and amateur photographers, to be used for educational purposes such as reports, Web pages, presentations, and bulletin boards. Photos are organized in over 30 categories, including: art (carvings, paintings, sculpture, statues), architecture, countries (more than 40), culture, flags, geography and maps, history, holidays, monuments and national parks, music, Native American, parts of the body, plants (cactus, flowers, garden, trees), religion, schools, science (astronomy, energy, fossils, geology), signs, space, tools and machinery, transportation (air, boat, car, train), United States (subcategory for each state), and weather (clouds, extreme, fall, fog, rainbow, sunrise, sunset, winter). Permission has been granted for teachers and students to use the images in this collection. Created by Tech4Learning, Inc. in partnership with Orange County Public Schools (Florida).

Project Center

http://www.eduplace.com/projects/

More than 70 collaborative classroom projects for use over the Internet, divided by four subjects: reading and language arts, math, social studies, and science. Reading and L.A. sample projects: Great State Mystery, Random Acts of Kindness, Playwriting in the Round, Weather Postcards, USA Quilt Project, Square of Life, Movie in the Making, Amazing Trees, Museum Mania Treasure Hunt, Middle Grades Book Reviews, and Researching Sugar Gliders. Math sample projects: Snowy Math, Let's Sum up Weather, Having a Bubble Blast, Square of Life, Math Risk Game, and Dominant Traits. Sample projects for science: Seasons Across America, Global Water Sampling, Robotics on the Web, and many more. Created by Houghton Mifflin. K–12.

Reference Desk

http://www.refdesk.com/

Great for teaching students to find quick facts, Reference Desk would make a great home page, because it has over 1,000 links on one page. Headline News contains all the links to the popular news sites around the world: AP, Reuters, UPI, network TV, CNN, and more. Reference Resources contains dozens of "quick fact" references: Facts Encyclopedia, search engines, facts subject index, and more. Facts-At-A-Glance contains over 100 popular sites that people are always needing to find: area code finder, airline flight tracker, perpetual calendar, CIA World Fact Book, all kinds of dictionaries and encyclopedias, vital records, human anatomy, state and local governments, and dozens more. Other categories are weather, sports, just for fun, and subject categories. This site is a "must have" for general reference in the classroom. Created by Refdesk.

Rubric for Student Designed Pages

http://www.essdack.org/tips/webpagerubric.html

Easy-to-use assessment rubric to evaluate web pages designed by student groups at the conclusion of an assignment. Categories to be evaluated: layout and design, graphics, information, navigation and links, working together as a group, and following classroom guidelines. Four levels in each category with a point assignment; add points together to get a percentage score. Created by Tammy Worcester, Educational Service Center, Kansas.

Teaching With the Web

http://130.218.134.31/web/teaching.htm

Hundreds of links, some for students and others for teaching resources. Hundreds of themes that involve teaching with the Internet, divided into four grade levels. K–2 sections features mostly animal themes, plus holidays, seasons, math, plants, alphabet, senses, and transportation. Gr. 3–5 section has nearly 50 themes: lots of animals, plus art, deserts, explorers, landforms, human body, earthquakes, government, and more. The middle school and high school sections are divided into the major subjects (math, language arts, etc.). Created by Cheek and Redish, Educational Technology Center, Kennesaw State University (Georgia). K–12.

TeAch-nology

http://www.teach-nology.com/teachers/lesson_plans/

Search over 17,000 technology-infused lesson plans, teaching ideas, and worksheets in all the subjects. Sections for arts and humanities, computing, health, holidays, language arts, literature, math, music, P.E., science, social studies, special education, and world languages. The Computing section has more than 50 links, plus sections for computing subject matter and Web quests. Computing Subject Matter has links for desktop publishing, journals, using technology in the classroom, lesson plans, online projects, and presentation software. Web quests explains all about Web quests and has a list of them for all subjects, or you can make your own with the Web quest generator. Created by Teachnology, Inc. K–12.

Technology and Media

http://www.lessonplansearch.com/Technology_and_Media/index.html

Over 120 technology lesson plans and resource links, divided into four grade levels (high school has the most). When you click a lesson title, your browser will take you to another site where that lesson is stored. If you need *Adobe Acrobat Reader*, to view/print PDF files, there's a link at the top of the page to download it. At the bottom is a search box to find specific lessons by keyword. Sample title lessons: Cyber Seas Treasure Hunt, Holiday Postcards, TV Violence, Gender issues in Stories, Human Body Field Trip, How to Analyze News, News and Newspapers, and Learning to Use Software. Created by Lesson Plan Search. K–12.

Other Features: Lesson Plans Search (**www.lessonplansearch.com**) contains lessons for all the major teaching subjects plus secondary subjects like music, dance, drama, and health/P.E. You can click on the Pen Pals link to connect with other teachers and schools that are looking for classes for penpal and post card exchanges.

World News Online

http://www.nytimes.com/learning/

One of America's most reputable newspapers brings world news online to students in a form they can read, understand, and discuss. Updated daily, the site features: today's news summary, a news quiz, On This Day in history, snapshot of the day, conversation starters related to daily news headlines, and more. Developed by New York Times in partnership with the Bank Street College of Education. Gr. 3–12.

Don't Miss: Students can Ask a Reporter a question, and the NY Times will post selected questions and answers in the future. Also has a bio and photo of various Times reporters. Word of the Day gives definitions and usage. Also look for the archive of previous vocabulary words.

Notes:

INTERNET HOW-TO'S

Basic Computer Skills for Students

http://www.bonnydoon.santacruz.k12.ca.us/apple_core/techless/techless.html

This Macintosh-based site allows beginner and intermediate students to learn and reinforce computer skills. It begins with the basics (mouse skills, selecting, moving, copying, and pasting) and ends with spreadsheets and word processing using *ClarisWorks*. All links will download a file unless it's labeled as "sample." You can also download files from "sample and download" pages. "How-to" links will download simple illustrated instructions suitable for student handouts. Students helped to create and to maintain this site. Created by Bonny Doon Union Elementary School District (California). K–12.

Basic Guide to the Internet

http://library.albany.edu/internet/internet.html

A one-page summary of the components of the Internet: World Wide Web, e-mail, Telnet, FTP, e-mail discussion groups (listservs), usenet news, FAQs, chat and instant messaging, and MUDs. Each section explains the purpose of that component, its benefits and drawbacks, and how they are used. Several have links for additional reading. Created by University at Albany Libraries (New York).

Other Features: Click on **Back to Internet Tutorials** to see more links about the basics of the Internet, research guides, search engines and subject directories, browsers, and software training. You will also see underlined links in the summary that will take you to additional tutorials and background information.

HTML Beginner's Guide

http://archive.ncsa.uiuc.edu/General/Internet/WWW/index.html

Many people use a beginner's guide like this one as a starting point to understanding HTML (hypertext markup language), which is the code used to create Web pages. This guide contains several versions: printable version will appear as text-only; very clean and fast if you need to print it. The other two versions are full length (similar to text-only except it appears in the browser window) or three-part version (three smaller files in sequence). Major section headings: getting started (terms to know), HTML documents (HTML editors, tags explained), markup tags (head, title, body, headings, paragraphs, lists), character formatting, linking (URLs, mail-to), inline images (graphics, colors, sounds), tables, fill-out forms, troubleshooting, and for more information (style guides, online resources). Created by National Center for Supercomputing Applications, University of Illinois at Urbana-Champaign.

Internet 101

http://www.internet101.org/internet101.html

This site was created as an introduction for those who want to know about Internet basics without reading a lot of instructions. Simple explanations of complex subjects is the best part of Internet 101. It explains how the Internet developed, from 1960s military application to the popular broadcast media it has become today. Illustrations show how a Web browser combines text, pictures, sound, and video together. There are also sections on e-mail, newsgroups, chat rooms, newsgroups, e-commerce, file sharing, and viruses. Created by Scott Cottingham.

Don't Miss: The section on viruses provides excellent advice on protecting your computer investment, plus the difference between viruses and hoaxes. At the bottom of the page, there are links to several sites where you can find out about specific viruses in online encyclopedias as well as the latest virus making the rounds.

Other Features: Terminology has an extensive list of basic terms you will encounter as an Internet user, with easy-to-understand definitions.

Internet Tutorial

http://www.centerspan.org/tutorial/net.htm

Although created for busy doctors, this site can be used by anyone who needs an overview of how the Internet and its components are organized. What Is the Internet explains how it works, the history of the Internet (interesting), what kinds of information is available, how people use it, and Internet components. What Is the Web explains the history of the Web, what makes it unique, what the Web empowers you to do, and a quick tour of a typical site. How To Connect discusses hardware, software, service providers, etc. Surfing For the First Time explains Web indexes (like Yahoo) and browser tools. Troubleshooting provides help when your connection won't work or if a site won't load. Other Features explains e-mail, usenet groups, mailing lists, chat, and virtual reality.

Created by CenterSpan, American Society of Transplant Surgeons.

Don't Miss: Internet Quiz at the end allows you to take a multiple choice quiz and test the knowledge of what you learned. Teachers who monitor this feature can take anecdotal notes about what concepts need additional reinforcement or practice.

Searching the Web Tutorial

http://www.sc.edu/beaufort/library/bones.html

It's frustrating to most people to enter a keyword or two into a search box, and receive 16,000 links in reply. Furthermore, trying to read the Help or Search Tips information in search engines can leave some people even more confused! A South Carolina library created this tutorial called Bare Bones 101, with very short, succinct lessons you can read in a few minutes. Lessons explain things like subject directories, library gateways, search strategies, Boolean logic, basic search tips, and troubleshooting. Several of the lessons examine the most popular search engines with tips and tricks. Created by University of South Carolina, Beaufort Library.

Linda's Teacher Training for Developing Web Sites

http://mywebpages.comcast.net/ljbm/index.htm

This site was created by a retired high school educator (who came back out of retirement) who is also a top-notch web site creator and designer. Linda created this web site to train teachers how to create a basic web site using HTML or *Netscape Composer*. It has tips and directions on planning, building, and decorating a web site from scratch. She starts with the basics of HTML and works up from there; also provides lots of links for more information.

Having a teacher-made web site can have multiple purposes: a way to communicate with students and parents, to help students focus on specific information through the links provided, to present a lesson or web quest, and to present classroom activities and assignments. Students can download and email assignments back to the teacher, and those who have extended absences can keep up with their assignments through a teacher-made web site. Linda's Teacher Training site was recently featured as a web resource in *NEA Today*. Created by Linda MacCleave, Henrico County Public Schools, Virginia.

WebTeacher

http://www.webteacher.org/winexp/

An interactive, self-paced tutorial that provides both basic and intermediate instruction and in-depth information for K–12 teachers and students about the World Wide Web. WebTeacher was designed to help teachers understand the Internet and be able to use it in the classroom. Web Primer contains the basics of how web browsers, menus and controls, Internet addresses, domain name system, sending and receiving e-mail, Telnet and FTP, search engines, and newsgroups and mail lists (listservs). Web Tutorial is for intermediate users and those who completed the Web Primer section. It contains info on how to build a Web page, how to manage image, sound, and movie files, Java applets, and advanced topics like style sheets and CGI scripts. Created by National Cable Television Association and Tech Corps.

WEB QUESTS AND SCAVENGER HUNTS

Introduction to Webquests

http://webquest.sdsu.edu/

If you're not familiar with the concept of Web quests, this is the site for you. It has four levels: elementary, grade 3–4, middle school, and middle/high school. Any of these levels will allow you to explore the concept, see examples, and learn how to create a web quest for your students. According to Bernie Dodge, who developed the Web quest model in 1995 at San Diego State University, Web quests are "designed to use learners' time well, to focus on using information rather than looking for it, and to support thinking at the levels of analysis, synthesis and evaluation." Created by Bernie Dodge, San Diego State University. K–12.

Introduction to Scavenger Hunts

http://www.teachersfirst.com/summer/webquest/quest-a.shtml

Similar to the Web quest, a scavenger hunt allows you to explore different Web sites, seeking answers to questions. This narrative site is a good introduction for teachers. The explanations go slow, in easy-to-understand language. Click **Next** at the bottom to see the next page. Sections of this site: organization, before beginning (think about its purpose), designing, searching (steps to finding the components), reviewing (checking URLs, site's intent), organizing, packaging, trying it out, and presenting the results to students. Lots of examples along the way. Created by Network for Instructional TV, Inc. K–12.

Links to Scavenger Hunts

http://www.stemnet.nf.ca/CITE/integrationideas.htm

Click Scavenger Hunts to see more than 20 links leading to hundreds of scavenger hunts you can assign to your students. Choose one that involves a topic or theme you are teaching, and let the Web present the information so students are participating in their own learning. Themes on this site: animals, treasure, references and facts, weather, holidays, history, and many more. A few of the links may not be active. Created by a teacher at Gander Academy, Newfoundland, Canada.

TechTrekkers Scavenger Hunts

http://www.techtrekers.com/scav.htm

More than 250 ready-to-use scavenger hunts have already been created for you and your students in all subjects and at all grade levels. Hunts are divided into subject categories: English and literature, history, math, science, and general. Students may hunt for answers online and record them on a separate sheet for assessment, or teacher may reproduce the hunt and distribute to students. Choose one that supports a topic or theme you are teaching. Students learn more effectively when they are actively participating in their own learning. A few of the links may not be active. Created by Debbie Rollins, educational consultant for PBS and other organizations. Gr. K–12.

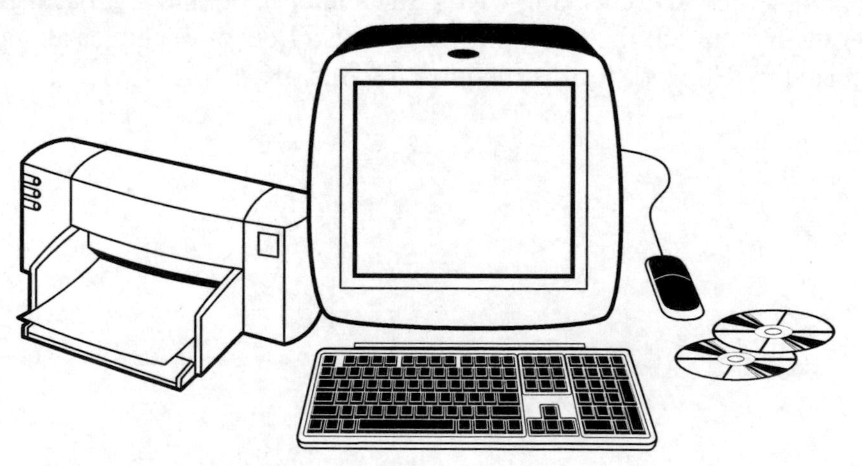

Scavenger Hunt Articles

Animals of the World:

http://www.education-world.com/a_lesson/lesson068.shtml

Ants:

http://www.education-world.com/a_lesson/lesson087.shtml/

Black History:

http://www.education-world.com/a_lesson/lesson052.shtml

Inventions:

http://www.educationworld.com/a_lesson/lesson120.shtml

U.S. History 1930s:

http://www.education-world.com/a_lesson/lesson079.shtml

Education World has posted several articles that combine background information for the teacher, along with a hunt for students. Teachers can read the articles to become familiar or assign the hunts to students. Some have different levels: beginner and experienced Internet users. Many of the questions are keyed as to grade level, so you can choose which questions or hunt to assign. Be sure to check all the links in the hunt before assigning to students, to make sure they're still active. You can use the hunt as is, or type a handout with the questions and URLs, choosing which questions you want to use. Created by Education World, Inc.

TeAch-nology Web Quests

http://www.teach-nology.com/teachers/lesson_plans/computing/web_quests/

Over 1,000 Web quests, grouped by subject category: general (on home page), language arts, math, science, social studies, plus an easy generator to make a printable Web quest. Each Web quest mostly follows the same format: introduction (what students will learn), task (what you want students to do), resources (the links to find information), process, evaluation, and conclusion. Some Web quests are simple (finding answers to questions) while others involve writing reports with information found. Created by Teachnology, Inc. K–12.

Technology Lessons

http://www.kent.wednet.edu/curriculum/tech/lessons/

More than 60 technology lesson plans written by experienced teachers, grouped by grade level. You will see a title (click it to view) and brief description of each. K–3 sample titles: Number Writing, Shape Match, Zoo Search, 100th Day, About Me, Frames and Arrows, Weather, Let it Snow, Internet Evaluation, Pet Survey, Tall Tales, Wanted Poster. Each lesson plan follows the usual format of purpose, materials, procedures, resources (links) and assessment. Gr. 4–6 samples: Fictional Genre, Native American Comparisons, Technology Experts, Totems, Body Systems, Fitness, Biographies, Political Cartoons, U.S. History Timeline, Country Reports, Planets. Created by teachers at Kent School District (Washington state). K–6.

Web Quests, All Subjects

http://www.allabery.com/courses/webquest/

More than 70 Web quests written by teacher education students at Old Dominion University. Well-organized page lists all the links in order by grade level, then grouped by subject—lots of science topics but also social studies and language arts. Sample of topics: deserts, African safari, bats, bones, Civil War, butterflies, animal habitats, rocks, solar system, American Revolution, Edgar Allen Poe, mythology, algebra, Anne Frank, recycling, marine animals, managing stress, and many more. Created by Allabery Technical Solutions. Gr. 1–12.

WebQuests

http://sesd.sk.ca/teacherresource/webquest/webquest.htm

This site offers over 1,200 Web quests compiled and divided into subject categories. Nearly all the web quests include rubrics, so students know exactly what is expected. Subjects with the most quests are: science (500+), social studies (450+), language arts (250+), and math (140+). You will need to check all the links in the hunt before assigning to students to be sure they are age-appropriate and working properly. Created by Saskatoon East School Div. No. 41 (Canada). K–12.

Don't Miss: Special section for K–2 teachers with dozens of scavenger hunts that are appropriate for beginning Internet students. Check out the link to Bernie Dodge's WebQuest page, because he is widely acknowledged as the creator of the Web quest concept. Check the top of the page too for virtual field trips, scavenger hunts, student publishing, and tutorials.

Web-Based Projects

http://oncampus.richmond.edu/academics/education/projects/

These webquests and projects (over 100) were written and designed by University of Richmond (VA) students preparing to become teachers, created for an integrated technology course. Subjects covered: art, English, foreign language, math, science, and social studies—for elementary through secondary students. These webquests, which follow the original model and format created by Bernie Dodge, were developed as cooperative learning projects. Each student in a group takes on a role. Once students have carried out their research, they come back to their groups and teach their peers what they have learned. The group then reflects on this material and together completes a task that includes all roles and perspectives. Hosted by University of Richmond, Gr. K–12.

Webquests by Subject Area (K-12)

http://www.plainfield.k12.in.us/hschool/Subject.htm

A nice collection of more than 150 webquests for teachers to use, organized by subject area: English/language arts, math, science, social studies, and miscellaneous. The science and social studies categories are especially comprehensive. Under each subject, you will see a list of the webquests and the grade level. Click on the title of the webquest to view it.

Some of the sample titles are: Do You Haiku?, Fairy Tales Around the World, Anne Frank, Little House on the Prairie, Mission Possible, Endangered Species, Journey of a Monarch Butterfly, Dinosaurs, Weather, Rainforests, Nutrition Mission, American Time Travel, Mexico, Medieval Times, Civil War, Crisis in the Balkans, Bill of Rights, Vietnam, Great Depression, Voting Machine, Computer Lab Detectives, March Madness, Banned Books, Safe Driving, School Uniforms, and many more.

If you want to see the same list organized by grade level, click the link at the top that says Sort by Grade Level. Compiled by Indiana University graduate students led by Jackie Carrigan. K-12.

Notes:

Sample Report Guidelines

Any time students are using the Internet for research, it is important to give them guidelines and let them know how their work will be assessed. Following is a sample lesson plan for a state report that can be modified to suit the project in other curriculum areas.

Topic: U.S. State Report

Grade Level: 3-6

Procedures

Researching the report—Using encyclopedias, library books, the Internet, and other sources available, perform the research necessary to gain information on these facts.

Look at a map of your state and draw an outline for use in your report. You may find outlines at this website:

http://www.abcteach.com/Maps/mapsTOC.htm

Writing the report—These are the elements that you need to include in your report. You may either write the report by hand, or type it into a document or PowerPoint presentation.

Layout	Points	Contents
Cover page	2 points	This page should include the name of your state, a color illustration, and your own name.
Table of contents	2 points	Create this based on what you have chosen to include in the report.
Page 1	4 points	Draw a map of your state. Label the capital, important cities, and major landmarks.
Page 2	14 points	Information sheet on State Facts.
Page 3	4 points	Information sheet on Geography.
Pages 4 & 5	3 points per page	Information sheet on Sports, Tourist Industry, Landmarks, Famous People (choose 2 topics)
Page 6	8 points	Write a paragraph for each of these 4 topics: State history, location and region in America, reasons people should visit, the most interesting fact you learned.

Creating a Bibliography: If you used information in your report that came from a source written by someone else, you need to give credit to your sources. A list of the sources of information is called a Bibliography. Remember, any information written by someone else cannot be used word for word. You must write the information in your own words. To copy someone else's writing is called "plagiarism."

The bibliography should be the last page of your report. Here is the format for citing your sources, followed by an example of each.

Books:

Author (last name first), Title (underlined), City, Publisher copyright date.

Phillips, Vicky. *Writer's Guide to Internet Resources.* New York, NY: Macmillan, 1998.

Magazines:

Author (last name first). Title of the article (in quotation marks). Title of the magazine (underlined),

Date (day, month, year), page number of the article.

Gleick, Elizabeth. "Read All About It." *Time*, October 21, 1996, p. 3.

Encyclopedias:

Title of the article (in quotation marks). Title of the reference book (underlined), edition, date published.

"Interpreting the News." *Encyclopedia Brittanica*, vol. 29, 1996.

Internet:

Name of company or organization sponsoring the website. Title of page (in quotation marks). Date (if known). URL address (underlined).

abc Teach Network, © 2003. "State Facts."
http://www.abcteach.com/States/StateTOC.htm

CITING SOURCES

NoodleTools Quick Cite!

http://www.noodletools.com/quickcite/citwww3.html

This is an excellent resource for examples of how to cite a reference or resource. Examples include sources such as newspaper articles, email messages, Online discussions, professional web pages, personal web sites, magazine articles, books, CD-ROMs, and interviews. The bibliographic style is simplified to help the young student learn this important aspect of researching. The student chooses what type of medium he wants to cite, clicks on the link, and an explanation and example appears.

Yahooligans! Teacher's Guide

http://www.yahooligans.com/tg/citation.html

This site stresses the importance of giving credit to the original authors of information collected for a report. A trusted source of age-appropriate information, Yahooligans! has cleverly broken this information down by grade level. Click on the link to the grade level that you teach, and you will find simple and clear examples for the format appropriate to citing electronic sources. The font is large and clear, with plenty of white space for easy viewing. A particularly helpful aspect of this site is that it provides examples of how to give credit for visual information as well, including pictures, sounds, and videos gathered from web sites.

Best Sites for Teaching SECONDARY SUBJECTS

FINE ART AND THEATER ARTS

Art Lessons and Activities

http://www.lessonplanspage.com/Art.htm

In addition to providing a large number of lesson plans on fine arts, drawing and creative writing, this site also cross indexes lessons through other subjects. Teachers may search the database or browse by grade level and subject. Lesson plans exist in various areas such as drawing, painting, sculpture, crafts and art history. Created by EdScope LLC. K–12.

Other Features: Lesson Plans Page has hundreds of lesson plans and activities on all the other subjects, also grouped by grade level.

Drama and Literature

http://www.english-teaching.co.uk/

Site features more than 1,000 pages of free lesson plans. All can be downloaded in *Adobe Acrobat* PDF format. KS3 (key stage 3) is a section with dozens of lessons grouped by poetry, prose, drama, nonfiction, speaking and listening, and writing. You'll even find Harry Potter material (under prose). The drama section is particularly well stocked with a heavy emphasis on Shakespeare. You can browse by age group or subject matter. You must register to download some plans, but registration is free and the form takes less than a minute to fill out and process. Created by Free Resources for English Teachers.

Don't Miss: Samples contains a nice collection of free lessons, so you can check the quality of the material before registering: adverb poem, animal farm prose, multiple exercises in examining a poem, and resource sheets for *Macbeth* and *Merchant of Venice*.

Gateway

http://www.thegateway.org/SubjectBrowse.htm

A huge site with more than 10,000 social studies lessons for all grade levels. On the main page, click Arts to jump down to that section to see almost two dozen categories including architecture, art therapy, careers, computers in art, dance, drama/dramatics, film history, informal education, instructional issues, music, photography, popular culture, process skills, technology, theater arts and visual arts. When you click a category, you'll get about a dozen listings on each page. Each listing contains the title, a detailed description and grade level for each lesson. When you click on each title, you will see a database entry for that lesson, so you'll need to click the title once again to see the actual content. Lessons are linked to a variety of sites, and they feature photos, illustrations, sound files, reference materials, maps, and more. Created by the U.S. Department of Education and the ERIC Clearinghouse. K–12.

Photo Image Library

http://www.pics4learning.com/

Thousands of free photographic images that have been donated by students, teachers, and amateur photographers, to be used for educational purposes. Unlike many Internet sites, permission has been granted for teachers and students to use all of the images donated to this collection. Photos are organized in over 30 categories, each with many subcategories. Categories pertaining to fine art include: art (carvings, paintings, sculpture, statues), architecture (bridges, buildings, castles, fountains, interior), and backgrounds and textures. Many of the other categories can be used for all kinds of art projects, including artistic presentations, web pages, collages, and representational art. Created by Tech4Learning, Inc. in partnership with Orange County Public Schools (Florida).

Teacher's Desk: Drama

http://www.teachersdesk.com/lessons/lessons_theater_drama.htm

The drama section at Teacher's Desk features several good lesson plans dealing with the nuts and bolts of putting on a play. Lessons cover dialogue and dialects, warm-ups, environment, focus, character analysis, and a unit that takes five days to teach over all aspects of theater production. The plans themselves are in text format which makes them easy to download and modify. Links to all of the drama lesson plans are grouped together on one page for easy navigation. Created by Teacher's Desk. K–12.

Other Features: The site also features links to educational software downloads, homework help, a literature club and bargains on educational books.

TeAch-nology: Arts and Drama

http://www.teach-nology.com/teachers/lesson_plans/arts/drama/

This site provides a huge number of links to resources in almost every subject and discipline imaginable. The arts and drama section offers a guide to more than 20 other drama lesson plan sites on the Internet. Links are gathered on one page for easy access. Sample titles: Action Drama, Dramatic Feelings, Ethnic Folk Dancing, Exploring Disability, Julius Caesar, Death and Drama of The Pigman, Music of the 1920s, and Theater for Younger Children. A brief description makes finding the required lesson plans a quick, simple task; click on the title to view the full lesson. Created by Teachnology, Inc. K–12.

Other Features: Free worksheets, ask the experts area and a variety of tools and tutorials.

Utah Museum of Fine Arts

http://umfa.dev.verite.com/?id=MTAw

This series of fine art lessons is based around items and exhibits found at the Utah Museum of Fine Arts. However, access to the museum isn't necessary in order to conduct the lessons. Topics covered include African art, medieval manuscripts, materials of art, subjects of art, ancient Egyptian art and modern art. The lessons are designed to help students learn about the civilizations that created the work as well as the art itself. Created by the Utah Museum of Fine Arts. 9–12.

Other Features: Virtual tours of the museum and its exhibits.

Visual Arts Lessons

http://www.lessonplansearch.com/Visual_Arts/index.html

This site provides more than 60 lesson plans centering upon the visual arts. The plans may be browsed by grade level, although beyond that art lessons are simply arranged in alphabetical order rather than being subdivided by discipline. Primary (K–2) and middle school has the most lessons, not as much for high school. Some of the topics here: marble painting, fun craft recipes, mosaic magnets, bugs, Medieval castles, meaningful masks, name drawings on a grid, monsters in literature and film, pointalist portraits, ad agency project, weaving, and Chinese paper art. Created by Lesson Plan Search. K–12.

Other Features: Lesson plans are available for a variety of subjects, a searchable database, rubrics and season themes.

Notes:

MUSIC

American Music Education Initiative

http://lessons.usamusic.org/viewlessons.lasso

The National Music Foundation designed this site to identify, recognize and support the creative educational accomplishments of teachers who use American music in the classroom. The organization does this by holding an annual competition to find the best lesson plans focusing on American music. Selected plans are then archived on this Web site and made available free of charge to music teachers. As a result the database holds hundreds of lessons plans handpicked by fellow music teachers. Each plan on the main index contains a notation telling whether it was a winner, finalist, semi-finalist or honorable mention. Created by the American Music Education Initiative of the National Music Foundation. K–12.

Lesson Plans Page: Music

http://www.lessonplanspage.com/Music.htm

This site features a wealth of lesson plans arranged by grade level. In addition to browsing the lessons alphabetically by grade level, teachers may also search the database by keyword. Lesson plans cover everything from the basics of music to advanced theory. One of the nicer features is that links are provided for tying music education plans in with other subjects such as language arts and social studies. Created by EdScope LLC. K–12.

Other Features: Lesson Plans Page has hundreds of lesson plans and activities on all the other subjects, also grouped by grade level.

Lesson Plan Search: Music

http://www.lessonplansearch.com/Music/index.html

This site provides more than 50 music lesson plans for grades K–12. It also features a wide variety of links to general resources for music education.

Music at School

http://www.musicatschool.co.uk/

Maintained by a British secondary school music teacher, this site provides hundreds of worksheets, lesson plans and online activities for music teachers. Music at School offers teachers instant access to some worksheets the author has created and used effectively. It also allows pupils to research extra information and revise classwork without taking away valuable worksheets. The site itself loads quickly and is easy to navigate. Along with classroom resources it offers a few articles on the importance of teaching and studying music. Created by Music at School. K–12.

Other Features: Homework help and online lessons.

Resources for K-12 Music Educators

http://www.isd77.k12.mn.us/resources/staffpages/shirk/k12.music.html

This site has valuable resources for music educators and students of all areas and educational levels. The main page has a long, comprehensive index of links to other websites for music educators, or you can jump to the section you want by clicking one of the buttons at the top: band, choral, orchestra, classroom, and all music. Every kind of music-related resource you can think of is here: journals, membership associations and organizations, teaching resources and lesson plans, music history, arts and music societies, music libraries, databases, downloadable music sheets and songs, care of instruments, lyrics, and more. Created by Minnesota teacher Cynthia M. Shirk. K-12.

Music Notes

http://musicnotes.net/

A supplemental music curriculum developed by elementary music teachers for teaching all children how to read music. Music Notes believes the single most important aspect of education is language development. Music teachers can develop these skills through music's language, especially during the formative elementary years. Although paid membership allows full use of the program, there are dozens of sample lessons and a trial membership available at no cost. Click **Teachers** (left sidebar) then go to the bottom and click **Teaching Index** to view dozens of sample lessons you can print and use. K–8.

Other Features: Click on **Workshops** (left sidebar) to view seminars and workshops held in their offices in Cumming, Georgia. Click **Schools** to see a list of schools around the world (though it's mostly U.S.) that have joined the program and from whom you may wish to get feedback and recommendations.

Music Lesson Plans

ttp://www.lessonplansearch.com/Music/index.html

This site provides more than 50 music lesson plans for grades, divided into four grade levels: K–2, 3–5, 6–8, 9–12. The K–5 categories are more comprehensive than the middle and high school categories. The main page also features a wide variety of links to general resources for music education such as: finding rhythm, understanding the blues, making your own music, music and minerals, music themes, and songs for instruction. At the bottom is a search box, where you can enter a keyword to search for specific lessons. K–12.

Other Features: To view PDF files (some links have these), you will need *Adobe Acrobat Reader*, and a link is available at the top of the page to download it.

New York Times Daily Lesson Plan: Music

http://www.nytimes.com/learning/teachers/lessons/music.html

These lesson plan units use recent New York Times articles as springboards for examining important curricular topics in interesting and exciting ways. Lessons are listed in reverse chronological order, from the most recent to the oldest. The site is free, fast and easy to navigate. Teachers have the ability to search by keyword or browse by subject or age range. Created by the New York Times. K–12.

Other Features: The News Snapshot and Daily Quote are nice features that help bring current events into the classrooms. The subject featured changes depending upon the photo or quote chosen.

Rock and Roll Hall of Fame

http://www.rockhall.com/programs/plans.asp

Using John Lennon's "Imagine" to study the Protestant Reformation and comparing Mark Twain with David Bowie are just a couple of the unique ideas you'll find among the lesson plans developed by the Rock and Roll Hall of Fame (Ohio). These resources are intended to stimulate student interest and creativity, to develop higher order thinking skills and to promote interdisciplinary learning. The program also offers teacher workshops and inservices. It's a definite must if you're looking for fresh, innovative ways to introduce music into other subjects or just approach musical studies from a slightly different perspective. There are some schools and/or parents who might find some of the material inappropriate, depending on educational, political, and societal views, so that needs to be kept in mind prior to teaching. Created by the Rock and Roll Hall of Fame. K–12.

Other features: Information on the museum, inductees and rock music in general.

Blank Sheet Music

http://www.blanksheetmusic.net/

Stylish site with free sheet music you can print and use in your music class. Formats include single stave (including no clef, treble, bass, various strings, percussion) and double staves (including piano or guitar). You can chose from several options before printing: ruler between staves, lighter or darker, size of lines, etc. On the left side, click Digital Scores to see all kinds of sheet music for Christmas, Broadway, classical, jazz, rock, and more. K–12.

Teaching Ideas & Suggestions

http://www.teachnet.com/lesson/music/general/

Although there aren't many lessons here, what is there contains valuable ideas and suggestions for teachers of music. The lessons include slurs-ties-phrases for lower brass instruments and researching families of instruments (using the Web). Teaching suggestions include how to use classical music in the classroom (impacts all the subjects), setting the mood for creative writing, and cartoons and classical music. TeachNet encourages music teachers to submit lesson plans for this section. Created by TeachNet. Gr. 4–12.

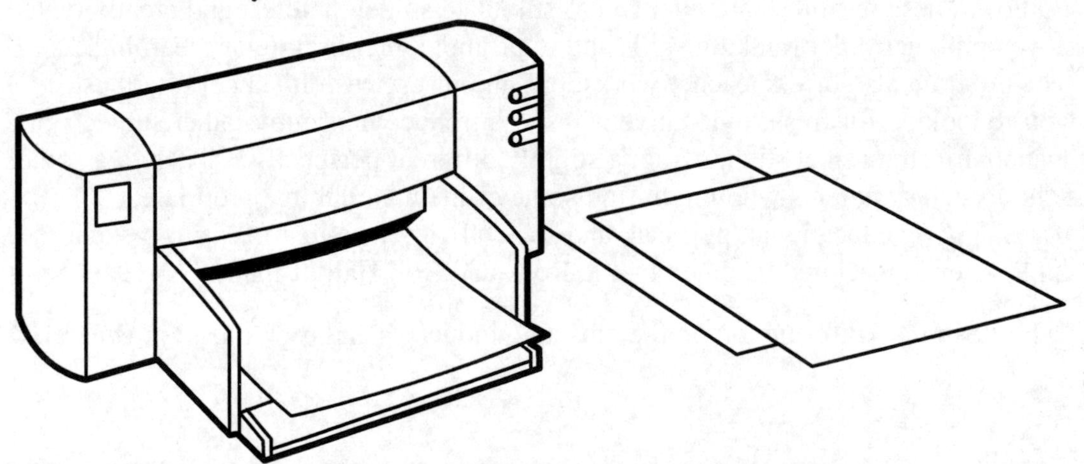

Treasure Trove of Music

http://www.treasure-troves.com/music/

A professional encyclopedist has assembled over this resource more than a decade with assistance from the internet community. The main categories listed are chords and notes, intervals, musical instruments, musical notation, scales and notes and time signatures. Each main category contains in-depth discussions of numerous entries. You can also search by keyword or browse the alphabetical listing. Although this site doesn't contain any lesson plans, it does provide quite thorough scholarly explanations of musical terms. Created by Eric Weisstein. K–12.

Other Features: Other Treasure Trove topics include astronomy, biography, books, chemistry, math, music, physics and science.

Notes:

PHYSICAL EDUCATION AND HEALTH

Discovery School—Health Lessons

http://school.discovery.com/lessonplans/health.html

Aimed at middle and high school students, this site has dozens of formal lesson plans, with objectives, materials needed, procedures, discussion questions, and assessment. Some sample lesson titles: Addiction, Cruel Schools (bullying), Resolving Conflicts, Teen Pregnancy, Depression, Digestion, Safe Driving, and Sexual Harassment. Sponsored by Discovery.com. Gr. 6–12.

Awesome Library

http://www.awesomelibrary.org/health.html

This site links to lesson plans, books, papers, and discussion lists for Health, Nutrition, Personal Care, Physical Education, Prevention, Sports and Recreation. Well organized and fast loading text and graphics. Sample lesson plan topics: body systems, fitness, illegal drug use, nutrition, personal care, and safety. The Medical category includes lots of subtopics: aging, asthma, babies, cancer, children, diseases and conditions, fitness, headaches, health news, medication, obesity, prevention, seniors, and sleep disorders. Physical Education has their lesson plans by grade level. Created by Dr. E. Jerry Adams and the Evaluation and Development Institute. K–12.

Other Features: Sections for children, teens, parents, librarians, and the general community.

Health Teacher

http://www.healthteacher.com/lessonguides/default.asp

Lesson guides on Alcohol and Other Drugs, Community and Environmental Health, Injury Prevention, Mental and Emotional Health, Nutrition, Personal and Consumer Health, Physical Activity, Family Health, and Sexuality and Tobacco. Site is nicely organized in an easy-to-read matrix of lessons and activities. Sample K–5 topics: safe use of medicine, air and breathing, be safe, drugs and goals don't mix, choosing friends, and hazards to health. Sample Gr. 6–12 topics: marijuana, psychoactive drugs, advertising, choices and consequences, alcohol's effects, and steroids. Can browse by grade or subject and has a teacher support section. Created by WebMD. K–12.

Don't Miss: The Teacher Support area has information on health literacy and NHES skills.

Lesson Planz

http://lessonplanz.com/Lesson_Plans/Health/

Well organized and fast with more than 130 lesson plans grouped by grade and subject. Gr. K–5 have the most selection. Sample K–5 topics: eating right and nutrition, five senses, anatomy, balanced meals and healthy snacks, dental health, emotional puppets, bad dreams, and illness and prevention. Sample Gr. 6–12 topics: food labeling, magazine ads and teens, cardiovascular fitness, nutrition, resistance skills, parenting styles, cultural awareness, and coping with loss. It is also possible to search by theme in order to put together a group of linked plans. An easy menu allows teachers to quickly check for the most recently added and top rated plans. A random lesson plan link is also available for those wanting help in brainstorming. Created by A to Z Teacher Stuff. K–12.

Don't Miss: There's a link for a dozen worksheets and printable pages: coloring pages for maps and famous historical figures, geography theme pages, and puzzles and word searches. Some files are *Adobe Acrobat* PDF.

PE and Health Lesson Plans

http://www.lessonplanspage.com/PE.htm

These nearly 1,000 lessons were contributed by practicing teachers, so they are practical lessons that work. Lesson Plans Page has a nice search engine, where you choose the grade level (PreK–1, 2–3, 4–5, 6–7, junior/high school, multiple/other), then you see a lengthy list of lessons and activities. Click on the one you want to view in detail. The results are organized by category: Games and Relays, Health and Fitness, Sports, plus connections to various subjects (language arts, music, science, etc.). This site is different than most because the titles of lessons are descriptive. More than just a title, they explain the purpose of the activity or lesson. Each lesson has the name and email address of the person who contributed it, so you can contact that person for more information or questions. Created by Lesson Plans Page. PreK–12.

P.E. Central

http://www.pecentral.org/

Resources on the site include health and physical education lesson ideas, ready-to-print assessment ideas, adapted P.E. information, classroom management ideas, job center, professional and conference information, bookstore, links to other health and P.E. sites, and information about best practices. Lesson plans are written for K–12 but preschool suggestions are also available. The site is well organized with a searchable database and a well-designed system for browsing. Created by P.E. Central.

Don't Miss: Instant Activities and Warm Ups, featuring dribbling, fitness, jumping and landing, kicking and punting, rhythm and dance, striking with implements, throwing and catching, traveling, volleying, and more.

Other Features: Assessment ideas and other instructional resources.

Sports Media

http://www.sports-media.org/

Click Database, then Lesson Plans, to view an alphabetical list of hundreds of quality lesson plans and activities contributed by PE teachers across the country. However, to be able to use the database at no cost, the Sports Media site asks that teachers submit at least five lesson plans or activities. Teachers who don't want to submit lesson plans will be asked to pay a fee. All other parts of the web site are available at no cost. Sample of lesson plan titles: aerobics patterns, basketball drills, circuit training, dance lines, fitness testing, nontraditional gymnastics, indoor games, jump rope games, kickball rules, parachute games, pickleball, safety tips, soccer volleyball, table tennis, and much more.

Other Features: Teaching tips, professional articles, P.E. teacher forums, and chat are also available so you can communicate with colleagues across the world.

Notes:

FOREIGN LANGUAGE

EdSitement

http://www.edsitement.neh.gov/tab_lesson.asp?subjectArea=2

This site features language plans and teaching resources for French, German, Greek, Italian, Japanese, Latin, Russian, Spanish and several other languages. Each subject's page is broken down into a four main sections. The first is a link of Web sites which offer lesson plans and materials for the language. Next is a collection of lesson plans which can be downloaded at Edsitement. A collection of at-home activities follows. The final area of each subject is a listing of other learning activities. You can search the database or browse by subject. A particularly nice feature is the site's lesson plan calendar which provides a schedule of lesson plans for the entire month. Created by the National Endowment for the Humanities. K–12.

Don't Miss: A particularly nice feature is the site's lesson plan calendar which provides a schedule of lesson plans for the entire month.

Education World

http://www.education-world.com/foreign_lang/

The Foreign Language Center at Education World offers a variety of resources for teaching English as a Second Language, French, German, Spanish and Latin. A particularly nice touch is the drop down menu that lists foreign language standards for every state in the U.S. In addition to the lesson plans hosted on the site, links are provided to valuable resources for creating new lesson plans. Created by Education World. K–12.

Don't Miss: Each lesson plan area also includes a "tool box" which provides teachers with a quick gateway to useful teaching tools. In the foreign language area, the tool include a drop-down menu of online dictionary, translators, and bilingual games

Foreign Language Lesson Plans and Resources

http://www.csun.edu/~hcedu013/eslsp.html

A professor emeritus who teaches secondary education students maintains this site. Although he doesn't offer any on-site lesson plans, the collection of Spanish and French links and resources he offers is fairly impressive. Resources include: Spanish sites, association for teachers of French, info for Latin teachers, beginner level Japanese, basic Spanish, Chinese information page, and much more. Created by Dr. Marty Levine, California State University-Northridge. K–12.

Other Features: In addition to linking to lesson plans, the site also features Web-based learning resources and information on museum exhibits (quite a few in Mexico) which are helpful in the study of languages.

ePals Classroom Exchange

http://www.epals.com/

Remember writing to a penpal when you were a kid, and waiting a month (or months) to get a reply? Technology has changed all that! ePals is the 21st century way of making friends in countries that you might be studying. Click Find Classrooms to view profiles for certain countries and age groups—there are more than 83,000 profiles featured. The benefits of such cross-cultural communication are numerous and far reaching. ePals is dedicated to helping students from around the world connect and interact with each other by email and other forms of electronic communication such as voice, video or chat. Registration and membership is free, and each account allows an educator to create up to 35 monitored email accounts for students. For speakers of other languages besides English, the site can be viewed in French, Spanish, German, Portuguese, Japanese, Arabic, and Chinese (click the appropriate tab). Hosted by ePals Classroom Exchange, Inc. K-12.

Other Features: Click Projects (then choose which age group) to see ideas of how you can incorporate ePals into your curriculum. One suggestion is an ePal Book Club, where kids from around the world talk about their favorite books and authors.

French Language Course

http://www.jump-gate.com/languages/french/

This friendly online French course is intended to allow students to understand written French (newspapers, articles, magazines, signs on the road during your next trip in France, etc.) and to write a letter to a French friend or penpal. The lessons are organized in a course index, some with sound files. The first lesson contains pronunciation guidelines while later lessons feature adjectives, plurals, comparing, and French expressions and idioms. Students can practice their skills at reading French by clicking the links at the bottom to look at a current issue of Le Monde, a well known French newspaper. Created by Jacques Léon at Jump Gate. Gr. 9-12.

Gateway to Educational Materials

http://www.thegateway.org

Click Browse Subjects (left side), then click Foreign Languages, to view more than 1,400 foreign language lesson plans. The categories are: alphabet, bilingualism, careers, cultural awareness, grammar, history, informal education, instructional issues, linguistics, listening comprehension, process skills, reading, speaking, spelling, technology, vocabulary and writing. When you click a category, you see a list of lesson summaries with a title, a detailed description, grade level. Clicking the title takes you to the actual lesson plan. Lessons are linked to a variety of sites, and they feature photos, illustrations, sound files, reference materials, maps, and more. K-12.

IRC Spanish Language Plans

http://www.fhsu.edu/irc/spanish/spanish.html

Index of links for teachers interested in Internet resources for teaching Spanish as part of an instructional resource program. The page is divided into two sections for lesson plans and for Spanish Internet resources. You will find links for Spanish lessons on the Web (bilingual), links to foreign educators, a Maya quest for teacher use, online lessons, translation dictionaries, language exercises, vocabulary builder, and more. Created by the Instructional Resource Center, Fort Hayes State University (Kansas).

Other Features: Pointers to a variety of other foreign language resources are also given.

Japanese Online

http://www.japanese-online.com/

As a language resource site, Japanese Online is a gathering place for anyone who has interest in Japanese language and culture. Free Japanese language lessons and sound files, an online Japanese-English dictionary, and examples of Japanese junior high school math placement test questions. Each lesson includes a conversational dialog, a translation of the conversation, vocabulary used within the conversation, grammar points, and cultural issues. Some lessons require you to have Japanese character sets for your monitor—you can download the extensions needed from this site. Created by Pacific Software Publishing, Inc. K–12.

Don't Miss: Type an English or Japanese word in the Online Dictionary to get it translated.

Other Features: The math questions are interesting and more challenging than traditional English problems. Answers are multiple choice—click to see if it's correct. Sound files are available to hear the question being read in English (using Real Player). Each tells how much time would be given for a Japanese child to answer.

Online Translations

http://www.systransoft.com/

Cistern provides instant online translation. Just enter the text you'd like translated in the box on the main page, then select the languages involved and press the translate button. Available languages include English, French, German, Italian, Portuguese and Spanish. The system can translate back and forth from any of the listed languages. You can also enter a Web site address in the text box to have the site translated as you browse it. While machine translations aren't as good as human translations, this is useful if you want to get the general meaning of a Web site or document. Created by Symantec.

Other Features: It is possible to download demo versions of the software or use it to add translation boxes to your own Web site.

Tina's French Café

http://www.tinasfrenchcafe.com/

Although the site was designed for parents who home school their children and who need French language lesson plans, the site is available for school teachers and parents as well. It provides 16 brief lesson plans designed for adults working with a single student. The site also provides a number of downloadable quizzes and links to shareware and other resources that the author has found valuable in home schooling her children. The most useful software links are probably those for French language text-to-speech software which will allow children to highlight French words and hear them pronounced correctly. Created by Robert and Tina Brown. K–12.

Don't Miss: A free English/French dictionary is also included in the download area.

Tongue Twisters

http://www.uebersetzung.at/twister/en.htm

How can a clam cram in a clean cream can? That tongue twister is one of nearly 400 that will get kids reading, talking, working, and laughing at each other. This is actually an international collection, and there are links to see tongue twisters in nearly 100 different languages. Click on 1st International Collection of Tongue Twisters to see the list of languages. Great idea for foreign language students! Created by Michael Reck, Waldenbuch, Germany. K–12.

Verbix Languages

http://www.verbix.com/languages/index.asp

While it doesn't provide any lesson plans, Verbix is an excellent resource for creating plans and for teaching languages. This site allows online conjugation of verbs. Just select the language you're interested in from the extensive list on the main page, type your verb into the text box and press "Go." While many languages are available for free online conjugations, others require downloading software. Created by Verbix.

Other Features: You can also download the software in order to use the program offline on your own computer.

Notes:

INTERNATIONAL CULTURE

Ask Asia

http://www.askasia.org/teachers/

The Asia Society helps teachers introduce high-quality course content on Asia into their classes. From social studies to language arts this site provides lesson plans tailored to help students understand Asia. The instructional resources section includes lesson plans, readings, maps, photographs, drawings and time lines. While the site contains a number of lesson plans about Asia in general, it also provides plans on specific Asian cultures in an effort to break up the stereotype that all Asians are alike. Plans are broken down into the sub-categories Asian American, Central Asia, China, India, Indonesia, Japan, Korea, the Middle East, Philippines, Singapore, Taiwan and Vietnam. Created by the Asia Society. K–12.

Don't Miss: The resource center locator provides university, museum and non-profit information sources about Asia in your area.

Developing Literacy Through Hispanic Culture

http://library.thinkquest.org/50035/index_e.html

Students will learn to write a book report, poetry, and character sketch in order to appreciate Hispanic history and culture. Each of those three sections includes how-to's, examples from students, and assessment guidelines. You will also find teacher guidelines for developing a literacy program through Hispanic culture, a glossary, links to other Web sites, and a discussion forum to connect with other teachers. Created by ThinkQuest, a nonprofit organization offering education activities that use technology. Gr. 4–8.

The Discovery Channel

http://school.discovery.com/lessonplans/

The Discovery Channel's teacher resource section features hundreds of original lesson plans written by teachers for teachers. You may use the pull-down menus on the site to browse by subject, grade, or both. The site is well-designed and easy to navigate. It also provides blurbs showing the most recent and most popular lesson plans of the day. A quick glance at the geography section shows more than two dozen lesson plans involving world cultures. Other subject areas containing lesson plans involving international culture include world history, ancient history, contemporary studies and economics. Created by the Discovery.com. K–12.

Don't Miss: The site includes many tools such as an online clip-art gallery, puzzle gallery, lesson planner and worksheet generator.

Global Cultures

http://www.worldtrek.org/odyssey/teachers/lessons.html

The Odyssey provides two kinds of lesson plans—those to be used with the Trek (virtual tour of a country or region) or to be used independently. Egypt, Mali, Zimbabwe, Peru, Guatemala, and Mexico are the featured countries so far—others to be added in the future. Each country's themes and lessons are extremely detailed and would take a month or more to study. Each section contains objectives, suggested readings, activities, discussion guides, maps and illustrations, and assessment tools for each country theme. Sponsored by The Odyssey: World Trek for Service and Education. Gr. 9–12.

Other Features: The site includes a message board teachers may use for discussing their lesson plans and ideas.

National Council for Social Studies

http://www.socialstudies.org/resources/lessons/

This site contains a collection of lesson plans reprinted from the organization's official publication. All lesson plans are reproduced exactly as they appeared in the magazine complete with photos, charts and graphics. In order to do this, the plans are only available in *Adobe Acrobat* PDF format (link to download is provided). While some lessons focus on historic themes, there are also lessons on South Africa, Bosnia and Kurdistan. In addition to lesson plans, the teacher resources based on the general themes of culture; time, continuity and change; people placcs and environments; individual development and identity; individuals, groups and institutions; power, authority and governance; production, distribution and consumption; science, technology and society; global connections; and civic ideals and practices. Created by the National Council for the Social Studies. K–12.

Other Features: Information on the organization, membership and periodicals.

Native American Links

http://www.ameritech.net/users/macler/nativeamericans.html

Marilee has assembled several hundred links to sites celebrating Native Americans, organized by these topics: clip art, clothing, craft projects, folk art, games and legends, recipes, songs and dances, teaching aids and class projects, and miscellaneous tribe info. Click on the **paw print**, not the words, to see the link. There are over 100 links for all the tribe categories: Algonquin, Apache, Cherokee, Comanche, Haida, Hopi, Iroquois, Navajo, Plains, Pomo, and Sioux. Information is perfectly geared for elementary and middle school age. K–8.

New Years Around The World

http://www.proteacher.com/090098.shtml

No matter what countries or cultures you think of, at some point they all celebrate the beginning of a new year as a time of hope and new beginnings. ProTeacher has gathered dozens of activities, lessons, recipes, crafts, worksheets, and links for New Year's traditions from around the world. Featured cultures and countries: Greek, Diwali-Hindu, Jewish, Ecuadorian, Persian, Tet (Vietnamese), Cambodian, Iranian, and Chinese cultures. Created by ProTeacher.

Peace Corps

http://www.peacecorps.gov/wws/guides/looking/contents.html

The Peace Corps offers a variety of lesson plans designed to help students learn about other cultures. These plans fit into three main categories: defining culture, developing global perspectives and challenging assumptions. Each category is further divided by grade level for grades three through 12. These unique perspectives cover everything from understanding a culture's people to understanding their food. The Challenging Assumptions categories deal largely with overcoming prejudice and promoting understanding. All materials needed for each plan are available for downloading from links within the plans themselves. Created by the Peace Corps. K–12.

Other Features: Information about the Peace Corps and how to volunteer.

ProTeacher

http://www.proteacher.com/090031.shtml

Teachers may browse lesson plans by under the headings of ancient cultures, art history, holidays, around the world, and Native Americans today. These lessons feature formal lesson plans, foreign language activities, games, activities, worksheets, maps, cross-curricular themes, arts and crafts, and much more. Some of the cultures included are Middle Eastern, European, Asian, African, and many others. Click on Around The World to see lessons from Africa, Arctic, Asia, Australia, Oceania, Central America, Europe, Middle East, North America, and South America. Created by ProTeacher. K–12.

Other Features: The site also offers free membership registration that allows teachers to store their favorite lesson plans online in a personalized area.

Social Studies & Culture

http://www.edhelper.com/cat263.htm

EdHelper provides a large number of social studies lesson plans organized by subject and grade level, many of which involve non-American culture. In addition to worksheets and lesson plans, teachers will also find links to web quest projects. Subjects range all the way from archaeology to current events on a variety of international topics. Sample topics: American Revolution, archaeology, community service, under-developed countries, racial discrimination, the White House, individual differences, local and national governments, current events, conflict situations, and more. Created by EdHelper. K–12.

Other Features: EdHelper contains thousands of lesson plans and web quests on all the major and minor teaching subjects.

Teachers First

http://www.teachersfirst.com/

Teachers First offers a wealth of content on almost all subjects. Click on the Classroom Resources tab at the top of the page and select "Content Matrix" from the drop-down list. You'll be taken to an easy-to-read chart that breaks the available lesson plans down by grade level and subject. Once you've selected world cultures and your grade level, you'll be taken to fast, clean one-page index subdivided into the following topics: general sites, Africa, ancient history, Asia, China, Europe, India, Japan, Latin America and the Mid-East. Following any of the links in those sections will lead to even more lesson plans and Web resources. Created by the Network for Industrial TV, Inc. K–12.

Don't Miss: The Teacher's Lounge section isn't strictly academic but offers quite a bit of time and sanity-saving advice that isn't taught in school.

Notes:

PERSONAL VALUES AND CHARACTER

Moral Education

http://tigger.uic.edu/~lnucci/MoralEd/overview.html

The site offers a wealth of scholarly resources for professionals interested in the moral aspect of educational theory and practice. Although it does feature a handful of lesson plans (under Classroom Practices), the site focuses more on journal articles, book reviews, overview of moral development and education, and email discussion lists for educators. The main page (Overview) contains several summaries of educational philosophies held by Piaget, Kohlberg, Turiel, and Gilligan. Featured Articles is an excellent collection of more than two dozen full-text articles on the topic. Classroom Practices will be of most interest to teachers. It has classroom guidelines, how to lead a class discussion, plus sample lesson plans. Created by Dr. Nucci, University of Illinois at Chicago.

CHARACTERplus

http://info.csd.org/staffdev/chared/Lessons/

A project involving over 30 public school districts in the United States, this group provides resources to encourage cooperation between the school, home and community. Their web site offers many useful resources for character educators including lesson plans, student efforts, and links to other resources on the Internet. Lessons are divided into three grade levels. Sample elementary topics: peace pledge, flag dedication, and newsletter. Sample middle and high school topics: responsibility, citizenship, and a mural project. Created by Cooperating School Districts of Greater St. Louis (Missouri). K–12.

Core Knowledge

http://www.coreknowledge.org/CKproto2/resrcs/

Based on a program philosophy that schools need a specific, shared core curriculum in each grade to help children establish strong foundations of knowledge. Great site to browse and pick up ideas. Lesson plans are grouped by grade level for pre-school through eighth grade. This collection contains units and lesson plans developed by teachers in Core Knowledge schools and presented at recent national Core Knowledge conferences. Lesson plans can be downloaded in Adobe PDF format which allows teacher to print out the included graphics. They are not listed in any particular order; click on title to view. Plans judged as the "best of the best" by Core Knowledge teachers are marked with gold stars. Created by Core Knowledge Foundation. K–8.

Goodcharacter.com

http://www.goodcharacter.com/

This site provides discussion questions, writing assignments and student activities broken down into the themes of trustworthiness, citizenship, respect, honesty, responsibility, courage, fairness/justice, diligence, caring and integrity. The site also includes information on character in sports, service learning and key character organizations. Created by Good Character. K–12.

Don't Miss: The site also includes listings of character education organizations and public service groups students can volunteer to help.

Character Education Ideas

http://www.ilovethatteachingidea.com/ideas/subj_character_ed.htm

About two dozen detailed lesson plans and activity ideas help children learn about and reflect on the kind of people they want to be. Lessons are organized in a nice table that gives the title, grade level, and a brief description. Click the title to view it. Some of the titles are Fishin' For Good Friends (uses Rainbow Fish), Who Am I? Cards (team building), Character Trait Spotlight, Deck the Halls with Positive Behavior (holiday incentive), Flower for a Friend, and many others. Sponsored by I Love That Teaching Idea! K–6.

Other Features: The site has plenty of other teaching ideas, activities, and lessons for other subject areas—Art, Field Trips, Holidays, Math, Learning Centers, Reading, Science, Spelling, Writing/Language Arts, and many others. Click on the alphabetical links on the left side.

Character Education Partnership

http://www.ncpublicschools.org/nccep/lp/

This site has over 100 character-based lesson plans, incorporated into one of the following subjects: science, math, English, social studies, art, guidance, communication skills, and computer skills. Examples of English/language arts topics: characters in literature and life, compliments, voyage to values, puppet interview, writing an autobiography, poetry, problem solving in the adult world, and citizenship. Lessons are written in standard format: subject, time, objective, procedures and activity suggestions, and rubric. Created by the North Carolina Department of Public Instruction. K–12.

Don't Miss: The site also includes information about a U.S. government grant program for funding character education in public schools.

International Cultures

http://www.pbs.org/teachersource/soc_stud.htm

Correlated to more than 230 sets of state and national curriculum standards, the social studies area of the PBS Teacher Source site offers a multitude of lesson plans and activities focusing on international cultures. From archaeology and world history to current events, the site allows teachers to search by keyword or by using a combination of drop-down menus to narrow browsing by grade level and subject. Created by the Public Broadcasting System. K–12.

Saddleback Valley Schools: Character Education

http://www.svusd.k12.ca.us/resources/character/

Various teachers from within this California school district have put together a collection of their best lesson plans. Topic sections are cooperation, goal attainment, honesty, respect for law and order, responsibility, respect for cultural differences and respect for self and others. The Honesty and Respect for Self/Others sections have especially high-quality curriculum for Gr. 1–12, which all follow a standard lesson format. Lesson plans are given in a plain text format and can easily be copied. Created by the Saddleback Valley Unified School District (California). K–12.

Notes:

Best Sites for CLASSROOM AND STUDENT MANAGEMENT

CLASSROOM MANAGEMENT

Articles on Classroom Management

http://www.education-world.com/preservice/learning/management.shtml

Two dozen magazine articles posted by Education World. Sample topics include: adult praise for children, classroom computer rules, conflict resolution, first six weeks of school, classroom management experts, classroom discipline problems and solutions, homework hassles, recess success, rewards and punishments (several articles), Harry Wong speech, shy students, creating an atmosphere of cooperation, mini-lessons for spare minutes, and when to discipline. Created by Education World, Inc.

Other Features: Site has hundreds of resources for educators: subject and lesson plans, as well as resources for special educators (special education, vocational, and counseling).

Classroom Management Ideas

http://www.proteacher.com/030000.shtml

More than 40 contributions from experienced teachers with hundreds of ideas about classroom management: managing classroom jobs, beat the clock, bell work, breaking up a fight, file cabinet odds and ends, homework policies, manners madness, nonverbal signals, rewards, routines, and use of space in the classroom. Created by ProTeacher.

Don't Miss: Class Meetings has ideas for circle time, morning meetings, running meetings, problem solving, and success skills for students.

Other Features: Message Boards (right sidebar) contain the subject topics for all kinds of current discussions taking place (more than writing topics). Click to go there and read what others have posted—you can jump in and join the discussion too.

Common Misbehaviors in the Classroom

http://www.disciplinehelp.com/teacher/list.cfm?cause=All

Discipline Help describes 177 common misbehaviors seen in classrooms. Their approach is that before you can begin trying to change a child's behavior, you have to properly identify that behavior. The identification must be specific, so labels are given to the behaviors, not to or about the children themselves. Understanding the primary and secondary causes of the misbehavior is the first step to coming up with strategies and procedures to better handle it. Each "behavior label" has a description (attitudes and actions), what effect it has on others, actions (what is causing the behavior, needs being revealed), common mistakes teachers make in handling the behavior. Some of the 117 labels include the agitator, the blabbermouth, the class clown, the complainer, the disorganized, the dreamer, the fighter, the follower, the gossip, the immature, the know-it-all, the loner, the liar, the pest, the pouter, and many more. Solutions to handing these behaviors, which used to be posted at no cost on this site, are now available only with a subscription. K–12.

Discipline With Purpose

http://www.selfdisciplinedwp.com/

Child psychologist experts say there is a huge difference between discipline (external) and self-discipline. DWP is a program that schools can purchase that emphasizes and teaches students 15 self-discipline skills. Click on 15 Skills to see the list, which are in three groups: basic skills for K–3 (listening, following directions, sharing, social skills), constructive skills for Gr. 4–7 (cooperation, understanding rules, leadership, communication), and generative skills for Gr. 8–12 (organization, problem solving, serving others). The program shows the benefits of fewer discipline problems when implemented over the long run. Created by Discipline With Purpose. K–12.

Don't Miss: Research and Results shows several articles and summaries of research about how discipline is inseparable from teaching. Self-discipline must be an integral part of managing student behavior and attitude problems, according to DWP. Call and they will send a free copy of the "ABCs of Self-Discipline."

Educational Philosophies and Theories

http://www.funderstanding.com/about_learning.cfm

Contains links for numerous theories and educational philosophies developed by medical, health, educational, and university experts on these topics. Each topic you click provides basic definition, quick facts, and how it impacts learning (curriculum, instruction, and assessment). Topics discussed here: constructivism, behaviorism, Piaget's developmental theory, neuroscience, brain-based learning, learning styles (concrete and abstract, active and reflective), multiple intelligences, right brain/left brain thinking, communities of practice, control theory, observational learning, and Vygotsky and social cognition. Beautiful, organized site that is succinct and not overly academic. Created by Funderstanding.

Educational Philosophies: Conference Papers

http://www.bu.edu/wcp/MainEduc.htm

More than 50 professional papers presented at an international conference on philosophies in education. Files are in text-only format (viewed through your browser), for easy viewing and printing. Sample topics in the papers: corporate sponsored education, pedagogy in a technological era, gifted education, education and violence, education of the soul, humanities, rethinking education, liberal arts, critical thinking, ethics, social-cultural factors in youth education, and South Africa issues. Papers are organized in an index by author, affiliation, and title. You can also search by keyword. Created by The Paideia Project Online; hosted by Boston University.

Effective Classroom Strategies

http://www.adprima.com/managing.htm

Expert article about classroom management, room arrangement suggestions, setting expectations for behavior, managing academic work, inappropriate behavior, consequences, and effective praise guidelines. Article also contains information for teachers of ESL students. Look for the chart comparing effective praise with ineffective praise. The page is long so you'll have to scroll. Created by Dr. Robert Kizlik, Adprima System for Instruction.

Don't Miss: See the page devoted to mistakes often made by new teachers, such as standing in one place too long and beginning a new activity before getting students' attention. Also links at the bottom with suggested print resources for classroom management.

Harry K. Wong Summary

http://www.glavac.com/harrywong.htm

This site contains an excellent summary of the major concepts from Harry Wong's popular book, *The First Days of School: How to Be an Effective Teacher*. The book's premise: What you do on the first day of school will determine your success for the rest of the year. His book contains practical information about setting up procedures and expectations for nearly every routine activity in the classroom, from pencil sharpening to lining up. There are links to read a review of Wong's book as well as an interview the site's author conducted with Wong. Created by teacher, author, and speaker Marjan Glavac.

Honor Level

http://www.honorlevel.com/

A program being used by schools across the U.S. that provides a framework for student discipline—a blend of assertive and empathetic discipline that shows respect for the child. Eleven Techniques for Better Classroom Discipline has practical tips and guidelines to help teachers be effective and have control. One of those techniques is focusing—making sure the teacher has students' attention before talking. Otherwise, children think it is acceptable for them to continue chatting while teacher is talking. Four Steps to a Better Classroom Discipline has practical, real-world advice for teachers, by having different sets of rules for different students, depending on what level they are operating (determined by past behavior). Clean, well-designed site. Created by Budd Churchward, The Honor Level System: Discipline By Design.

How To's of Daily Routines

http://www.teachnet.com/how-to/manage/

Contributions about the day-to-day routines of running a classroom, posted by dozens of experienced teachers: attendance charts, banana bucks, bathroom breaks, great group behavior, starting the day, student whiteboards, thinking hats, tips for starting the day, hats in the building, using whiteboards, and why kids tattle. Scroll down to see even more topics: assessment of reading, glue bottles, popcorn as a reward, sorting, point scales, student teams, when a student is sick, pets and animals, indoor recess, lining up, party jar, and more. Created by Teachnet.

Don't Miss: I Can't Wait—Bathroom Breaks, a humorous article filled with dozens of teacher ideas about handling the annoying problem of student bathroom requests.

Really Big List of Classroom Management Resources

http://drwilliampmartin.tripod.com/reallybest.htm

Say hello to Dr. Martin's recently streamlined collection of classroom management and discipline web sites, "still the biggest on the Internet." Originally created by Monmouth University graduate students who gave up one week of their lives scouring the entire Internet (well almost), this site has many of the best that cyberspace has to offer teachers. There are classroom management techniques tailored to elementary and secondary education, discipline ideas for new and experienced teachers, tips for handling special education, suggestions for getting organized, strategies for preventing behavior problems, sample classroom rules, ways of creating a caring community, and information on new products and services. There are even a few resources for those who question the basic premise of "classroom management." This site has it all! Compiled by graduate students of Dr. Bill Martin, Monmouth University, West Long Branch, New Jersey.

Learning Pyramid

http://lowery.tamu.edu/Teaming/Morgan1/sld023.htm

http://www.gareal.org/learningpyramid.htm

The Learning Pyramid concept is often taught in teacher education programs. The pyramid design is based on research that shows 90 percent of students retain information best by immediately using it or by teaching others, 76 percent by practicing what they learned, and 50 percent by discussing it with others. Lecture and reading appears to be the two least effective methods—only five and ten percent of students, respectively, retain information effectively with that method. There are some colorful pictures of learning pyramids you can view and print. Created by National Training Laboratories (Maine).

Learning Styles

http://7-12educators.about.com/cs/learningstyles/

Not all children learn the same way. About.com compiled this excellent list of links about different learning styles of which educators need to be aware. Learning Styles Assessment has tests and tools to help you evaluate your own and your students' learning styles. An article on the use of mnemonics is useful for visual learners. Learning Styles Theory has an overview of concrete versus abstract as well as active and reflective styles. Another article gives suggestions on nurturing the genius in each child. Be sure to click on the next page at the bottom to see more articles. Created by About.com. Gr. 7–12.

Management Strategies

http://www.inspiringteachers.com/tips/management/

This site is especially useful for new and beginning teachers, because often, the biggest obstacles they face when they first begin teaching is classroom management, discipline, and motivating students. There are several short, practical articles on how to give specific instructions (to avoid student misunderstandings), using routine procedures, how to conduct good planning (to prevent problems), and recording daily behavior with a clipboard (great for documentation with parents and administrators). Created by Inspiring Teachers Publishing, Inc. K–8.

Other Features: Site features lots of good resources for new and experienced teachers: mentoring, monthly features, professional and classroom resources, and community. Check monthly features, which usually has articles for new teachers on subjects from discipline to holiday celebrations. The site's authors welcome e-mail from new teachers with questions and comments.

Multiple Intelligence Online Class

http://www.thirteen.org/edonline/concept2class/month1/

An online class, where teachers can learn about theory and concept, then go to hands-on, practical demonstrations. Well-written narrative is friendly and explains the concepts in easy-to-understand narrative. Topics move sequentially: what is the MI theory, how it varies from traditional definition of intelligence, what multiple intelligences have to do with your classroom, how MI theory has developed since 1983 (when first introduced), what the critics say, benefits of using MI in your school, and application of MI theory to help students learn better. Nice use of illustrations, some of which have links to read more. The page is long, so you'll have to scroll to read it all. Created by Thirteen Ed Online and Disney Learning Partnership.

Multiple Intelligence Theory

http://www.teachers.ash.org.au/teachereduc/indexTE.html

Click on **Theories** (top) to see a pop-down menu, then choose **Multiple Intelligences**. Colorful, concise summary of Howard Gardner's famous theory (1983) in which he suggests that a person has at least seven different kinds of intelligence. Some of these intelligences are: linguistic (ability for using language for expression and communication), mathematical (ability for logic and math), and visual spatial (ability to represent the world in your mind). There is a section for educators that explains how to present materials and how to reach children through all their abilities. Article includes an example of how to use spelling activities that address all the intelligences. Created by Teacher Education, South Australia. K–12.

Whole Class Self-Monitoring

http://www.pb5th.com/selfmoni.shtml

An in-depth article about a behavior management system based on self-monitoring by students at regular intervals throughout the day. The whole class participates. Students monitor their own individual behavior and keep a frequency tally. Some of the tips for implementing this program: avoid wholesale stickers and treats, praise honest self-reporting by students, never change a mark a student has given him/herself, teach appropriate group interaction, gradually allow students to take over, teacher to keep a 3:1 ratio of positive to negative comments, inform parents what you're doing, and give it time to work. Created by teacher Fred Roemer, Tampa, Florida.

Notes:

DISABILITIES

ADHD Fact Sheets

http://www.chadd.org/webpage.cfm?cat_id=24

There is probably not a teacher who hasn't had a student with symptoms of or diagnosis of ADHD. Site features several high quality fact sheets compiled by a leading organization on Attention-Deficit Hyperactivity Disorder. Fact sheet topics include: ADHD as a disability, parenting a child with the disorder, medical management of children and adults, coexisting disorders, unproven treatments, educational rights, and ADHD in adults. The online fact sheets are abbreviated versions of a full series that is available upon membership. Created by CHADD (Children and Adults with Attention-Deficit/Hyperactivity Disorder).
Don't Miss: Research Studies has comprehensive information about current research into the disorder, funded research projects, and list of links to additional research, articles, and projects.

Children with Disabilities

http://www.math.ttu.edu/~dmettler/dlit.html

Suggested reading and book list for teachers and parents about kids with physical disabilities (cerebral palsy, hearing, visual impairment, spina bifida, etc.), developmental disabilities, mental illness, learning disabilities, multiple disabilities, and more. List is lengthy and organized by categories, so you'll have to scroll or use the Find feature in your browser using a keyword. Each listing has author, title, and brief description. Created by Donna Metler, Texas Tech University.

Dyslexia

http://www.dyslexiaonline.com/home.html

Updated regularly, this comprehensive site is dedicated to resolving the traditional misconceptions of dyslexia and related attention deficit and anxiety disorders. Features highlights recently published books and articles about this disorder. In The News has news headlines, national survey results, medical studies, and scientific research being conducted with autistic children and adults. You can also hear news interviews with the site's author (*AudioPlayer* is needed; download link provided). Created by Levinson Medical Center for Learning Disabilities.

Gifted Education

http://ericec.org/gifted/gt-menu.html

Includes fact sheets, article digests, articles, links to other resources, and searchable database by state. The FAQ (Frequently Asked Questions) has general information and links about all aspects of this topic: alternative assessments, classroom placement, curriculum compacting, early entrance to college, children with disabilities and giftedness, history of gifted education, best practices for teaching, longitudinal studies, legal issues, racial and ethnic minorities, and resiliency. Article Digests appear to be full-text with lots of good information on over 30 topics. Created by ERIC Clearinghouse on Disabilities and Gifted Education, U.S. Department of Education.

Other Features: Links to Other Resources features more than 50 well-researched sites by federally funded agencies, university sites, and miscellaneous sites. You can also search the database by state using the pull-down menu. Project Description explains about the searchable database and why so many states no longer offer special programs for the gifted. Dual Exceptionalities is a term that usually means gifted students with disabilities.

Inclusive Education

http://www.uni.edu/coe/inclusion/

When all students in a school, regardless of their disabilities, strengths, or weaknesses, become part of the general school community, that is considered "inclusive education." Site is designed for educators, special education teachers, parents, and anyone interested in the goal of inclusive education. Philosophy explains the benefits received by children with special needs, by teachers, and by society. Legal Requirements contains information about federal mandates including IDEA (Individuals with Disabilities Education Act), which requires that children with disabilities be educated in regular classroom settings. Site also has sections for teacher competencies, teaching strategies, decision making, and resources. Created by Department of Special Education, University of Northern Iowa.

International Center: Dyslexia

http://www.interdys.org/

Comprehensive site featuring conferences and seminars, technology, public policy issues, research, and general factual information. ABCs of Dyslexia includes what you can do, how to use the Web site, facts about dyslexia, definitions, common signs, and general information. Branch Services has a clickable map to find a centers all over the U.S. and some foreign countries. Technologies explains about assistive devices, which many teachers may find useful since an increasing number of students find these technologies invaluable. Established 50 years ago, IDA is an international, non-profit, scientific and educational organization dedicated to the study and treatment of dyslexia. Created by the International Dyslexia Association, International Office, Maryland.

Learning Disabilities

http://www.ldanatl.org/

Click Resources to see all that is available to educate and support teachers and those who work with children with learning disabilities: audiotapes, videotapes, books on tape, national organizations, government agencies, publications for professionals, recent publications, toll-free resources for adults, and Web links. LDAA is a non-profit organization of volunteers including individuals with learning disabilities, their families, and professionals. Created by the Learning Disabilities Association of America (Pennsylvania).

Other Features: Check the link for LDA's position on issues such as reading and learning disabilities, inclusion, violence in schools, and neurotoxicity levels. For example, the paper on reading and learning disabilities states that LDA's position is that no single reading method will be effective for all students with learning disabilities and that a combination of approaches is necessary.

Learning Disabilities Online

http://www.ldonline.org/

An interactive guide to learning disabilities for parents, teachers, and other professionals. ABCs provides definitions of Attention Deficit Disorder and learning disorders, types of learning disabilities, causes and theories, how to determine if a child has a learning disability, steps to take after diagnosis, and an explanation of IEP (individualized education plan). LD In Depth has links for dozens of subcategories, including: assessment, bilingual, family relationships, foreign language acquisition, math skills, nonverbal learning disabilities, processing deficits, speech and language, technology, and a section for teachers. Created by LDOnline and WETA.

Don't Miss: Ask Dr. Silver, where you can read questions and answers from a child and adolescent psychiatrist with 30 years of research behind him. You can also post a question for him.

National Center for Learning Disabilities

http://www.ncld.org/

According to NCLD, 2.8 million students are currently receiving special education services for learning disabilities in the U.S. The organization provides national leadership in support of children and adults with learning disabilities by offering information, resources, education, advocacy, and referral services. About LD has definitions, basics, fast facts, early and common warning signs, legal rights, in-depth information, and tips for parents and teachers. Sprinkled throughout the site's many departments are links to other resources and information.

Don't Miss: Get Ready to Read, which features a screening instrument that can help a parent or teacher see whether a young child (four or five years old) is learning the basics of reading.

Special Education Resources

http://seriweb.com/

A comprehensive collection of Internet information resources of interest to those involved in the fields related to special education. Categories include: general disabilities, disability products and commercial sites, legal and law, special education discussion groups, mental retardation, physical and health disorders, learning disabilities, attention deficit, speech impairment, special needs and technology, inclusion resources, university-based information, national organizations, autism, gifted and talented, and more. Site is continually updated with new resources and research. Created by Roseann Horner.

Behavior Home Page

http://www.state.ky.us/agencies/behave/bi/bi.html

The goal for most educators, parents, and other professionals is for all students to be successful in school and in life. To reach that goal, many have adopted a three-tiered model of behavioral support. Interventions on this site are organized in these three tiers: universal (school-wide), targeted (small groups or individual students), and intensive (wraparound) levels, to teach all students what they must do to be successful, not only in a classroom setting, but in everyday life. This site identifies and provides links to resources for each level of behavioral support. Compiled by the Kentucky Department of Education. K-12.

Other Features: Using "time out" to remove a child from an emotional or behavioral situation used to be a common practice among teachers as well as parents. Because of its tendency to be misused, many states are adopting guidelines for schools on how and when to use time out. Click on Time Out Procedures (left column) to view documents issued by Kentucky DOE to its superintendents and schools about uses and limits of time out.

Notes:

TALENTED AND GIFTEDNESS

Canadian Resources

http://www.acs.ucalgary.ca/~gifteduc/info-services.html

Nice collection of links for teachers and parents of gifted and talented children in Alberta, Canada. Center for Gifted Education Library has curriculum resources and professional reading materials. Articles by Centre Staff contains full-text articles written by experienced psychologists and professionals on topics like emotional sensitivity, perfectionism, acceleration, and individualized program planning. Reading List contains book descriptions for parents, and there's a similar reading list for teachers. Newsletters shows previous issues of the organization's online newsletters (*Adobe Acrobat* PDF format). Created by Centre for Gifted Education, University of Calgary.

Conference Papers

http://www.nexus.edu.au/teachstud/gat/papers.htm

Nearly 50 professional papers presented at a national conference on the education of the gifted and talented in South Australia. Files are in text-only format, for easy viewing and printing. Papers can be located by author, title, or keyword. Sample topics in the papers: acceleration, the new intelligence (caring thinking), gifted deaf students, underachieving gifted students, impact on self-esteem, establishing cluster groups, giftedness in disadvantaged schools, isolated Aboriginal gifted program, linking parents and teachers, perfectionism, questioning techniques, gifted minority students, talent in music, and thinking skills. Created by the Australian Association for the Education of the Gifted and Talented.

Gifted Kids in a Regular Classroom

http://www.kidsource.com/kidsource/content/challenging_gifted_kids.html

Most talented/gifted students are in regular classrooms, yet that instruction is generally not tailored to meet their needs, according to this article by Beverly Parke. She explains how regular classroom teachers can meet the needs of gifted students. Article features the steps to full service, characteristics of gifted and talented, role of the classroom teacher, program options to meet their needs, instructional provisions, references, and additional reading. Created by KidSource OnLine, Inc.

National Assoc. for Gifted Children

http://www.nagc.org/ParentInfo/index.html

A gifted person is one who shows a well-above average performance level (or special talent) in one or more areas. Sections include: who are the gifted (definitions, intelligence, meeting their needs), characteristics of various areas of giftedness (visual arts, leadership, creative thinking, general intelligence, and specific talent), and why gifted education needs to be supported. Refer parents of your gifted children here to learn more about how they can support their children with educational and environmental experiences. Created by National Association for Gifted Children, Washington, DC.

Multiple Intelligence Theory

http://www.teachers.ash.org.au/teachereduc/indexTE.html

Click on Theories (top) to see a pop-down menu, then choose Multiple Intelligences. Colorful, concise summary of Howard Gardner's famous theory (1983) in which he suggests that a person has at least seven different kinds of intelligence. Some of these intelligences are: linguistic (ability for using language for expression and communication), mathematical (ability for logic and math), and visual spatial (ability to represent the world in your mind). There is a section for educators that explains how to present materials and how to reach children through all their abilities. Article includes an example of how to use spelling activities that address all the intelligences. Created by Teacher Education, South Australia. K–12.

Notes:

BULLETIN BOARDS, AWARDS, WORKSHEETS

Award Certificate Generator

http://www.teach-nology.com/web_tools/certificates/

Follow the five easy steps to make personalized, colorful awards and certificates for students: pick a horizontal border, then a vertical border, pick a graphic (14 to choose from), then type in the student name, teacher name, and message you want to be printed. Click on "generate certificate" and it puts all the elements together for you. You can review it, go back to make changes if needed, or print it. You can print on color paper or quality embossed paper to add a special touch. Subjects elements (graphics) include: art, computers, English, P.E., math, science, social studies, plus female and male trophies, and generic ribbons and trophies. Easy to use. No plug-ins needed. Created by Teachnology.

Award Maker

http://www.schoolexpress.com/awards/name.asp

Enter student's name, click the type of award (140 different titles and messages). Samples of messages: ravenous reader, awesome attendance, great job, great penmanship, marvelous math, writers award, student council, great oral report, volunteer booster kid, BUG (bringing up grades), good sportsmanship, job well done, handwriting improvement, good behavior, and computer whiz. Then scroll to the bottom and "click here to choose a picture." Choose from 70 colorful, graphic images (kid-friendly cartoons and school images), then scroll to the bottom again and "click here to choose a border." Choose from several colorful borders, click to go to next screen and type a personal message. Then you're done. You can print the award and present it. No plug-ins needed to use this award maker. Created by School Express.

Bulletin Boards

http://www.theteacherscorner.net/bulletinboards/

Great ideas to jazz up bulletin boards contributed by teachers. Monthly Bulletin Boards has monthly sections, each with ideas for that month such as seasonal, holidays, and school-related events. Subject Bulletin Boards has about ten subject themes, each one with several ideas. Subjects featured include art, geography, history, library, math, music, and others. Theme Bulletin Boards has themes such as seasons, student work, motivation, sayings, special events, teamwork, and more. Bulletin Board Materials features ideas like making letters from laminated fabric, and backgrounds using wallpaper, tablecloths, and fabric.

Other Features: Each idea has the teacher's e-mail address so you can contact them for more ideas. Teacher's Corner also wants teachers to e-mail their favorite ideas so they can be posted on the site. Site also features a huge section with lesson plans for all subjects.

Bulletin Board Links

http://school.discovery.com/schrockguide/bulletin/

Discovery School has compiled a page of links to all kinds of sites; some are personal and some are organizations/companies. Examples of categories: ideas for library media specialists, displays for K–3 teachers, all seasons, music classroom, business education, and preschool. Also there's a section for links that have pictures and more ideas, divided by grade level: elementary, middle, high, and any. Created by Kathleen Schrock.

Other Features: You will also see a section of suggested reading list of books all about bulletin boards. Most of them link to Amazon.com. You can also note the titles that interest you, then check with Half.com (**http://www.half.com**) and see if anyone is selling a used copy.

Certificate Links

http://www.theeducatorsnetwork.com/utt/certificates.htm

This page contains links in two sections. Certificates, which features links where you can purchase or generate personalized certificates, contains a dozen categories: success, early childhood, high school, elementary, certificate maker, teacher and coach, achievement, appreciation, and more. The second section, Ready-Made Certificates has all different grade and subject levels, where you can find sites to print ready-made certificates, most of which are in full-color. Some of these topics are: fantastic, perfect attendance, best friend, fantastic work, team player, service to school, school spirit, history, music, French, Spanish, sports, geography, and several major subject areas. You can print these on nice quality paper, then personalize with student's name. Created by The Educators Network. K–12.

Certificates, Worksheets & Printables

http://atozteacherstuff.com/printables/

Excellent index to hundreds of links within the AtoZ Teacher website, featuring a variety of student activities, worksheets, games and puzzles, monthly themes, coloring pages, poems, story starters, center signs, and more. Just click on the category that interests you and you'll find even more classroom resources. Some of the categories are: 100th day of school, body organs theme, book printables, high frequency words, maps/geography, rhyming words, animals, word puzzles, and colorful center signs. Created by AtoZ Teacher Stuff. K-4.

Don't Miss: At the top of the site are links to other AtoZ valuable lesson plans and ideas: teaching themes, lesson plans, tips, articles, subjects, grades, discussion forums, and more. The lesson plans link has suggestions for K-12.

Tried-and-True Teacher Resources

http://hbogucki.staffnet.com/aemes/resource/resource.htm

This colorful site features a variety of resources for elementary teachers (grades 2 to 4): mini-programs you can download to practice math and language arts, games and puzzles, interactive activities and practice for students, project and assignment ideas, fact sheets and forms, reading contracts, quiz generators, and much more. Scroll down to see the entire list. Some of the resources require *Adobe Acrobat Reader* (free to download) to view the pages, such as a page of math facts to photocopy for students. Compiled by Mrs. Bogucki, Anne E. Moncure Elementary School, Virginia. Gr. 2-4.

Don't Miss: It's hard for a child to visualize how much a million really is. How to Make A Million (look under Forms and Logs) is a classroom project where students can create a poster that has a million dots on it. Teachers can print the pieces of the poster from the online instructions, and students can assemble it.

Kim's Korner Bulletin Board Ideas

http://kimskorner4teachertalk.com/classmanagement/bulletinboards.html

Are you out of bulletin board ideas? Kim's Korner has hundreds of ideas for any subject, any grade level, any type of classroom. Teachers have generously contributed the ideas and photos you will see here. If you need a fresh idea for your board's background, did you know you can use curtains, magazine pages, picture post cards, book covers, a tablecloth, wallpaper, or wrapping paper? These same materials can also be used for die cutting letters and shapes. That's just one idea you'll find here. Other categories of ideas include: borders, computer information, schedules and calendars, student baby pictures, trivia contest, question of the week, riddles and jokes, epal and penpal communications, first day activities, recommending reading, feature attractions, remember this. Created by Kim's Korner 4Teacher Talk. K-12.

Don't Miss: Link at the bottom to an Education World article, "Your Search for Bulletin Board Ideas is Over," which takes you to a story with dozens more links to photos and ideas from teachers around the world. Kim's Korner also has great links at the bottom to elsewhere in her site: classroom management, writing, grammar, and reading and literature.

Halls, Walls, and Bulletin Boards

http://gardenofpraise.com/bulletin.htm

This site offers a beautiful, well-organized collection of visual displays for hallways, classroom walls, and bulletin boards. School bulletin boards are an effective way to show visitors and parents what students are learning and doing. The site is organized by grade level, and each idea features color photos(s) and a description. There are two dozen ideas just in the Kindergarten section alone. Spanish and Accelerated Reader classes are also included. Once you click on a title, you can click the "Next" button to view the next one without going back to the index page. Sponsored by Garden of Praise. K–5.

Teaching Extras and Tools

http://abcteach.com/directory/teaching_extras/

If you have a color printer, this is the site for you! This colorful, fun site features all kinds of extras that teachers can use to make teaching more fun for students. In the bookmarks section, you can print colorful bookmarks for your students, from animals to 9/11, laminate them, and give out. No matter what the season or holiday, you'll find paper borders, which are blank or lined sheets with colorful borders on which they can write a letter or story. There are blank calendars for each month of the year, student awards and certificates, center and classroom signs, classroom helper graphics (more than 30 sets), book genre labels, field trip checklists, printable flashcards, signs for thematic use (like science and social studies), and much more. Created by ABC Teach. K–5.

Notes:

CLASSROOM SUPPLIES AND MATERIALS

ACE Educational Supplies

http://www.ace-educational.com

Online catalog of two stores in Florida. Full Line Catalog has dozens of categories: arts and crafts, awards, critical thinking, creative play, flannel boards, furniture and equipment, games, globes, incentives, manipulatives, maps, music, puzzles, multimedia education, multilingual, plan and record books, pocket charts, and resources for every subject. Scroll down to see a section to shop by grade. Created by ACE Educational Supplies, Inc. and C&M Webmasters. K–12.

Don't Miss: Activity Calendar has free printable calendars, one for each month. Choose a month, and each day has a general fun activity for students. Project Room contains ideas by subject of hands-on activities that reinforce teaching concepts.

Classroom Direct

http://www.classroomdirect.com

Company says it's the largest marketer of non textbook educational supplies and furniture for K–12 to offer discount prices and same day shipping. Search by category, age, or grade, or shop by category: across the curriculum, active play, arts and crafts, audio-visual, furnishings, games, library and reference, paper, markers and highlighters, room decorations, software, teachers' helpers, and technology teaching aids, plus materials for all the major subjects. Free shipping is offered on orders of $149 or more. One-year satisfaction guarantee on all supplies and traditional teaching aids. Created by ClassroomDirect.com

For Teachers Only

http://www.forteachersonly.com/

Attractive design, well-organized site for teaching supplies and games. Teachers can browse among categories such as: patriotic, teaching aids, fun and games, gifts, supplies, holidays, pencils, pop-a-points (mechanical pencils), sharpeners, erasers, and more. Teaching Aids include resource books and manipulatives. Fun and Games has many categories: pencils, games, licensed characters and teams, sharpeners and erasers, toppers, pencil boxes, stickers, and other goodies kids like to get. Pencils can also be personalized—great student gift idea. Company has been in businss since 1940, with a toll-free number if you want to do business over the phone. You can also track your order, using this handy feature on the site. Created by Atlas Pen and Pencil Corp.

Oriental Trading Co.

http://www.orientaltrading.com/

A favorite of many teachers, because most craft kits and other items are available in lots of six or twelve, which makes the cost per item reasonable when buying for large classroom(s). Online shopping features are easy to use. If you have a print catalog, enter the item on the home page (under Catalog Quick Order) and you're off and running. If you don't have a print catalog, you can browse the online catalog, which has lots of photos and good descriptions of sizes, colors, etc. Categories for shopping include: party, candy, themes, jewelry, plush toys and dolls, toys and novelties, costumes, crafts, home accents, stationery, religious, personalized items, and electronics. It takes less than five minutes to set up an account, choose shipping method, enter credit card info, and place an order. Created by Oriental Trading Company.

Really Good Stuff

http://reallygoodstuff.org

Online version of a store in Connecticut. Opened in 1991, all products are tested in the classroom and reviewed by teacher panels before they ever make it into their catalog.

Don't Miss: Free resources such as study guides (nearly 100 kits and reproducibles in *Adobe Acrobat* PDF format), stationery templates (Mac and PC versions), and online tools (calculators and chat rooms). Other Features: Daily specials, teachers lounge, and easy catalog request form.

Scholastic Teacher Resources

http://www.scholasticdealer.com/products/catalog.shtml

Online educational resources for teachers from a trusted-name, Scholastic, publisher of children's books, core curriculum, and supplementary learning materials. Main page has a searchable database—you can search by author or title (if you know it) or just leave it blanks, and it will list all titles. Or you can search by grade, curriculum, or category (or leave grade level blank to list all grades). Categories are book and tape kits, emergent, games, mini-books, month-by-month, series, skills, start of the year, and seasons. Curriculum includes all the major subjects.

Other Features: See sidebar for product reviews, monthly specials, alpha tales, teaching genre, and dealer listings. To open a dealer account, you'll need to contact a regional sales rep (click your state).

School Tools ABC

http://abc2z.com/schooltools-nc/

General supplies for the classroom and teacher activity books for every subject. Over 9,500 catalogs organized in categories: arts and crafts, awards, decorations, electronics and software, furniture, games, religious and inspirational, resource books, teacher essentials, workbooks, and subject categories. Catalogs are also organized in Areas of Special Interest, such as: calculators, carpets, character education, first aid, games, handwriting, homework products, library products, overhead products, P.E., plays, teacher stamps, telling time, testing skills, toys, videos, and more. Shipping charges are 15 percent of order. Created by School Tools, North Carolina.

SmileMakers

http://www.smilemakers.com/

Teachers are always needing inexpensive treats, giveaways, rewards, and incentives to motivate students and recognize their efforts. You'll find reasonable prices, which means good value. Candy and Gum category includes lollipops, bubblegum, tattoo pops, and gum. Holiday, neon, licensed characters, grade level, metallic, sports and patterned pencils and stickers are perennial kid favorites. Toys include backpack pulls, balloons, crafts, erasers, gliders, holiday and seasonal toys, jewelry, party favors, rings, sound toys, soft spike animals, sticky and stretchy toys, oversize clips, balls, and more. Created by SmileMakers. K–12.

Other Features: Teacher category includes craft kits, certificates and paper products, stickers, and pencils. Craft kits include items to make butterfly plant stakes, animal paper bags, frog note holders, photo holders. Click on **Specials** to see what's on the discount table. Request a Catalog will bring one to your door to peruse and share with colleagues.

Best Sites for STUDENT USE

GENERAL

700+ Amazing, Spectacular Sites for Kids

http://www.ala.org/parentspage/greatsites/amazing.html

A children's technology committee of the American Library Association developed criteria to select the most "amazing, spectacular, mysterious, colorful Web sites for kids and the adults who care about them." From arts, literature and language to people past and present, planet earth, science, and technology, the site is packed with fun, factual games and information for all ages. From George Washington to Jane Addams, learn about our country's founders and others who shaped the nation. Includes much of the information in Spanish. The first Children and Technology Committee of the Association originally compiled this site in 1997 for Library Service to Children, a division of the American Library Association; it is currently maintained and updated by the Great Web Sites Committee.

America's Library

http://www.americaslibrary.gov/

Meet Amazing Americans such as the inventors, politicians, performers, activists and other everyday people who made America what it is today. Jump Back in Time has links for periods of history, super sleuth game, send a postcard, and see what happened on your birthday. Explore the States has a clickable map plus pull-down menu to visit states. Join America at Play features links to America's favorite pastimes, sports, and hobbies. See, Hear & Sing allows visitors to see a movie, hear a song, or play a tune from America's past. The site contains many documents, prints, photographs, maps, recordings, and other materials from the past, some of which may be offensive today because of how times change. Created by Library of Congress, the largest library in the world and the America's official library.

Cyberkids

http://www.cyberkids.com

Publishes original creative work (poetry, stories, art, multimedia) and serves as an online community for kids under 13. Kids Connect is a safe place for youngsters to chat and communicate with their peers (registration required). There are more than 50 interactive games (Fun and Games) with names like: hit and missile, jellyfish splat, ladder mazes, blingball, sixes, and space waste. Most games will require Macromedia Shockwave (link to download provided). Funny Bone has jokes sent in by kids. Cyberviews has movie, book and product reviews. Launchpad has links, categorized by subject (museums, schools, entertainment, sports), to many other Internet sites of interest to kids. The Learning Center has several links to sites where your child can find homework help, online tutoring, and scholarship information. Finally, the "Shopping" section provides categorized links to sites that offer products for kids such as clothing, toys and games, and children's software. Site works better with PCs than with Macintosh computers. Created by Able Minds, Inc. Gr. 2–5.

Fun Brain

http://www.funbrain.com/kidscenter.html

Excellent site to bookmark as a classroom home page. Divided into 6 sections: game showcase (the most popular games), numbers (math games), words (grammar and alphabet games), universe, culture, and extra. Older computers may not have enough memory to run some of these games. Has something for K–6, pre-teen, parents and teachers. Teacher resource section offers assistance in tracking student progress and enriching curriculum. The Quiz Lab offers thousands of pre-made quizzes in ten subjects and allows students to take the tests online. Targeted flash cards can be made online and easily printed. Lab Inservice Kit and the Curriculum Guide aid teachers in find age-appropriate information for their class.

Students can enhance math skills, learn new words, travel the universe and test spelling online with games and quizzes designed for whatever age they choose. Site copyrighted by The Learning Network Inc. K–6.

Homeworkopoly

http://www.teachnet.com/homeworkopoly/

To play the game each day, the student must complete their homework from the night before and turn it in. If student does not have homework, he/she must skip their turn that day. Throughout the year the game keeps going. Great concept to motivate students! This game board is an *Adobe Acrobat* PDF file that you print out and assemble, and it even includes Chance and Community Lunchbox cards. You can also make minor changes to the squares. Each student has his or her own token to move around. Measuring 35 inches square, it's large enough to use on a bulletin board. Some squares earn special prizes, provided by the teacher of course. Created by TeachNet.com. Gr. 1-8.

Kids Puzzles

http://www.kidcrosswords.com/

This popular site gets over two million visits a month and for good reason. Many of the puzzles can be worked online or they can be printed and distributed the old-fashioned way. Various types of puzzles: scrambled words, crossword puzzles, picture builder, words with similar meanings, backbone, crostic crossword, bendable word searches, and more. Themes of puzzles cross all subjects: math, social studies, science, and popular children's literature. To see hundreds of more puzzles in the archive, click on Previously Published Puzzles at the bottom. Site is available in a Spanish version too (click Español). Created by Kid Crosswords.com. Gr. 4–8.

Other Features: Kid Reader has interactive, flashing puzzle pictures—each one leading to a painting, story, trivia, or famous book. Kids Outdoors has hundreds of links to outdoor activities, pictures, how-to's, sports, and places of interest. Puzzles for Grown-Ups (home page) will give teachers a fun break too.

NCES Classroom

http://www.nces.ed.gov/nceskids/

Run your mouse over the images in the picture and watch the chalkboard to see what's available (or click on words below). There are several games involving math concepts. What Are your Chances allows students to roll virtual dice, then see a chart and explanation about probability of dice rolls. Create a Graph allows students to choose from several types of graphs, then enter the data. Games and Activities has a math quiz, education quiz, college mascot matching game, word search puzzles, print a survey, color online, and learn a new word of the day. Crunch is an online magazine where kids can read about or give their opinions about all kinds of issues. Created by National Center for Education Statistics (Washington, DC). Gr. 6–12.

Other Features: For high school students, Find Your College is a good starting point to search for colleges and universities by state or by region. Over 5,600 colleges are listed, and information includes: tuition, enrollment, degrees and programs, library resources, financial aid, and campus statistics.

Photo Image Library

http://www.pics4learning.com/

Thousands of free photographic images that have been donated by students, teachers, and amateur photographers, to be used for educational purposes such as reports, Web pages, presentations, and bulletin boards. Photos are organized in over 30 categories, including: art (carvings, paintings, sculpture, statues), architecture, countries (more than 40), culture, flags, geography and maps, history, holidays, monuments and national parks, music, Native American, parts of the body, plants (cactus, flowers, garden, trees), religion, schools, science (astronomy, energy, fossils, geology), signs, space, tools and machinery, transportation (air, boat, car, train), United States (subcategory for each state), and weather (clouds, extreme, fall, fog, rainbow, sunrise, sunset, winter). Permission has been granted for teachers and students to use the images in this collection. Created by Tech4Learning, Inc. in partnership with Orange County Public Schools (Florida).

Puzzle Depot

http://www.puzzledepot.com

Entertain your brain with three galleries of entertaining games, complete with sound effects. Sample game titles: Penguin Plunge, Feed the Pig, Three-Card Monty, Balloon Pop, Jigsaw, Trivia, Ant Run, Solitaire Master, and more. There are also Trivia Teasers, Scrabble™ word list, Educational Puzzles (word finder and anagrams) and Online Crossword Puzzles to help students with vocabulary and spelling skills. A lookup utility gives helps if the player gets stuck on any of the word puzzles. Games work better in *Internet Explorer* than in *Netscape*. Some games require *Macromedia Shockwave* (link to download is provided). Teachers may want to monitor usage, as they are several gambling, wrestling, and lottery-type games. Site features a fair amount of annoying pop-up ads. Created by Add2Net.com, LLC. Gr. 3–8.

Touch Paint

http://www.touchpaint.com/

Great site to help beginning computer students to develop eye-hand coordination as they "paint" pictures. Dozens of detailed black-and-white drawings with a palette of 48 active colors; others can be mixed. Categories of pictures include flowers and plants, kids doing what they do best, music and musicians, people, and abstract art. Touch the color, then touch the drawing. The young artists can print their drawings to keep or e-mail them to friends. Older children and adults can use HTML code on a stock picture to create a customized drawing. Created by New Jazz Media Inc. K–4.

Youth Net

http://yn.la.ca.us/

A place where youth of all ages around the world can safely meet each other, and participate in discussions, interactive learning projects, and activities. There are interactive projects for students of all ages that are posted by month. Examples include: Holiday Celebrations, Weather Watch, Grammar and Spelling Marathons, Math Olympic Warm-Ups, Scientific Method of Research, Science Experiments, Victorian Letters and Lives, and a Role-Playing Game involving creative writing. Created by Richard Bisbey II, California.

Notes:

LANGUAGE ARTS

Finish the Story

http://www.funbrain.com/wacky/

Wacky Tales (similar to Mad Libs). Students choose from one of 20 stories, fill in blanks with the requested parts of speech, then click "make story," and they get to read the funny story they created. Reinforces use of nouns, verbs, and adjectives. Sample story titles: Joe's Frog, The Mummy, My Summer Vacation, Fred's Birthday Party, Frida the Cat, Riding My Bike, and many more. Parents links offers quizzes for age-appropriate behavior. Great for a first-time parent concerned about child's academic progress. Links to Funbrain and Quiz Lab for teachers and students. Created by The Learning Network Inc., the same company that gave us FunBrain. Gr. 2–5.

Other Features: Click on FunCards to find free e-mail cards that kids or teachers can send. Topics are birthday, job well done, great try, you're the best, how are you, you're a superstar, congratulations, have a nice day, and fantastic. Cards are easy to send, but an e-mail address is needed.

Definition Guessing Game

http://www.eduplace.com/fakeout/

There are two sections to this site: Students can guess the answers to given words, or they can submit creative answers for future game definitions. Fake Out is the definition guessing game—students are given a word and they have several definitions to choose from, some of which are purposely funny. The second section is where students can submit made-up definitions to words, and Houghton Mifflin will use some of them in future Fake Out guessing games. Three grade levels: K–2, 3–5, 6–8.

Don't Miss: Past Games shows a long list of words used in the previous several months (for each grade level), which students can also click to guess.

Grammar Gorillas Game

http://www.funbrain.com/grammar/

Sponsored by FunBrain, this interactive game makes it fun for students to practice nouns, verbs, and other parts of speech. Two levels: beginner and advanced. When the student clicks on the correct noun or verb, the gorilla gets another banana. A help feature pops up when the incorrect answer is given. A scorecard at the top shows correct/incorrect answers, or you can click **Start Over**.

Other Features: FunBrain has lots of interactive games in all different major subject areas—math baseball, grammar gorillas, tic tac toe squares, line jumper, bunny count, word turtle, the plural girls, and dozens more. Go to the bottom and click **Games** or **Kids**.

Library Kids Page

http://www.scpl.lib.fl.us/kids/

All kinds of links to other sites organized by area of interest, such as animals, astronomy, authors, dinosaurs, people, pets, sports, stories, zoo, and more. Book reviews by kids (click on **Books & Reviews**). Children can learn more about favorite authors then try some suggested activities or write down ideas for writing their own stories. Each author is different but most have activity ideas. Created by Seminole County Public Library System Youth Services. Gr. 3–6.

Random House

http://www.randomhouse.com/kids/

Games, activities, trivia, coloring pages, contests, and author information for Random Houses' most popular children's' titles: *Arthur*, *Berenstain Bears*, *Dragon Tales*, *Junie B. Jones*, *Magic Tree House*, *Sesame Workshop*, *Seussville*, *Star Wars*, *Sweet Valley*, and *Thomas the Tank Engine*. Each of the book title links take you to another mini-site. Kids get to read excerpts from books and learn more about the author. Parents are encouraged to teach their children the facts of life with the Parent's Guide. Lots of highlighted books and authors on the home page. Teacher's guides, reader's companions, and other teaching tools available by clicking **Teachers@Random**. Updated monthly. Created by Random House, Inc. K–3.

SpellaRoo Game

http://www.funbrain.com/spellroo/

This interactive game from FunBrain lets kids play spelling games with a kangaroo that is a better hopper than a speller. Two playing levels: beginner and intermediate. Students read a sentence, then click the word that is spelled wrong. When the wrong answer is chosen, a popup menu explains what to do. A scorecard at the top shows correct/incorrect answers, or you can click **Start Over**. Created by The Learning Network. Gr. 1-5.

Other Features: FunBrain has lots of interactive games in all different major subject areas—Math Baseball, Grammar Gorillas, Tic Tac Toe Squares, Line Jumper, Bunny Count, Word Turtle, The Plural Girls, and dozens more. Go to the bottom and click **Games** or **Kids**.

Teen Reading at SmartGirl

http://www.smartgirl.org

SmartGirl was started by a single woman in 1996 who observed, at that time, there were very few web sites or computer games for teenage girls. Today, the site is hosted by Institute for Research on Women and Gender at the University of Michigan, to give teen girls "a safe place online where they're in charge" and where they can grow and thrive in the company of other teenage girls. The main categories say it well: Speak Out, Express Yourself, and Spread the Word. Speak Out is where teen girls can share their opinions and thoughts in surveys on all kinds of topics, and they can view results of past surveys to see what other teens think. Express Yourself is a creative writing forum where girls can submit love letters, poems, or announce their accomplishments and achievements. All of those submissions are published online. Spread the Word is where teens share their reviews and opinions on products, movies, websites, books and more. Sponsored by the National Science Foundation and the University of Michigan. Gr. 6-12.

Tongue Twisters

http://www.uebersetzung.at/twister/en.htm

How can a clam cram in a clean cream can? This impossible tongue twister is one of nearly 400 that will get kids reading, talking, working, and laughing at each other. The site is actually an international collection, and there are links to see tongue twisters in nearly 100 different languages. Click on 1st International Collection of Tongue Twisters to see the list of languages. Great speaking and listening practice for ESL students and foreign language students as well as English speakers. Created by Michael Reck, Waldenbuch, Germany. K–12.

Wacky World of Words

http://www3.bc.sympatico.ca/teachwell/

Over 100 fun and funny activities to learn parts of speech, vocabulary, and mechanics of the English language. Letters, words, phrases, sentences, and more—it's fun to mix them, shake them, and turn them inside out. Award-winning site where students can have fun with words, rather than working uninspiring worksheets. Activities you will find: Compound Clues, Words Within Words, Numbletters, Alpha-Spells, Fractured Fractions, Rhyming Buddies, A-Z Lists, Anagrams, Similes, Oxymorons, Mystery Words, and links to similar sites. Updated regularly. Created by Alison Elkins. Gr. 4–12.

Notes:

MATH HELPERS

A+ Math

http://www.aplusmath.com/

The site was designed to interactively assist students in improving their math skills using a game room, flashcards, homework help, and worksheets. Word search puzzles reinforce math language skills. Students can create, print and find the solution to their puzzle and then print it. Games and puzzles range from basic algebra, geometry, fractions and counting money. Flash cards are easy to make and print for classroom use. Worksheets can also be easily printed and reproduced by teachers. Answers to puzzles and online worksheets are given so students can self-assess, and students can get online help with math homework too. There are even advanced math problems for the brave! Created by Aplusmath.com.

Ask Dr. Math

http://mathforum.org/dr.math/

Dr. Math is a question and answer service for math students and their teachers. Students can search the archives for previously asked questions, and if it's not there, they can send a question to Dr. Math. Questions must be in English and can be about homework, puzzles, and math contest problems. Answers are sent back by e-mail. The best questions and answers are entered into a searchable archive organized by grade level (elementary, middle school, high school) and topic (exponents, infinity, polynomials, etc.). Over 300 volunteer math teachers and professors are involved in this project. Sponsored by the Math Forum at Drexel University (Pennsylvania).

Counting Change Games

http://www.quia.com/jg/65704.html

This site offers three interactive games for practice with counting change: matching game, flashcards, and concentration (memory). Flashcards can be played with or without Java plug-in. Matching Game is where a student matches (by clicking) number of coins with total value. Flashcards allows practice with counting coin value—student can flip the card over to see the answer, skip it, or take the card out when it's correct. Concentration is similar to the matching game, except it's done by memory—turning over cards until you get a match.

Don't miss: Math Journey—travel to 30 world cities by answering math problems. In order to board the plane to each new city, the player has to correctly answer a math question. If you miss three questions, you miss the flight! Created by Quia Corporation. Gr. 2–4.

Fractions and Decimals

http://www.webmath.com/index2.html

Whether students need help with converting decimals to fractions (and vice versa) or calculating fractions, this is an excellent problem-solving site, because it is interactive. The student enters the problem, then clicks the "solve" button to get the answer. First, click on the category: Numbers, Decimals, Number Crunching, Fractions, or Scientific Notation. You will see a quick explanation of what the category means and how to do it, then you will see blank boxes in which you can enter digits to solve the problem. Not only does the solution give the answer, but there is also an explanation of how the answer was derived, just like having a teacher there!

Other Features: There is a pull-down menu at the bottom for about two dozen other interactive problem solvers, from Calculus to Geometry. At the top, WebMath offers help in other areas of math: Math for Everyone (finances, unit conversion), K-8 Math (basics, fractions, ratios), Algebra, Plots and Geometry, Trig and Calculus, and Miscellaneous (polynomials, statistics).

Fact Monster

http://www.factmonster.com/

This site includes everything from all-time top grossing kids films to profiles on each of the United States. Site includes an atlas, almanac, dictionary and encyclopedia. Subjects range from current events, history, math and science to weather facts and a spotlight section. Homework center offers handy tips on study, speaking, listening and writing skills. There is also the opportunity to see what questions other students have asked. Don't miss the chance to enter any date in time to find fun facts in history or notables birthdays. The Holiday Roundup offers insight and synopses of many world religions and their holidays. Great site to bookmark as a classroom home page, because there is so much to see and do. Created by The Learning Network. Gr. 2–8.

Prongo Math Games

http://www.prongo.com/games/

Although there are some blinking/flashing ads, it's still worthwhile for students to visit this colorful, educational site. Most of the games are math-related, and others are mazes, puzzles, pattern recognition, and word games. Games are organized by age level: 3–6, 6–9, and 9–12. Some of the game titles are Hungry Caterpillar, Memory Match, Batter's Up Baseball Math, 2-Player Math Game (addition), Guess the Number, Alien Code, and many more. Most games require *Macromedia Flash* (free to download). Created by Prongo.com, educational software manufacturer. PreK–6.

Don't Miss: Click Brain Teasers at the top for a fast-paced trivia game in various categories: human body, outer space, dinosaurs, inventors, United States, and other subjects. *Macromedia Flash* needed.

Math For Morons

http://library.thinkquest.org/20991/intro.html

ThinkQuest developed this humorous site for those students who get confused or lost in math class, sleep through the class because it's boring, think the teacher is going too fast, or some combination of the above. The site features tutorials, sample problems, and quizzes. The assumption is that the student knows the basic concepts and just needs some practice and reinforcement, or the student just needs a review of something learned long ago. This site is divided into four sections: Algebra (covers elementary algebra), Algebra II (covers intermediate algebra and basic trigonometry), Geometry, and Precalculus (covers advanced algebra). Created by ThinkQuest Inc.

Don't Miss: Formula Database, which has 150 basic math formulas, such as the equation of a circle, associative property, difference of squares, Pythagorean Theorum, trigonometry equations, temperature formulas, and much more.

AAA Math Help

http://www.aaamath.com/

Students can choose their grade level or go directly to the math topic with which they need help, although clicking the grade level seems to give a more detailed list of topics to choose from. Topics include the four basic operations, plus comparing, equations, exponents, geometry, money, percents, ratios, estimation, mental math, graphs, patterns, place value, and several others. Created by AAA Math, K–8.

Don't Miss: Click Really Cool!! at the top to see some really cool pictures, such as earth from different satellite locations, the Smithsonian Institute, National Geographic, and more.

Other Features: Click Index of Exercises to see a lengthy (alphabetical) list of all the math topics and practice problems on the entire site. It includes interactive problems so students can practice online without paper and pencil. Ask Dr. Math (at the top) is an archive of questions and answers that previous students who visited the site have asked.

Math.com Homework Help

http://www.math.com/

Sometimes students needs more help than a textbook can give. From basic math to advanced topics, this comprehensive math site offers homework help, easy-to-understand explanations, illustrations and pictures, and practice problems for all the math subjects. Choose from: basic and everyday math, pre-algebra, algebra, geometry, trigonometry, calculus, and more. Created by Math.com, LLC. K–12.

Don't Miss: Need a calculator? Click Calculators and Tools to use an online calculators that are as fast as hand-held models. Basic calculator, scientific calculator, and trigonometry calculators—they are all here. Each math section has useful tables and formulas that can be printed and saved.

Plane Math

http://www.planemath.com/activities/pmactivitiesall.html

Practical math applications for aeronautic situations. Flying section features: how to design a flight path, how planes lift off, build a kite, and aircraft capacity. Pioneer Flight has an animated video with sound, and it features movie clips and trivia grab bag. Plane Math Enterprises welcomes students to join a flight training program, where they learn about aircraft design and basics of flight. Some games require *Macromedia Shockwave* plug-in (link to download is provided). Created by InfoUse and NASA Ames Research Center. Gr. 9–12.

Middle School Math Goodies

http://www.mathgoodies.com/lessons/

Over 50 self-directed, interactive activities on these topics: introduction to statistics, pre-algebra, probability, integers, percentage, number theory, circumstances and area of circles, and perimeter and area of polygons. Click the "x" under Shortcut to view the lesson. Student reads the information on the screen, then enters answers in the boxes. Pages are filled with colorful illustrations as well as "moveable" images: dice that roll, spinners that spin, etc. Don't miss the online tutoring assistance if you need to challenge a gifted student. To print, follow instructions at the top of the puzzle page. Browser must have Java Script. Entire site is also available in French. Created by Mrs. Glosser's Math Goodies, Inc. Gr. 5–8.

Don't Miss: Click **Puzzles** to view crossword puzzles and word search puzzles in all the same math topics as above. Teachers can print these and copy for students. There is also a solution page for each.

Purplemath—Algebra Resource

http://www.purplemath.com/

"How do you REALLY do this stuff?", commonly asked by algebra students, is the reason why this site was created. The first section, Algebra Modules, has practical tips, hints, examples, and points out common mistakes that students make. This site explains in easy-to-understand language basic, intermediate, and advanced algebra topics—from factoring numbers to inverse functions. If a student doesn't remember how his/her teacher wants homework done, Homework Guidelines (a.k.a. "how to suck up to your teacher") has guidelines like: keep your work neat, use correct paper size, number the problems, work in pencil, etc. Site created by Elizabeth Stapel, Western International University (Arizona). Gr. 6–12.

Other Features: Other Links has dozens of algebra sites for students in categories like tutoring, quizzes, lessons, math anxiety, software, and study tips. Math study skills self-survey allows students to self-assess and see where they still need practice.

Math Lesson Plans

http://school.aol.com/teachers/lesson_plans/browse.adp?cat=16000010

Here's a site no math teacher should be without, no matter what level he or she teaches, since AOL@ School has it all. A collection of more than a thousand math lesson plans are organized by category: algebra, applied math, arithmetic, business math, calculus, functions, geometry, measurement, patterns, probability, statistics, and trigonometry. Clicking on any of the categories shows an alphabetical list lesson plans from math sites all over the Internet. Each listing gives a brief description of what is taught and grade levels. Click the bold, underlined title and your browser will open a new window with that lesson plan. America Online uses a team of education professionals from several national membership associations to review the sites used. Created by AOL@ School. K-12.

Notes:

MATH PUZZLES AND GAMES

Brain Benders & Puzzles

http://www.coolmath4kids.com/puzzles.html

As soon as you reach this page, the bouncy number string that follows the cursor all over the page will entertain you. Kids will have fun taking the genius quizzes, packed with trick questions ("Does England have a fourth of July?"). There are about a dozen math puzzles, riddles, and games, beginning with easier ones, with harder ones near the bottom. Sample game titles: Alphabet Soup (riddle), Number Fun, How Many Triangles?, Karen's Age (prime numbers), and Corner Riddle. Created by CoolMath.com. Gr. 1–12.

Brain Binders

http://www.teachnet.com/brainbinders/

Sounds easy until you try it! There are nearly 50 colorful puzzles that you print, cut out, and fold to match the finished picture. The goal is to fold the puzzle into a flat shape with a solid color on each side. The level of difficulty increases as you work through the four levels, from two to five folds. Printing the *Adobe Acrobat* PDF file works much better than printing from the Web page, because you'll have more control over the finished size. TeachNet is temporarily sponsoring this site. The URL may change in the future, but there will most likely be a link to redirect you if/when that happens. Created by Teachnet. Gr. 2–8.

Cool Math 4 Kids Games

http://www.coolmath4kids.com/games/

As soon as you open this page, the bouncy number string that follows the cursor all over the page will entertain you. Dozens of online, interactive games are divided into two sections: Thinking Games (that need a math mind) and Mindless Games (not really math related, so teacher's permission should be obtained first). Some of the thinking games are Memory, Lemonade Stand, Lunar Landing, 3D Maze, Crab Race, Marbles, Word Search, Concentrate, and Lights Out. No plug-ins are needed to play these games, but you need to make sure Java is enabled on your browser (look under Tools, Internet Options). A few of the games indicate that one browser (*Netscape* or *Internet Explorer*) works better than the other. Created by CoolMath.com. Gr. 2–12.

Fun Brain Numbers

http://www.funbrain.com/numbers.html

This is a great site to use as a home page for math class, because even older-model computers can handle most of the games. Soccer Shootout, Math Car Racing, What's the Point, Operation Order, Number Cracker, Power Football, Line Jumper, and Change Maker are a few of the titles. Most of the games have varying levels of difficulty—from easy to super brain. Created by The Learning Network. Gr. 2–8.

Don't Miss: Quiz Lab is a free, online database of assessment quizzes in ten subjects. Teachers select quizzes for students to use in the classroom, library, or at home, or you can also create your own. Quizzes are graded by Fun Brain and sent to you by e-mail. The database keeps track of most frequently missed questions, score averages, and other assessment data. You must register to use Quiz Lab. Fun Brain also has games in other subject areas, like Words, Universe, and Culture.

Math.com Games

http://www.math.com/students/puzzles/puzzleapps.html

Math can be used to play lots of games, and Math.com has assembled this collection of challenging math games from around the world: Peg Solitaire (also known as Hi-Q), Fiver, Hare and Hounds (also called the military game), Tower of Hanoi, Tac-Tix, and Hex-7 (popular in the 1940s). There is also a maze generator that generates and solves mazes using three different algorithms. These games require that your browser have Java enabled. If you can't see the games, click the indicated link for help and/or to download what is needed. Created by Math.com.

Weekly Brain Teaser

http://www.eduplace.com/math/brain/

Each week (Thursday) one new math brainteaser is posted—many of them have pictures, cartoons, or puzzles. The solution appears a week later on the same page. Typical third-grade question: "You have a sheet of 20 postage stamps, connected in 4 rows, with 5 stamps in each row. Using the least number of tears, how many times must you tear the sheet to get all the stamps apart?" Typical seventh-grade questions are more involved, using graphs, columns, and patterns. Three grade levels. Created by Houghton Mifflin. Gr. 3–8.

Notes:

SCIENCE

Fun and Games

http://www.explorescience.com/

When you reach the Explore Science site, click on **Fun and Games** to see several interactive games involving fun science concepts. Design a snowflake online, instead of the old-fashioned method of paper and scissors. In Black Hole, your job is to get the ore buckets from your ore cannon to the stations that are surrounded by black holes. A Real-Time Histogram allows you to gather data while clicking your mouse every two seconds, which creates a histogram while you're clicking. Sight Vs. Sound Reflexes lets you test your response time to different types of input. Requires *Macromedia Shockwave* plug-in (link to download). Created by Explore Learning.

Insect Fun

http://www.uky.edu/Agriculture/Entomology/ythfacts/entyouth.htm

Ideas and activities for teachers, students, and bug lovers. Bug Food has recipes (ants on a log, ant treats, butterfly mouth parts, pretzel spiders) and stories of real edible insects around the world. What Is It? features photos of insects, and students are to identify the mystery bugs—novice and expert levels—hints provided too. Send guesses to the e-mail link provided. Insects All Year features stories and pictures of insects for each month of the year. August shows how cicadas sing. January shows insect winter hideaways. Bug Fun has arts and crafts projects (bookmarks, paper mache, art and ornaments) and games and jokes (bug quotes, riddles, trivia, puzzles). Insect Stories features oddball and unusual explanations. Created by University of Kentucky Entomology Department. Gr. 1–5.

Kids Go Wild

http://wcs.org/5675/kidsgowild

Colorful site for animal lovers. Wild Animal Facts has links to learn everything from survival habits to the weird and wacky habits of kids' favorite animals (birds, reptiles, mammals, and invertebrates). Wild Arcade has games including jigsaw puzzles, concentration (memory and matching), nature paint, and amazing trivia. Some games require *Macromedia Shockwave* (link to download provided). Wild News gives news updates from around the world about endangered species, new discoveries, and animal events. Conservation Kids has many links about animals that are threatened with extinction and the efforts being made to understand and protect them, including the field efforts of Conservation Kids (fee to join). Created by Wildlife Conservation Society.

Kids Planet

http://www.kidsplanet.org/

Get The Facts has animal fact sheets, with high-quality photos, on more than 50 species, divided by world regions: North America, South America, Europe, and Africa. Wild Games has two sections (for younger kids and older): concentration and matching, guessing the sounds, fly around, picture puzzles, animal quiz, and word searches. Games require *Macromedia Flash* plug-in (link to download provided). The Web of Life is a 30-page story as told by a common garden spider—colorful illustrations and easy-to-read text. Click page number to go to next page. Cool Stuff has pages to print and color and wildlife adoption projects. Defend It has dozens of ideas of practical suggestions for kids who want to take action to help protect our world's wildlife population. Created by Defenders of Wildlife. Gr. 1–5.

Dog Breeds Index

http://pets.yahoo.com/pets/dogs/breed_guide/alphabetical/

Many boys and girls are crazy about dogs or have dogs at home. Yahoo's alphabetical index contains 150 common breeds of dogs. This is a perfect site to research dogs for an animal project, science report, or follow-up activity to related literature. Each one shows a photo, general appearance, ownership information, characteristics, temperament, did you know" facts, and links to more sites about that particular breed. Dog breeds are also grouped by categories: herding, hounds, sporting, non-sporting, terriers, toy dogs, working, and miscellaneous. Created by Yahoo! Inc. K–5.

Other Features: For students interested in other kinds of pets, click "Pets" at the top to see similar information about cats, fish, birds, horses, and other pets like reptiles, amphibians, and the small, furry variety.

NASA Coloring Pages, Games, Puzzles

K–4 Coloring Pages:
http://kids.msfc.nasa.gov/puzzles/coloring/

Gr. 3–8 Games & Puzzles:
http://kids.msfc.nasa.gov/Puzzles/Games

Forty coloring pages with detailed line drawings of space shuttles, satellites, aircraft, space station, rockets and blast off stages, astronauts, and the solar system. Easy-to-print and photocopy for classroom use, no plug-in needed. Interactive space-theme games includes ones such as Photo Scramble, Word Games, Riddles, Mazes, Galaxy Hunt, connect the dots, Mars lander (like the old moon lander game), and concentration (memory game). Created by National Aeronautic Space Administration. K–8.

Physics Easy Start

http://www.gcse.com/science/physics/menu.htm

According to the site, if you're no good with physics or not sure where to begin, this is a great place to get started. Begins with the easy stuff, gets a little harder, then ends with the more complex topics. Earth and Beyond includes: earth and moon, eclipse, force of gravity, solar system, planets, stars, and the sun. Electricity includes: atoms, cells, circuits and their symbols, current, Ohm's Law, resistance, static, and voltage. Easy Start was created to teach basic science and physics for secondary students in the United Kingdom to pass the general exam. Created by General Certificate of Secondary Education, United Kingdom. Gr. 10–12.

Other Features: If you're looking for something specific, click on Physics Index or Glossary.

Ranger Rick's Kids Zone

http://www.nwf.org/kids/

Lots of interactive games, stories, and outdoor activities to heighten student awareness of wildlife and habitats around the world. Some of the concepts reinforced: habitats (grasslands, cave, forest, swamp), migration, water cycle, and shapes. Games has dozens of interactive games using sound effects, music, and movement: Wacky Wildlife Stories, Jigsaw Puzzles, Rhymes, Quiz Yourself, Did You Know?, Riddles, Matching Games, and Summer Fun Activities. Cool Tours has information and illustrations about common habitats like water, wetlands, public lands and parks, as well as a section on endangered species. Outdoor Stuff has outdoor activities, nature camps, summer fun, and Earthsavers Club. Reader's Corner has subscription magazines. Some games require *Macromedia Flash* plug-in (link provided to download). Created by National Wildlife Federation.

Search for Intelligent Life

http://www.seti.org/epo/fun_n_games/games/

Design a research project to help answer the age-old question, "Is there really intelligent life out there?" First, assemble a team of scientists, then send a probe to the stars or search the skies using Earth telescopes. Since the universe is pretty darned big, focus your search to the Milky Way, Earth's neighborhood, or the Andromeda galaxy. Next you will decide what you are searching for: something visible like a giant light or something not visible, such as sound waves. Lots of vocabulary and outer space concepts along the way. Created by SETI Institute (Search for Extraterrestrial Intelligence), a nonprofit corporation that conducts research into search for life in space. Gr. 5–8.

Don't Miss: FAQ with answers to questions like: Is someone hiding aliens? and What happens if we find something? (**www.seti.org/faq.html/**)

Yuckiest Body Functions

http://yucky.kids.discovery.com/flash/body/pg000029.html

Hosted by reporter Wendell the Worm, this "gross yet cool" site will fascinate kids with body functions they've always wondered about: bad breath, belches and gas, snot and boogers, dandruff, zits, ear wax, spit, hiccups, funnybone, body odor, gurgling stomach, and yes, pee and poop. Sound effects, trivia, and links to body systems. Worm World has more about Wendell, plus information on worms as recyclers, all about earthworms, and other cartoon worms for fun. Roach World is similar, with a peek into the world of roaches (diary of a roach, getting rid of them in your home, roach fact book, quiz, and glossary). Warning: sound file of scurrying roaches will likely gross out most people. Use caution when allowing students to view this site, because the classroom will get loud, giggly, and excited. Created by Discovery Communications, Inc. Gr. 2–6.

SOCIAL STUDIES

GeoBee

http://www.nationalgeographic.com/geobee/

The GeoBee Challenge is an online game to test geography knowledge in a fun way. Each day five new questions are posted. Students can click on a link to see previous days' questions, or click Play The Game to play that day's challenge. Each year thousands of U.S. schools in the participate in the National Geographic Bee, hosted by Jeopardy's Alex Trebek. Students in grades four through eight are eligible to participate in the national competition, but anyone can play this online game. Created by National Geographic Society. Gr. 2–6.

Geography Game

http://www.funbrain.com/where/

This is the game where your mind is a map, according to this FunBrain-sponsored site. Student picks a map and level of difficulty (five levels) to begin. Choose from a continent or world region: U.S., Africa, Asia, Europe, North America, South America, and worldwide. Level One is where student identifies which country or state is highlighted (multiple choice). Level Five is where student identifies which country or state and fill in the capital. Student identifies the correct country, state, or answer to the question. Choose a continent or go worldwide to play. There is also a two-player version. Created by The Learning Network.

GeoNet Game

http://www.eduplace.com/geo/

The premise for this game is that a group of aliens traveling through our solar system have discovered Earth, and they want to take over. If enough people prove they know a lot about Earth, especially geography, the aliens will leave us alone. There are two levels of difficulty, and as students play, they progress through levels such as GeoNet advisor, expert, and champion. Questions cover more than just geography—also physical systems, human systems, environment, and uses of geography. Sponsored by Houghton Mifflin. Gr. 4–8.

Homework Help

http://www.nationalgeographic.com/homework/

Need to know how much sharks eat, why witches were burned in 17th century Salem, or how fireworks work? National Geographic Society has provided rich resources in six subject areas, to help students with background research for topics. Categories and samples in each: animals (cats, manatees, sharks, turtles, Great Barrier Reef), history/culture (Pearl Harbor, Lewis and Clark, mummies, Salem witchcraft, urban sprawl), maps/geography, photos/art, and places (Alaska, Antarctica, New York, Yellowstone, flags and facts).

Middle Ages

http://www.learner.org/exhibits/middleages/

What was it really like to live in the medieval or Middle Ages? Most people think of knights in shining armor, banquets with wandering minstrels, kings and queens, bishops and monks, and glorious pageantry. Good background information for students as they study this period in history. Sections to click: Feudal Life, Religion, Medieval Homes, Clothing of the Various Classes, Health and Hygiene, Arts and Entertainment, Town Life and Commerce, and links to other Internet resources. Each section contains a narrative and includes a link at the bottom to read even more on that topic. Site is a partnership between the Annenberg Foundation and Corporation for Public Broadcasting. Gr. 6–12.

Notes:

FOR THE YOUNG SET (K–2)

Back Porch Activities

http://www.agr.state.nc.us/markets/kidstuff/backporch/book.htm

Learn about North Carolina commodities with puzzles, word searches, mazes and coloring pages. The Back Porch was the name of an exhibit at a North Carolina State Fair, and the pages were part of an activity book. Sample page titles: Cattlemen Color-by-Numbers, Pork Pyramid, Honeybee Crossword, Hidden Peanuts, Potato Plant Parts, Pine Needle Fill-in-the-Blanks, Pecan Maze, Christmas Tree Code, Scrambled Vegetables, Chef Tomato, and lots of coloring pages. Created by the North Carolina Department of Agriculture. K–4.

Disney Playhouse

http://disney.go.com/park/bases/playhousebase/today/flash/

Kids will see their favorite Disney television shows, such as "PB & J Otter," "Rolie Polie Olie," "Bear in the Big Blue House," "Stanley," "Book of Pooh," and "Mouse House Jr." Each area (TV show) has games, puzzles, music, books, and activities. All of the games teach basic concepts, such as matching, colors, seek-and-find, animal characteristics, compare-contrast, plus computer skills of clicking and dragging, eye-hand coordination, etc. To view the full pictures, sounds, and interactive capabilities, many of the games need plug-ins such *Shockwave*, *Flash*, *RealPlayer*, and *Apple QuickTime*. Go to Disney's Help section for information on how to download these plug-ins. Created by Disney.

Other Features: Older kids will find plenty of games, music, and other activities by clicking on **Kids** (on the monorail at the top).

KidsCom Jr.

http://www.kidscomjr.com/flash_index.html

Described as the safe site for young kids, with kids' games, educational games, online coloring books, and ways to learn Internet safety, all geared for little kids and preschoolers. Interactive games with sounds effects feature same and different, matching, and Internet safety. Art has a coloring book, paint pad, building blocks, and goofy faces. Meet the host characters and send them a message in Friends. Created by Circle1 Network. Gr. PreK–2.

Random House

http://www.randomhouse.com/kids/

Games, activities, trivia, coloring pages, contests, and author information for Random Houses' most popular children's' titles: *Arthur*, *Berenstain Bears*, *Dragon Tales*, *Junie B. Jones*, *Magic Tree House*, *Sesame Workshop*, *Seussville*, *Star Wars*, *Sweet Valley*, and *Thomas the Tank Engine*. Each of the book title links take you to another mini-site. Kids get to read excerpts from books and learn more about the author. Parents are encouraged to teach their children the facts of life with the Parent's Guide. Lots of highlighted books and authors on the home page. Teacher's guides, reader's companions, and other teaching tools available by clicking **Teachers@Random**. Updated monthly. Created by Random House, Inc. K–3.

Touch Paint

http://www.touchpaint.com/

Great site to help beginning computer students to develop eye-hand coordination as they "paint" pictures. Dozens of detailed black-and-white drawings with a palette of 48 active colors; others can be mixed. Categories of pictures include flowers and plants, kids doing what they do best, music and musicians, people, and abstract art. Touch the color, then touch the drawing. The young artists can print their drawings to keep or e-mail it to a friend. Older children and adults can use HTML code on a stock picture to create a customized drawing. Created by New Jazz Media Inc. K–4.

Notes:

Best Sites for NEW TEACHERS

GETTING STARTED

Back to School Ideas

http://www.yesiteach.org/lesson2.htm

This page offers educators a collection of activities for the beginning weeks of school. Shared by experienced teachers, these lesson plans include ideas such as me in a bag, open house fun, back to school kits, giving tree, name games, slide show, and more. The lessons focus on students in grades K–5. Since the site specializes in back to school plans, the lessons tend to be grouped around holiday and vacation themes. These include Valentines Day, St. Patrick's Day, Easter, Mother's Day, winter holidays and the end of the year. Created by The Florida Education Society's Young Educators Association. K–5.

Don't Miss: The Kids are Funny section offers a variety of humorous stories about students. Teachers submitted all stories.

Beginning Teacher's Handbook

http://www.learnnc.org/newlnc/carepak.nsf

This online database provides timely tips and strategies for beginning teachers and the professionals who support them. Teachers may use the keyword search feature to find help on a specific issue. They may also browse the database for information included under the general subject areas of getting started, physical environment, classroom management, professional educator, advice from the field and resources. Created by the North Carolina Teacher's Network. K–12.

Other Features: This handbook is part of the North Carolina Teacher's Network's Web site. Visiting the main site will provide a wealth of other resources from lesson plans to links to other education sites.

Beginning Teacher's Toolbox

http://www.inspiringteachers.com/home/newteachers.html

This excellent starting point for new teachers features tips pages, articles, message boards and links to lesson plan sites. In addition to classroom and professional resources, the site also provides free Web site hosting and web-based e-mail for teachers. Created by Inspiring Teachers. K–12

Don't Miss: The free classroom toolkit package is a utility collection includes tools for creating and grading exams, maintaining a grade book and creating a variety of documents including progress reports and report cards.

Books for Beginning Teachers

http://www.theteacherspot.com/teacher_books.html

This site, created by two veteran teachers, provides a recommending reading list for beginning teachers. The list of recommended books is divided in two categories: top sellers and new recommendations. The site also includes great links to other teacher resources, including all the major subjects, puzzles, posters, email lists, role playing, educational software, teacher books, student behavior, and much more. There is a link at the bottom to see a listing of Newbery award winning books from 1922 to the present. Created by David and Wendy Timmons. K-12.

Don't Miss: A link for First Years (at the top), which is a link to an email discussion list for student teachers, interns, and beginning teachers with less than three years experience. Simply send an email to join the list.

Great Expectations

http://www.positiveparenting.com/resources/feature_article_018.html

This friendly article offers helpful hints for beginning teachers by author and consultant Jane Bluestein, Ph.D. Bluestein has worked with thousands of educators, counselors, administrators, health-care providers, criminal justice personnel and parents. Her down-to earth speaking style, practicality, sense of humor and numerous examples make her ideas clear and accessible. This article focuses on the main things Bluestein feels beginning teachers should want to accomplish during their first days as a teacher. The major themes revolve around having the students behave and the classroom run smoothly, having the students succeed and being accepted as a member of the faculty. Created by Jane Bluestein. K–12.

Management Strategies

http://www.inspiringteachers.com/tips/management/

This site is especially useful for new and beginning teachers, because often, the biggest obstacle they face when they first begin teaching is classroom management, discipline, and motivating students. There are several short, practical articles on how to give specific instructions (to avoid student misunderstandings), using routine procedures, how to conduct good planning (to prevent problems), and recording daily behavior with a clipboard (great for documentation with parents and administrators). Created by Inspiring Teachers Publishing, Inc. K–8.

Other Features: Lots of good resources for new and experienced teachers: mentoring, monthly features, professional and classroom resources, and community. Check monthly features, which usually has articles for new teachers on subjects from discipline to holiday celebrations. The site's authors welcome e-mail from new teachers with questions and comments.

Math Teachers

http://people.clarityconnect.com/webpages/terri/terri.html

Children learn mathematics in different ways and at different rates says Terri Husted, a 20-year teaching veteran and author of this site. She created this site to give new math teachers ideas and suggestions for teaching. Her basic advice is to keep a balance between teaching skills, concepts and problem. The result is a colorful, comprehensive site that is easy to follow and includes 20 pages with resources for new math teachers. The site includes information on making connections with students, classroom management, multicultural lessons, math myths, and sites for math projects. Created by Terri Husted. K–12.

Other Features: There are many links to other resources on the Internet.

Middle School Teacher Help

http://www.middleweb.com/1stDResources.html

MiddleWeb's site for teachers who are new to the middle school world. It contains an excellent, well-organized list of links: discipline and classroom management, books for new and restless teachers, general resources for the new teacher, when you're ready to dig deeper, and much more. Created by the Focused Reporting Project. Gr. 6–8.

Don't Miss: Scroll down until you see A Middle School Teacher Reflects on Her First Five Years. A Missouri, language arts teacher kept a personal diary, and you can read her thoughts, questions, and lessons learned as she ponders her chosen career. Go to the bottom to review previous diary entries or the entire index. Also sign up for MiddleWeb's weekly e-mails featuring middle grade news and articles of interest. They do not share their mailing list with anyone.

National Association of Beginning Teachers

http://www.inspiringteachers.com/nabt/index.html

This membership association is dedicated to giving new teachers the tools they need to complete their jobs. Its goal is to help them develop the skills necessary to succeed in the classroom and encourage them to remain enthusiastic as they face the challenges of the future in the classroom today. Information on joining the NABT is provided on the site; dues are inexpensive compared to other educational organizations. Membership includes a quarterly magazine, classroom management book, and conferences and workshops. The association is dedicated to new teachers. Created by the National Association of Beginning Teachers. K–12.

New Teacher Resources

http://www.teachersfirst.com/new-tch.shtml

Well-organized site dedicated to new teachers, including classroom, professional, and site resources. Several articles on the main page: ten tips for student teachers, mentoring for new English teachers, helpful hints for beginning teachers, ideas for new math teachers, and do's and don'ts for middle school teachers. Classroom Resources features web resources and lesson plans, organized in matrix with about two dozen subjects, divided by elementary, middle, and high school. Professional Resources features an index of links for teaching strategies (mentoring, multicultural resources, career planning, education standards, and using technology), special education, and professional development. Site Resources has lots of links to sites where you'll find even more ideas for new and beginning teachers. Created by the Network for Instructional TV, Inc., a nonprofit learning technologies corporation that works with hundreds of U.S. schools. K–12.

What to Expect Your First Year

http://www.ed.gov/pubs/FirstYear/index.html

This online book from the U.S. Department of Education was published in September 1998 for the purpose of helping beginning teachers know what to look for during their first year in the classroom. You can read the book online in your web browser or download a version that can be read with *Adobe Acrobat.* A link to download the free *Acrobat Reader* is also provided. The book includes tips and strategies from veteran teachers and other experts, ideas on how principals and administrators can help new teachers and a checklist of important tips and ideas. (Click "next" at the bottom to see the next chapter.) Created by the U.S. Department of Education. K–12.

A New Teacher's Survival Guide

http://hannahmeans.bizland.com/

More than 25 years ago, Hannah Means still remembers her first day of teaching, because she felt so unprepared. What she wanted was a mentor—someone who would help her if she made mistakes, or better yet, to give her guidance so that she wouldn't make mistakes in the first place. Hannah's web site is an attempt to be that mentor to beginning teachers. Her online "book" is divided into five chapters, starting with how to prepare before school begins, and continuing with grading and links to other resources.

Her style is friendly and supportive, as though she were a friend sitting across from you at lunch, explaining how to survive as a teacher. Her second chapter, what to do on the first day of school, has lots of good advice, such as greeting children at the door, asking them questions during attendance, having a classroom bill of rights, assigning numbers to help organize the children, deciding on classroom jobs, and creating a "Who am I" bulletin board. Compiled by Hannah Means, a 25-year veteran (now retired) teacher, Connecticut. K-5.

Teacher's Helpers: Organization, Resources & Tips

http://www.theteacherscorner.net/resources/teachhelp.htm

A comprehensive collection of resources and ideas that will help interns, student teachers, and beginning teachers in their day-to-day classroom operations. Links for classroom organization, management, materials, students, and teacher. All ideas were submitted by experienced teachers, with links for their email addresses if you want to ask questions. Some of the ideas you will find are: easy ways to keep anecdotal records, keeping student papers organized, cleaning blackboards, keeping a daily schedule to keep students informed, keeping students on time, using conduct cards and behavior management reports, keeping materials handy, storing markers and pens, items to include in centers, and recycling classroom materials. Created by The Teacher's Corner. K-12.

Teacher Vision

http://teachervision.com/lesson-plans/lesson-6494.html?egs080603

General site for new teachers with certificates to print, lesson plans, cross-curricular themes, classroom organization, dealing with parents, rubrics and other resources. Lesson plans may be browsed by grade level or subject. You can also search the online database by keyword. In addition to awards, certificates and planning forms, the "printables" area also contains a library of maps that may be printed out for use in the classroom. Created by the Learning Network. K–12.

Other Features: You can also subscribe to their New Teacher Newsletter. This newsletter offers tips and links to new items and timely resources. There is no charge for subscribing.

27 Tips for Starting the Year Off Right

http://www.vtnea.org/ti-1.htm

Get organized, learn their names, and find a buddy are just a few of the tips found in this list. Many tips such as "get parents involved" may sound like simple, common sense. Others, such as calling each child's parents before school starts to introduce yourself, might be an unfamiliar idea to someone new to the field. The site also lists links to opportunities for Vermont educators, advice for parents and support for students. Created by the Vermont National Education Association. K–12.

Notes:

JOB SEARCH AND INTERVIEW TIPS

Education Jobs

http://www.nationjob.com/education/

A database of teaching and education jobs. Jobs range from kindergarten to higher education. You can search by geographic region, education, job duration and minimum salary. You can also register to have new job openings that match your search criteria e-mailed to you when they appear. Created by NationJob Network. K–12.

Other Features: The Job Seeker resources area contains links to various useful tools. In addition on continuing education opportunities and business opportunities, they offer suggestions for reference checking and creating and distributing resumes. You can also find resources for comparing salaries in different areas.

How to Find a Teaching Job

http://K–6educators.about.com/education/K–6educators/library/howto/htjob.htm

This page offers a quick summary of the steps involved in finding a job as an elementary teacher. Modeled after a lesson plan, it states the project is difficult and the time required will be five to 10 hours. The summary lists 13 steps and three tips. It also gives a separate list of related resources on the site. Created by About.com elementary education guide Beth Lewis. K–6.

Other Features: This is part of the About.com system that features channels on literally hundreds of subjects. This makes it a good starting point for a variety of subjects.

National Educators Employment Network

http://www.teachersatwork.com/

This electronic employment service is designed to match the professional staffing needs of schools with teacher applicants who can fill those positions. The nationwide, online database provides an efficient and economical way to overcome the geographical limitations of recruitment and reach the most desirable teaching candidates. Created by WWWebtech Networks. K–12.

Don't Miss: The resource section offers links to job fairs, resume writing services, salary calculators and other tools for teachers in the process of looking for new jobs.

National Teacher Recruitment Clearinghouse

http://www.recruitingteachers.org/channels/clearinghouse/sitemap.htm

This is a national, nonprofit organization dedicated to building a qualified, diverse corps of teachers across the United States. Finding out where teachers are needed and how to conduct a job search are just two of the many resources you will find here. The main categories are Why Teach, which features several teachers talking about their experiences; Become a Teacher, which has licensing requirements by state, job search information, and teacher shortage areas; Successful Teaching, which has classroom tips and resources and how to stay motivated; and Profile Pages, which includes current teacher requirements and job search, mid-career changes, paraprofessional resources, plus information for college students and high school students who are thinking about teaching as a career. The search engine for job searching is thorough and has state-by-state requirements, plus areas to enter what you are looking for. Teachers can search through thousands of teaching jobs in the Job Search area, which includes over 800 job banks. Sponsored by the National Teacher Recruitment Clearinghouse, based in MA in 1986.

Preparing for Interviews

http://www.middleweb.com/MWLISTCONT/MSLinterviews.html

This page is a transcript of a listserv conversation about preparing for middle school job interviews. The conversation began with one teacher asking what kind of questions she should ask during the interview to make sure the school was the kind of place she wanted to teach. Numerous teachers and administrators responded with advice. In addition to the advice itself, the transcript provides those who are new to e-mail discussion lists with an idea of what to expect when they join one. Created by the Focused Reporting Project. Gr. 6–8.

Other Features: The listserv is part of the Middleweb.com site. Visit the main site for much more information about issues of interest to middle school teachers.

Principals Offer Advice

http://www.educationworld.com/a_admin/admin222.shtml

Having a plan, a portfolio, and a good attitude is a must for first-time job seekers, say principals across the U.S. in this article. The article was authored by Gary Hopkins with input from more than 25 principals. Its purpose is to help new teachers prepare themselves for their first job interview. Created by Education World. K–12.

Other Features: This article is part of the Education World Web site. Visit the main site for lesson plans, message boards, educational site reviews and other resources for teachers. A teacher's online reference library is also provided.

State License Requirements

http://www.inspiringteachers.com/preparation/States.html

Provides links to every U.S. state department of education, with certification requirements and/or teaching standards. This is a particularly valuable resource for teachers who are thinking about moving to a new state. It can also be useful for students who would like to shop around for the best state to attend college with an eye toward becoming a certified teacher. Created by Inspiring Teachers Publishing, Inc. K–12.

Other Features: The Inspiring Teachers site offers a wealth of information for teachers. Areas covered include mentoring, teacher preparation and classroom and professional resources. It's also a good place to look for lesson plans.

State Certification Requirements

http://www.uky.edu/Education/TEP/usacert.html

This site provides a quick, pull-down menu with a link to every state's department of education. This site will be particularly useful for students trying to decide where they should attend college while pursing their teaching degree. It is also useful for certified teachers considering a move to another state. Created by the University of Kentucky College of Education. K–12.

Other Features: The site also provides links to job openings at schools in all 50 states. This is a good way to check job availability and pay salary ranges in different states.

Teaching Jobs

http://www.k12jobs.com/

This site is designed to bring educators and potential employers together. The listing of available jobs ranges from kindergarten through high school. Openings at vocational schools are also listed. The site is well organized and easy to navigate with separate sections for employers and job seekers. Created by K–12 Jobs. K–12 and vocational schools.

Other Features: In addition to the job search function, the site offers information on job fairs, salary comparisons, education resources. There is also a service for making resumes available to prospective employers who search the database for teachers.

Teacher's Employment Network

http://www.teachingjobs.com/

Job seekers will have to register to use the site, although they can post a resume and browse job listings at no cost. Hundreds of educational jobs are posted by more than 23,000 schools and 1,200 school districts registered to use the site. The job search interface is well designed and easy to use. Select the state you're interested in and view the available jobs. The free search displays contact information needed to apply for the job by snail mail or phone. The resume form allows teachers to enter a huge amount of information that will be available to prospective employers that are searching the database. The site offers a free weekly e-mail newsletter. Created by Teaching Jobs.com. K–12.

Notes:

PORTFOLIO ORGANIZATION

Electronic Portfolios

http://www.eduscapes.com/tap/topic82.htm

Electronic portfolios are a creative means for educators to organize, summarize, and display artifacts, information, and ideas about teaching and/or learning. Often, portfolios are required to show progress and growth of a teacher's professional development over a period of time. This site shows how portfolios have progressed from traditional, three-ring binders to digital and electronic formats which allow much more flexibility through the use of sound files, images, web pages, and other electronic features. The site is organized into categories: electronic portfolio articles and websites, professional educator articles, electronic portfolio links, sample portfolios, webquests, and software and project-specific sites. Created by eduScapes.

Portfolio Organizers and Ideas

http://www.abcteach.com/Portfolios/portfolioTOC.htm

This helpful resource provides teachers with a library of colorful portfolio covers. Teachers can personalize their subject and special interest covers, dividers and evaluation sheets. All materials can be downloaded and printed free of charge. The site also offers a number of creative ideas for dressing up portfolios. Site also offers easy to follow directions for creating a portfolio using the materials on the site. Created by ABC Teach. K–12.

Other Features: This area is part of ABCTeach.com. Visit the main site in order to find lesson plans, theme units, games, puzzles and other resources for teachers.

Samples of Online Portfolios

One of the best ways to get a feel for creating an online portfolio is to take a look at those used by other educators. The following sites will provide a glimpse at some of the portfolios used by student teachers and experienced teachers:

Bellarmine University (KY):
http://education.bellarmine.edu/portfolio/students.htm

University of Virginia:
http://curry.edschool.virginia.edu/class/edlf/589_004/sample.html

Iona College (NY):
http://www.iona.edu/faculty/dgoldsby/portfolios/portfolios.htm

Northern Illinois University:
http://www.fcns.niu.edu/portfolios/fcse_portfolios_fall2000.html

Arizona State University:
http://www.west.asu.edu/achristie/eportfolios/main.html

Kelly Mandia's portfolio:
http://www.mandia.com/kelly/portfolio.htm

Selling Yourself

http://www.teachnet.com/how-to/employment/portfolios/

Whether you're a veteran or beginning teacher, a well-organized portfolio is a "must," because it represents a summary of your teaching abilities. Teachnet says not only is a portfolio an essential tool during the hiring process, but it's also valuable for unexpected district or school job shake-ups. Getting Organized explains what kind of binder to use, how to archive and save items, and using dividers to organize the contents. Elements of a Good Portfolio has a checklist of items that should be in the portfolio: resume, letters of recommendation, educational philosophy, personal goals, samples of student work, assessments and tests, committees and projects, photos, videotape, etc. Tips include: keep it simple and not lengthy, review it on a regular basis, keep a camera handy in your classroom, put copies (not originals) in it, and use clear covers. Created by Teachnet.

Tammy's Technology Tips for Teachers

http://www.essdack.org/tips/

No matter what your technology challenge may be, Tammy's site may have the answer for you. The major sections on this site are Instructions (general directions for computer activities), Related Web Sites (other sites created by Tammy, including one on electronic portfolios for students), Presentations (*PowerPoint* slide shows and handouts from Tammy's many workshops and trainings), Online Resources (interactive databases you can use, including meal recipes for busy teachers!), and Other Resources (software and resource books). Compiled by Tammy Worcester, technology trainer and educator, Hutchinson, Kansas.

Don't Miss: Christmas Capers with the Computer (look under Related Web Sites). From making package tags and invitations on your printer to finding holiday digital clip art, this page will keep you busy for hours as you investigate all the links and ideas for the holiday season.

Notes:

PRESERVICE & STUDENT TEACHERS

Community for Student Teachers

http://www.inspiringteachers.com/home/studentteachers.html

This community of educators offers support to new, student and substitute teachers through print and online resources. The site provides practical tips, articles, inspiration and information about becoming a teacher. Lesson plan links and mentoring services are also available on the site. Created by Inspiring Teachers, Inc. K–12.

Don't Miss: The free classroom toolkit package is a utility collection includes tools for creating and grading exams, maintaining a grade book and creating a variety of documents including progress reports and report cards.

Daily Journal Software

http://www.cci.unl.edu/Software/StudentJournals/StudentJournals.html

This free download provides Macintosh-based software that is useful for student teachers who need to make daily diary entries as they work in schools. The software was designed to make it easier for student teachers to transfer the information in the diary back and forth with their sponsor via the Internet. Created by the University of Nebraska-Lincoln. K–12.

Other Features: While the software itself is free, users may purchase a manual and training videotape.

Middle School Do's & Don'ts

http://www.teachersfirst.com/do-dont.htm

Treat students like responsible young adults and they will rise to the occasion, and be consistent with your expectations and consequences. There are just two pieces of advice from this list of do's and don'ts for beginning middle school teachers. The list was compiled by a veteran teacher in order to help others through their first year in the classroom. Created by The Network for Instructional TV. Gr. 6–7.

Other Features: This list is part of the Teachers First site. Visit the main site for a variety of resources, lesson plans, ideas and tools for teachers. There's an excellent matrix of lesson plans and Web resources for middle school teachers (and others too) under Classroom Resources, divided into 27 subject areas.

Preservice Educators Center

http://www.educationworld.com/preservice/

This site is designed to help student teachers and students who are just beginning to think about becoming teachers. Information is available to help in choosing a university, find a graduate program and getting financial aid. There are also sections designed to help new teachers with their job searches as well as helping them get their classrooms running smoothly when they find a job. Created by Education World. K–12.

Other Features: This article is part of the Education World Web site. Visit the main site for lesson plans, message boards, educational site reviews and other resources for teachers. A teacher's online reference library is also provided.

Resources for Education Majors & Student Teachers

http://www.abcteach.com/StudentTeachers/StudentTeacher.htm

This site offers beginning teachers a little bit of everything: lesson plans, monthly themes, portfolio advice, graphic organizers, links to other sites and more. Teacher Resources has center and classroom signs, job chart cards, theme signs, classroom labels, desktop name tags, hall passes, and lots of general forms. Month to Month has teaching ideas, poems, puzzles, and activities for each month. The site is colorful and well designed. Resources are grouped by themes and subject matter, but it is also possible to search the entire site by keyword. Created by ABC Teach. K–8.

Don't Miss: The special request section is a new feature, where teachers can e-mail questions or requests for lesson plan ideas. Site members will provide the ideas and post them on the site to help for everyone to see.

Secondary Student Teachers

http://educate.educ.indiana.edu/cas/tt/v3i1/v3i1toc.html

This online publication is designed to help secondary student teachers with instruction. The book has several chapters designed to prepare student teachers for the high school classroom. Issue address in the publication include common concerns, building rapport with students and your cooperating teacher, icebreakers and alternative teaching experiences. Several case studies are also included. Created by Center for Adolescent Studies, Indiana University. Gr. 9–12.

Other Features: Back issues of Teacher's Talk are available from the main site. Various issues address other aspects of teaching and education.

Student Teacher Survival Handbook

http://www.teachergroup.com/

This 174-page comprehensive book was written by an experienced substitute teacher, who prefers it to regular teaching. Although the book was written with secondary teachers in mind, the information can be adapted to primary levels. About The Handbook will tell you why the book was written, how it is organized, and how substitute teaching differs from any other job. Get The Handbook takes you first to a page that explains how to download it. It was written in *Microsoft Word* and converted to *Adobe Acrobat* PDF format (link provided to download). Click the book icon to open it. Depending on your computer's memory, it might take a minute to open this large file. Read it online, or print and put the pages in a binder. Although the author has sold this book for $20 in the past, he points out that value is subjective. He provides his address and says if you find it of value, send a check for whatever amount it is worth to you. Created by Dennis Heinrich.

Student Teaching Handbook

http://coe.etsu.edu/stguide/STmanual.pdf

In case your college or university does not provide a written handbook for student teaching, this one will provide you with general guidance, in terms of expectations, ethics, duties, professional appearance, classroom management, schedule, relationship with your supervisor, and evaluation. Of course, you would need to learn from your advisor what is expected for your specific situation, but this handbook will give you some ideas questions to ask when it's time. Student teaching is an important job, and in most schools, student teachers have just as much legal liability and risk as certified classroom teachers. You will need *Adobe Reader* to read this PDF file. It is large but opens fairly quickly. Compiled by East Tennessee State University, College of Education.

10 Tips for Student Teachers

http://www.teachersfirst.com/tenpoints.shtml

Visit school before it starts and review the curriculum. These are just two tips on this top 10 list compiled by a 16-year veteran teacher. This list was compiled from his own experience as someone who frequently acts as a mentor to new teachers. In addition to the 10 main tips, the list also provides eight bonus tips which point down to the advice "remember to go for the extras." Created by the Network for Instructional TV. K–12.

Other Features: This list is part of the Teachers First site. Visit the main site for a variety of resources, lesson plans, ideas and tools for teachers. The New Teachers' section is especially helpful for student teachers.

Notes:

SUBSTITUTE TEACHERS

Substitute Teacher Guide

http://www.bozeman.k12.mt.us/personnel/sub/

Even if you're not subbing in Montana, this site is a "must read" because it contains a wealth of valuable information for all substitute teachers at any grade level or school. It's a well-organized design—the left column has all the links, and each time you click, the text appears in the larger window on the right side. Here is what you will find there: checklists before, during, and after the school day; classroom management guidelines, crisis intervention (if a student is out of control), discipline, exercising professional judgment, expectations, how it leads to getting a permanent job, sub reports to leave for the teacher, resources, Internet links, legal responsibilities, sponge activities, reading styles and strategies, special needs students, and much more. Site developed by Bozeman School District #7, with portions contributed by San Diego Country Office of Education and Utah State University. K-12.

State by State Substitute Requirements

http://subed.usu.edu/sma/documents/subrequirements.pdf

If you plan to substitute teach in the U.S., this is a valuable document for you to read. It is a large database of information that tells for each state: whether a college degree is needed to sub, whether verification is needed, academic background, fingerprint or background check, initial validity period and whether it is renewable, and renewal requirements. *Adobe Acrobat Reader* (free to download) is needed to view the document. Compiled by the Substitute Teaching Institute, Utah State University, Utah.

Substitute Survival Tools Article

http://www.education-world.com/a_curr/curr260.shtml

Are you a substitute, or thinking about becoming one, and wondering whether you'll survive the challenges that lie ahead? If so, *Education World* has written this detailed article especially for you. You've signed up to be a substitute teacher, and now you're wondering whether it was really such a good idea? Will you be able to control the students? Will you understand fifth-grade math? Will the teacher leave detailed plans? Will it be as bad as you've heard it can be? The kind of substituting experience you have is pretty much up to you, say the substitute teachers that *Education World* talked to. All you have to do to survive, they say, is be prepared, be professional, and never let them (the students) see you sweat! Songs, games, lesson activities, and templates to help a sub survive even the most difficult experience! The article also includes a dozen links to other resources and tools to help subs survive. Published by *Education World*. K–12.

Substitute Teacher Homepage

http://www.csrnet.org/csrnet/substitute/

"If something can go wrong, it will," begins the introduction to this site. Created to survive "blisters" and enjoy the blessings of substitute teaching, this site has hundreds of excellent links to other sites that will help subs not only to survive but to seize the day. Lesson plans and activities that can be adapted by substitute teachers for temporary assignments. Created by Dennis Mills, Ph.D., Christian School Resource Net. K–12.

Other Features: In addition to links designed specifically for substitute teachers, there are also links for individual subjects. Resources are divided into sections about language arts, social studies, math, foreign languages, the arts, and science.

Substitute Tips

http://www.nea.org/helpfrom/growing/works4me/relate/subs.html

This site contains ideas posted by teachers with their e-mail addresses. Each tip also features the e-mail address of the teacher who submitted it. These tips are divided into four main sections: lesson plans, seating charts, student cooperation and little extras. The nice thing about these tips is that they are tips for regular teachers who would like to make life a little easier for their substitutes. Created by the National Education Association. K–12.

Other Features: This is part of the NEA Works for Me Web site. Visit the main Web site for tips on teaching techniques, managing your classroom, getting organized, and using technology.

Tricks of the Trade

http://www.qnet.com/~rsturgn/index.html

This online book was written by an experienced substitute teacher. The book shows a definite sense of humor as it discusses a typical day in the life of a sub. Some of the normal events during the sub's day include preparing for battle, facing the gatekeeper and developing power tricks. The chapters are easy-to-read and informative. Created by Mr. Sturgeon. K–12.

Don't Miss: The Useful Information for Substitute Teachers section includes helpful information about what to take to school when substitute teaching, what to do before class, what to do after class ends, why substitute teachers do what they do, and who becomes substitute teachers.

Phil's Place for Subs

http://mav.net/phil/subbing.shtml

These ideas should help you get more out of substitute teaching than just a paycheck. Some of them may even reduce your SQ (stress quotient). The author shares tips from experienced substitute teachers. The tips themselves are divided into several sections: before, during, after and career tips. Created by Philip J. Hess. K–12.

Don't Miss: The long list of teaching resources is a central part of Phil's Place. The links are arranged in alphabetical order and cover everything from art resources to weather information. Click the "Random" link to be sent to a random list of teaching resources. This can be useful if you're brainstorming for ideas.

Notes:

Best Sites for MISCELLANEOUS STUFF

BACK TO SCHOOL

Back to School Teacher Tips

http://atozteacherstuff.com/Tips/Back-to-School/

A nice collection of categories to begin a new school year with nearly 100 ideas contributed by experienced teachers. Including bulletin boards, meet the teacher, parent communication, calming first day jitters, first day of school activities, icebreakers, making students feel welcome, and organization and record keeping. Click any of those categories to see a dozen or so practical ideas that work. You could spend hours browsing all the ideas this site has to offer. Created by A to Z Teacher Stuff.

Other Features: Lots of other links at the top to explore: Lessons, Articles, Discuss, Printables, Subjects, Grades, and Themes. Excellent, well-organized website for educators of all subjects and grades.

ProTeacher Back to School

http://www.proteacher.com/030005.shtml

There are a myriad of things to think about for the first days and weeks of school, not the least of which is setting a business-like tone for the rest of the school year. ProTeacher has compiled an excellent collection of links with first day checklists, great activities for the first several days of school, getting to know you activities, first day lesson plans, setting up your room, structuring the class for learning, fall bulletin boards, icebreakers, rules and routines, school bus safety, and things you must do before school begins. Setting Up Your Classroom has lots of suggestions about what kinds of learning areas teachers should consider for their classrooms. A few of the links are not active, but overall, worth a look. Created by ProTeacher.

First Days of School

http://www.education-world.com/a_lesson/lesson074.shtml

Article that features 14 great ideas for the first several days of school, submitted by teachers around the world. The ideas are no in particular order. Here is a sampling of some of the ideas: teacher goes first and writes three true and one false statement about him/herself, and students see if they can guess. Then they each do the same and share them with the class throughout the day. Another idea is a kind of bingo game, where the squares have phrases that could be true about students (visited Florida this summer, has a little brother). Students get signatures in the squares. Students create a "who am I" riddle book about themselves, and other students guess who the person is. For older kids, have them put themselves in alphabetical order, as a way to learn names. Created by Education World.

Notes:

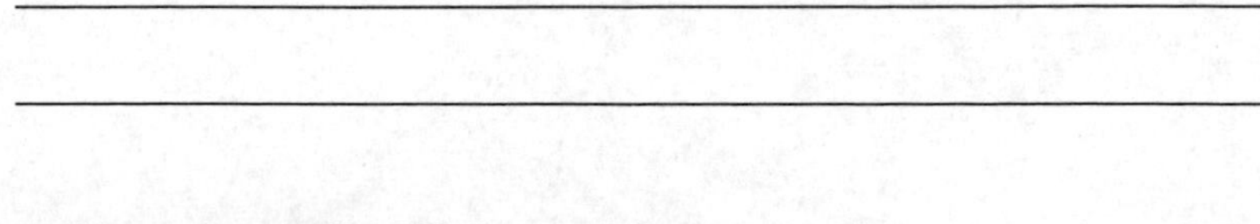

100th DAY OF SCHOOL

100s and 1000s Project

http://www.horshamps.vic.edu.au/100s_and_1000s.htm

This project was an initiative of an Australian school to recognize the beginning and end of the century and millennium. Students created lists of words, such as dollar, centurion, centimeter, thousand, liter, and millisecond. They created an online quiz with questions such "give the word that means a number with 100 zeroes" and "what's the measure of a temperature divided into 100 parts." They also found words in other languages, such as cientas, centum, and centaine. They made a list of things that can be purchased for 100 cents in the school cafeteria, such as two vegemite sandwiches or ten large licorice sticks. The school is still seeking e-mail help from visitors to fill in missing pieces of their project. Created by Horsham Primary School, Victoria, Australia.

Celebrate the 100th Day in 100 Ways

http://www.education-world.com/a_lesson/lesson149.shtml

Education World's article offers you the best 100 ideas for celebrating the 100th day of school. Try one…or 100…with your students! The article is one long list of 100 ideas and activities, many of which have links to other sites to complement that idea. Some of the suggestions are: plant 100 seeds with your students, have students collect 100 cans of food and donate to a soup kitchen, challenge kids to learn 100 new words, ask kids to count to one hundreds by twos (or by fives, etc.), measure the amount of water from 100 melted ice cubes, read "One Hundred Is a Family" by P.M. Ryan (other titles are suggested too), create a cookbook of 100 favorite recipes, have kids put 100 words in alphabetical order…whew! And that list was only in the top 50 suggestions. Posted by Education World. K-3.

100 Day Special Activities

http://www.siec.k12.in.us/~west/proj/100th/act.htm

Lengthy list with more than one hundred ideas involving arts, P.E., science, math, writing, and spelling. Lots of food and snack ideas; arranging the small pieces into graphs and arrays, poems and songs, tons of activities and games. Some of the more creative ideas are: say hello in 100 languages, exercise 100 times and then have 100 seconds of silence, trace children's feet and tape 100 footsteps down the school hallway, make an "aquarium" of blue gelatin with 100 red candy fish inside, collecting 100 coins and donating them to charity, clip 100 paper clips together and use it to measure things, students draw pictures of themselves at age 100, put together 100-piece jigsaw puzzles (very easy to find), make a class list or book of 100 things to be thankful for, estimate how much space 100 kernels will take up once they are popped, decorate white t-shirts or painters' hats with handprints to mark the occasion, make a necklace with any kind of cereal with holes (100 pieces of course), or read the book "100 Hungry Ants" and act out some of the activities. Ideas were contributed by teachers from across the country. Compiled by Tammy Payton, Loogootee Community Schools, Indiana.

Day 100

http://www.yesiteach.org/hundred.htm

A long list of ideas submitted by teachers. Some of them include: have a 100 piece snack (ten pieces of ten items like goldfish, popcorn, fruit loops, etc.), guess how far a paper chain with 100 links will then and then create it, make a picture with 100 macaroni pieces, let students calculate on what day they will reach 100 years old, flip a coin 100 times or roll a dice 100 times and graph the results, see how many times you can find "100" in the newspaper, and bounce a ball 100 times on a piece of paper without missing (good one for P.E. class). At the bottom of the page is a link to see even more 100-day ideas. Created by Florida Education Association's Young Educators Source.

100th Day Activities

http://www.globalclassroom.org/100days.html

A nice collection of 100th day of school ideas, mostly math related. This is a long list of ideas so you'll have to scroll and read. Many of the ideas came from other teachers from around the world, some ideas are posts copied from discussion lists, and other ideas were posted by students. One teacher asked the students to make word problems that have 100 as the answer. This was not as easy as some of them thought! Another suggestion (for the cafeteria) was to give a small treat to the 100th student in line for lunch. A great math idea is to toss a coin 100 times (probability) and graph the results. List what $100 will buy…use newspaper ads for help with prices. How many lire or pesos (or other foreign units) would equal to $100 in U.S. currency? Created by Patricia Weeg, Global Classroom. Gr. 3-5.

Printables, Worksheets, and Lessons

http://atozteacherstuff.com/themes/100days.shtml

Easy-to-print worksheets featuring grids where students can write to 100 by various multiples. Lesson ideas include: making a 50/50 book, where students compile 50 pairs of opposites, making a book of 100 items. Another idea is to release 100 balloons into the air that day, then map the final destinations (when residents call the school to report a found balloon); get local permits first. Kindergartners love to read a particular story that features 100 pancakes; a follow-up activity is to make 100 (small) pancakes in class, in ten stacks, and eat them with yummy toppings. Dozens of links to other sites for even more ideas. Created by A to Z Teacher Stuff. K–3.

Recommended Books

http://www.amazon.com/exec/obidos/ASIN/059025944X/themathforum/107-9115100-1563742

Suggested books you can purchase from Amazon.com on the topic of 100th day of school. Many of these same books can also be purchased used from private individuals on sites such as **http://www.half.com**. Some of the suggested titles: 100th Day Worries, Fluffy's 100th Day At School, One Hundred Is a Family, Roller Skates!, From One to One Hundred, and Miss Bindergarten Celebrates the 100th Day of Kindergarten. Created by The Math Forum and Amazon.com, Inc. K–2.

School Celebrations

http://www.yahooligans.com/around_the_world/holidays/100th_day_of_school/

Yahooligans has compiled a list of links to schools around the country, complete with photos, to show how they celebration 100 days. One school had their second graders draw pictures of how they will look when they are 100 years old, along with examples of their work. Another class made pictures with 100 pieces of cereal while other pictures show youngsters counting beads and working on a 100-piece puzzle. Some links on this page are not active, but overall, still worth a look. Created by Yahoo! Inc.

Teacher2Teacher FAQ

http://mathforum.com/t2t/faq/faq.100.html

In many classrooms, counting the days of school has become an important math ritual. It's a good way to develop the concept of base ten, looking for patterns, learning about factors and multiples, calendars and days, graphs, etc. Many primary teachers begin the first day of school with a single straw, adding a straw each day, bundling ten single straws every ten days (which teaches regrouping), until the 100th day has ten bundles of straws. This site is filled with teachers' questions, answers, ideas, discussions, and suggestions, with links to each subject of conversation. You will also find literature connections, reading list, and resources on the Web. Created by The Math Forum, a site for discussions, suggestions, and lessons from math teachers all over the world.

Notes:

HOLIDAYS

Holiday and Monthly Bulletin Boards

http://www.theteacherscorner.net/bulletinboards/

Great ideas to jazz up bulletin boards contributed by teachers. Monthly Bulletin Boards has monthly sections, each with ideas for that month such as seasonal, holidays, and school-related events. Subject Bulletin Boards has about ten subject themes, each one with several ideas. Subjects featured include art, geography, history, library, math, music, and others. Theme Bulletin Boards has themes such as seasons, student work, motivation, sayings, special events, teamwork, and more. Bulletin Board Materials features ideas like making letters from laminated fabric, and backgrounds using wallpaper, tablecloths, and fabric.

Other Features: Each idea has the teacher's e-mail address so you can contact them for more ideas. Teacher's Corner also wants teachers to e-mail their favorite ideas so they can be posted on the site. Site also features a huge section with lesson plans for all subjects.

Traditions, Customs and Holidays

http://www.pumpkinandcompany.com/pac/teachers-web-resource_t2.htm

Hundreds of links to activities, lesson plans, web quests, games, and ideas on American and foreign customs and traditions. Links are for both teachers and students. Most of the links are for American holidays however. You'll find: The North Pole, Christmas Advent Calendar, Symbols of the Season, Santa's Memory Quiz, Games and Activities, Christmas in Australia, Traditions in the United Kingdom, Groundhog Day links and activities, Folklore and Tales from Great Britain, Halloween Games and Activities, Ghost Stories, History of Thanksgiving, and a Thanksgiving Web Quest. Scroll down to see a section called Travel Guides where you can take virtual tours around the world.

Other Features: If you look at the left column, you will see a lengthy list of all kinds of general teacher resources on all kinds of subject areas, including animals, cinema, civilization, dictionaries, games, geography, history, idioms, Ireland, lesson plans, lyrics, museums, news, pen pals, phonetics, poetry, puzzles, quizzes, sports, stories, texts and exercises, web quests, and writing.

Holiday and Seasonal Activities

http://abcteach.com/contents/holidaystoc.htm

Hundreds of worksheets, maps, math and language activities, patterns, puzzles, flashcards, vocabulary and spelling, coloring pages, report forms, and history around the theme of international holidays and seasonal events. This list includes: back to school, Cinco de Mayo, Christmas, Chinese New Year, Easter, Father's and Mother's Day, Grandparent's Day, Halloween, Hanukkah, Kwanzaa, Martin Luther King, New Year's, President's, St. Patrick's Day, Thanksgiving, Valentines, Veterans Day. Click Month to Month to see even more ideas and activities. Due to different seasons in different countries, activities you need may be in a different month. Created by ABC Teach. K–4.

Notes:

GAMES, PUZZLES, GENERATORS

Kids Puzzles

http://www.kidcrosswords.com/

This popular site gets over two million visits a month and for good reason. Many of the puzzles can be worked online or they can be printed and distributed the old-fashioned way. Various types of puzzles: scrambled words, crossword puzzles, picture builder, words with similar meanings, backbone, crostic crossword, bendable word searches, and more. Themes of puzzles cross all subjects: math, social studies, science, and popular children's literature. To see hundreds of more puzzles in the archive, click on Previously Published Puzzles at the bottom. Site is available in a Spanish version too (click Espanol). Created by Kid Crosswords.com. Gr. 4–8.

Other Features: Kid Reader has interactive, flashing puzzle pictures—each one leading to a painting, story, or famous book. Kids Outdoors has hundreds of links to outdoor activities, pictures, how-to's, sports, and places of interest. Puzzles for Grown-Ups (home page) will give teachers a fun break too.

Math Practice Worksheets

http://www.rhlschool.com/computation/

RHL School has hundreds of basic skill worksheet generators, and every time you click to create a worksheet, you get a new one. Categories are: addition, subtraction, multiplication, and rounding (nearest ten and hundred). Choice of two- and three-digit problems, and with regrouping and without. You must supply an e-mail address to view sheets or get answers. RHL does not share your address with anyone else. You must supply an e-mail address to view sheets or get answers. Easy to print and photocopy. Created by RHL. Gr. 3–6.

Brain Boosters

http://school.discovery.com/brainboosters/

What is the next letter in the following series? A C F H K M ___ . This is an example of the kind of brain teasers you'll find at Discovery School. There are nearly 200 puzzles, riddles, and brain teasers for students of all ages. They are organized in categories: Categorization, Lateral Thinking, Logic, Number and Math Play, Reasoning, Spatial Awareness, and Word and Letter Play. Unfortunately, the question and answer are right there together, on the same page, so there's no mystery to finding the solution. However, since there are so many, enough to use one a day for an entire school year, teachers can use them for Brain Booster of the Day, without giving away the answer. By the way, the answer to the problem above is P (you can find an explanation under Next Letter, Please). Created by Discovery School.com. Gr. 2–8.

Touch Paint

http://www.touchpaint.com/

Great site to help beginning computer students to develop eye-hand coordination as they "paint" pictures. Dozens of detailed black-and-white drawings with a palette of 48 active colors; others can be mixed. Categories of pictures include flowers and plants, kids doing what they do best, music and musicians, people, and abstract art. Touch the color, then touch the drawing. The young artists can print their drawings to keep or e mail it to a friend. Older children and adults can use HTML code on a stock picture to create a customized drawing. Created by New Jazz Media Inc. K–4.

Puzzle Maker

http://www.puzzlemaker.com/

One of the most popular puzzle generator programs on the Internet, and with good reason—its easy to use and you can save your puzzles in puzzles in a personal account (free) to use over and over. Create your own customized word search, crossword, word search, math puzzles, and hidden messages using Discovery School's popular site. Great way to reinforce vocabulary, spelling words, or basic concepts in any subject. Click on the pull-down menu to choose which puzzle, click "go," and the program opens up with step-by-step instructions. After entering the words you want, you can create a printable version, or you can click and save it to an account. Each time you click "create a printable version," it rearranges the words in a different design. When you see the one you click, save it. The only disadvantage to this generator is it does not create a word bank, which most primary students need—you can make your own and paste it in. Created by Discovery.com. K–12.

Spelling, Vocab, Math Worksheets

http://www.edhelper.com/

Over 5,000 worksheets: spelling, vocabulary, and all levels of math. Spelling worksheets include existing word lists and practice sheets or you can generate your own (if you subscribe). Language arts worksheets: finding words, filling in the missing letter, respelling, unscrambling words, circling correctly spelled words, and missing vowels. The crossword puzzle creator is available without subscription. Hundreds of math worksheets and puzzles: operations, sequences, decimals, integers, money, time, fractions, percents, ratios, measurement, geometry, probability, algebra, statistics, trigonometry, and word problems. You'll need to be a subscriber to use some of the worksheet generators but not all. You'll also find special vocabulary, spelling, and word problems during holiday times. Created by EdHelper. Gr. 1–12.

Word Searches

http://www.stmary.k12.la.us/words/

Dozens of puzzles on all subjects, already created, ready for teachers to print and use. Categories: art, computers, English, foreign languages, government, history, holidays, math, places, science, and sports. Also links to sites with more puzzles. Kids category has the most puzzles: baseball, birds, computers, Columbus, farm, fishing, fruit, horses, oceans, pioneers, school, space, seasons, holidays, weather, and more. Created by St. Mary Parish Schools (LA). No plug-in needed. All grades.

Word Search Wizardry

http://thinks.com/wordsearch/ws.htm

More than 200 word search puzzles on all different topics. Click a topic to see the puzzle, and student can work it online, by clicking and dragging to highlight words. A new puzzle is generated each time the topic name is clicked. If your computer is older or does not support Java, you can print them out, photocopy, and let students work them the old-fashioned way. Puzzle categories (with some of the more educational subtopics): art and entertainment (musical terms, instruments), books and literature (books of the Bible, authors, playwrights, Nobel winners), food and drink, home, leisure, living things (lots of animals), boy and girl names by alphabetical letter (25 of those), occupations, people, sports, world wide (countries, capitals, cities, languages), word play (palindromes, silent letters), and potluck (miscellaneous). Simply designed site, easy to use. Created by Thinks.com Ltd. K–12.

Other Features: Site features dozens of other games, puzzles, family fun, word play, trivia, contests, quotes, sounds, toys and games, software, images, books, and more (see sidebar). Teachers will need to supervise since some links are not necessarily educational.

Worksheet Generators

http://teachers.teach-nology.com/web_tools/work_sheets/

Word Scramble allows teachers to create sheets with up to 999 scrambled words—great activity for spelling practice. Word Search Creator also works great and is very fast. Type in up to 20 words, click "make word search" and you have a printable puzzle in seconds. There is an Elementary Word Search Maker that works the same way, but it makes up to six words with large fonts for easier viewing. The Web Quest Generator is a tool to help teachers build their first Web quest. Complete the form with subject title, title of Web quest, choose a graphic image, then type in the text boxes what the task is and what Web sites to use. Generate the form, print it, and photocopy for distribution to students. Crossword Puzzle is cumbersome, because you determine how the words are arranged, and you must also enter your own clues so they exactly match the word placement, which is difficult since there are no numbers in the grid. Created by Teachnology.com.

Notes:

TOOLS AND MISCELLANEOUS

Clip Art

http://school.discovery.com/clipart/

Add simple graphics to your worksheets, puzzles, or Web site. Hundreds of clip art pieces in 19 categories: art, awards, food, language arts, letters and numbers, math, music, science, seasons, social studies, sports, students, teachers, and technology. PC users right click to save to your hard drive. Mac users click and hold to view options. Color and black/white images. Created by Discovery.com.

Coloring Pages

http://www.thecrayonhouse.com/books.asp

Thousands of pages that can be colored individually or compiled into books. Categories: neighborhoods (circus, daily activities, school, church, mazes), refrigerator art (seasons, dinosaurs, heroes, animals, miscellaneous topics), color and learn, holidays (21 including multicultural and standard holidays) , color me dictionary, occasions (birthday, wedding, baby, life topics), and calendar. All of the pages can be viewed and printed from the browser or with *Adobe Acrobat Reader*, the latter of which gives a better quality image. Many of the pages have an option to view thumbnails, so you can see miniature versions, before clicking and viewing the larger images. Created by The Crayon House, Inc. K–3.

Handwriting for Kids

http://www.geocities.com/creadman/handwrite/

Learning to write numbers and letters are very important tasks for kids. All students can improve their writing skills with lots of practice, and this site contains worksheets that model cursive and manuscript with blank lines for practice. Letters, numbers, words, and sentences. Created by Yahoo! Inc. Gr. K–3.

Label the Diagram

http://www.EnchantedLearning.com/label/

About 100 black-and-white diagrams and maps for students to read and label. Each diagram has definitions, vocabulary, student instructions, plus a separate link for answer sheet. The main page has all the diagrams in alphabetical order or you can click on the categories: biology (animals, human anatomy, insects, plant life cycle), animals (mostly anatomy diagrams), planetary (Earth and solar system, moon phases, water cycle, volcano), human anatomy (heart, brain, eye, skin, skeleton), plant anatomy and life cycle, geography (continent and country maps, compass rose). Created by Enchanted Learning. K–6.

Mini-Lessons

K–5: http://yn.la.ca.us/cec/cecmisc/cecmisc-elem.html

6–8: http://yn.la.ca.us/cec/cecmisc/cecmisc-interm.html

9-12: http://yn.la.ca.us/cec/cecmisc/cecmisc-high.html

Over 80 miscellaneous mini-lessons were developed and contributed by a consortium of experienced teachers. Teachers from all grade levels, who wrote these lessons, gathered from 14 states during 1995 summer workshop at Columbia Education Center. The lessons aren't in any particular order, but each has a descriptive title and grade level designation. When you click on a lesson, they are in text format, which makes them quick to print. It's an excellent place to browse if you're looking for general ideas. You can also find this same set of lessons on Columbia's site: **http://www.col-ed.org/cur/**. Created by Webmaster.

Photo Image Library

http://www.pics4learning.com/

Thousands of free photographic images that have been donated by students, teachers, and amateur photographers, to be used for educational purposes such as reports, Web pages, presentations, and bulletin boards. Photos are organized in over 30 categories, including: art (carvings, paintings, sculpture, statues), architecture, countries (more than 40), culture, flags, geography and maps, history, holidays, monuments and national parks, music, Native American, parts of the body, plants (cactus, flowers, garden, trees), religion, schools, science (astronomy, energy, fossils, geology), signs, space, tools and machinery, transportation (air, boat, car, train), United States (subcategory for each state), and weather (clouds, extreme, fall, fog, rainbow, sunrise, sunset, winter). Permission has been granted for teachers and students to use the images in this collection. Created by Tech4Learning, Inc. in partnership with Orange County Public Schools (Florida).

Primary Lesson Plans

http://www.schoolzone.co.uk/resources/primaryplans.htm

Over 240 lesson plans aimed at K–5, about half of which came from U.S. Department of Education's AskERIC. Covers all curriculum areas but unfortunately, lesson plans are not in any particular order or categorized. The list is long so you'll have to scroll or use the Find feature in your browser to locate a keyword. Some links are inactive but overall, site has hundreds of ideas and activities for elementary students. Created by Schoolzone Ltd., Oxford, United Kingdom. K–5.

Rubric Generator

http://rubistar.4teachers.org/

Rubistar is a tool to help teachers who want to use to rubrics but don't have time to develop them from scratch. Categories include: oral projects (interview, storytelling, debate, role play), products (time line, map, poster, brochure, display), multimedia, science (lab report, science fair), research and writing (story, letter, group projects), work skills, and math (graphing, problem solving). Select the subject or project, enter teacher's name and project name, then select areas that you want to include on the rubric from drop-down menus. When you make a selection, a range of appropriate criteria pop up under a numerical scale or a descriptive scale. Choose which criteria and/or edit any of the wording you want. Then press a button and the rubric is created and ready to print. Read the tutorial to find out how to change categories, headings, and content. Rubrics available in Spanish. Created by High Plains Regional Technology in Education Consortium. K–12.

Shape Books to Write/Color

http://www.abcteach.com/Shape%20books/SHAPEmenu.htm

Large pictures to print individually or make shape books. Shapes include: animals, buildings, flowers, fruit, holidays, insects, money, nature, people, transportation, and more. Shape books are books, journals, poems that are shaped like the topic of your book, and the story is written on the shape pages. Staple or bind together with yarn. Created by ABC Teach. K–3.

Student Art Gallery

http://www.artsonia.com/teachers/

Display your students' art on the Internet, which helps promote student pride, self-esteem, and multicultural understanding. Artsonia claims to be world's largest student art museum, showcasing 25,000 pieces of artwork from thousands of K–12 schools in more than 90 countries. To see the art gallery, click Museum. You can search the gallery by type of project, by school, or by country. Free membership allows up to 50 pieces of artwork to be posted for one year. Paid memberships offer more benefits. You don't have to be an art teacher to participate. The site encourages cross-curriculum projects combining art with other subjects. Visitors can leave written comments. Click View Project Ideas to browse ideas and lesson plans from other teachers—click the project title to see details. Created by Artsonia LLC. K–12.

Notes:

REFERENCES & RESOURCES

Educational Links

http://rcan.org/schools/links.html

Hundreds of links to popular sites, mostly in America. Categories are: government (White House, U.S. Post Office, Library of Congress), libraries and museums (Louvre, Smithsonian, Field Museum of Natural History, National Holocaust Museum, N.Y. Public Library), schools (search for any U.S. university by state), news media and television (network T.V., New York Times, Boston Globe, list of online newspapers), religion (Dead Sea Scrolls, Vatican, Bible Browser), various international and national education associations, sports, links to lesson plan sites, subject categories, and much more. Created by Roman Catholic Archdiocese of Newark (NJ).

FBI's Ten Most Wanted

http://www.fbi.gov/mostwant/topten/tenlist.htm

Started in 1950 by the (U.S.) Federal Bureau of Investigation in partnership with the news media, the Ten Most Wanted List features individuals who have a lengthy record of serious crimes, are considered to be a particularly dangerous menace to society, and likely to be apprehended with nationwide publicity. There are usually around 500 names on the entire list at any given time, and less than ten names have ever been women. Osama Bin Laden is/was on the list for terrorist attacks against America. The list would be a good reference material for a social studies theme on criminal justice. Gr. 6–12.

Biographies

http://www.biography.com/

Short biographies of over 25,000 people, living or dead, compiled by the same company that produces the popular "Biography" television show on Arts & Entertainment (A&E) Network. Students type in the name of the person they want to find in the white search box on the home page. Most of the popular searches are celebrities. Be sure to click Classroom (at the top) to find lesson plans, teaching ideas, and ways to use A&E in the classroom. You can also request a free copy of Idea Book for Educators, a biannual newsletter.

New York Times

http://www.nytimes.com/learning/

One of America's most reputable newspapers is committed to bringing world news to students, in a form they can read, understand, and discuss. Updated daily, the site features: today's news summary, a news quiz, On This Day in history, snapshot of the day, conversation starters related to daily news headlines, and more. Created by the New York Times Company in partnership with the Bank Street College of Education. Gr. 3–12.

Don't Miss: Students can Ask a Reporter a question, and the NY Times will post selected questions and answers in the future. Also has a bio and photo of various Times reporters. Word of the Day gives definitions and usage. Also look for the archive of previous vocabulary words.

Quick References

http://www.lib.jmu.edu/quick/

This site contains links to look up brief facts and quick information. Includes links for almanacs, awards and prizes, biographies, careers, colleges and universities, countries and regions, dictionaries and thesauri, directories, encyclopedias, libraries, maps, news, statistics, style manuals, time and calendars, and many more. Created by James Madison University Libraries.

ProTeacher Reference Desk

http://www.proteacher.com/150000.shtml

ProTeacher has compiled a list of useful links to dictionaries, encyclopedias, news/weather, telephone/addresses, language translation, library references, weights and measures, and writing. Created by ProTeacher.

Reference Desk

http://www.refdesk.com/

Great for teaching students to find quick facts, Reference Desk would make a great home page, because it has over 1,000 links on one page. Headline News contains all the links to the popular news sites around the world: AP, Reuters, UPI, network TV, CNN, and more. Reference Resources contains dozens of "quick fact" references: Facts Encyclopedia, search engines, facts subject index, and more. Facts-at-a-Glance contains over 100 popular sites that people are always needing to find: area code finder, airline flight tracker, perpetual calendar, CIA World Fact Book, all kinds of dictionaries and encyclopedias, vital records, human anatomy, state and local governments, and dozens more. Other categories are weather, sports, just for fun, and subject categories. This site is a "must have" for general reference in the classroom. Created by Refdesk.

Smithsonian Encyclopedia

http://www.si.edu/resource/faq/start.htm

Colorful encyclopedia, with entries grouped by letter, provides kids with answers about the Smithsonian and links to resources on subjects from art to zoology. Examples of entries: B has biodiversity, birds, books, botany, bugs, and butterflies. When you click an entry, you can see all kinds of background information and resources: information sheets, links to more sites, puzzles, photographs, interactive games, and trivia. Created by Smithsonian Institution.

Don't Miss: Kids' Castle (look under K), for kids 8 to 14, features articles written about the things that interest kids today: sports, history, the arts, travel, science and air and space, all with great photos. Message boards are filled with questions to get kids from all over the world talking to each other, plus fun and challenging games and contests.

Virtual Reference Desk

http://www.lib.purdue.edu/vlibrary/

Scroll down and click Virtual Reference Desk. Nicknamed THOR (THe Online Resource), this site is an excellent university-based library reference desk, featuring dictionaries, almanacs, encyclopedias, currency exchange rates, language translators, technical dictionaries, acronym finders, thesauri, maps and travel information, phone books and area codes, reference sources (news archives), science data (periodic tables, weights and measures), selected government documents (federal and state), time and date calendars (plus time zones), country codes, and postal abbreviations. Created by Purdue University Libraries (Indiana).

Other features: Click Resources to view links to other university library materials, such as science databases, Internet gateways, electronic journals, news and weather, libraries around the world, Federal Register, reading rooms, and other reference desks.

Librarians' Index to the Internet

http://lii.org/

Bookmark this site if you want to have your own personal library! The site is researched, compiled, and maintained by librarians. Updated each week with the newest sites on the Internet. The main categories are: Arts, Crafts & Humanities; Business, Finance & Jobs; Education & Libraries; Government & Law; Health & Medicine; Home & Housing; Internet Guides, Search Tools & Web Design; News, Magazines & Media; People; Ready Reference & Quick Facts; Regional; Science, Technology & Computers; Society & Social Issues; and Sports, Recreation & Entertainment. Each of those categories has subcategories. You could spend days, weeks, months even, and never look at all this site has to offer. There is also a section on new sites added that week, which you can request to receive by email, as well as current themes. A program of the Library of California. K-12.

PROFESSIONAL ORGANIZATIONS

Joining a membership association or professional organization is considered by most career experts to be an excellent way to learn and grow, both personally and professionally. For teachers and educators, such groups provide benefits such as:

- keeping abreast of industry news and trends
- networking with fellow colleagues to share ideas and stories
- attending training and development events
- receiving magazines or newsletters
- participating in continuing education classes
- purchasing discounted materials and products
- investing in credential or accreditation activities
- learning about job openings before they "go public."

Here is a partial list of the most popular education-related organizations (and their Web sites). Often your school or administrator will pay the annual dues from a professional development budget.

General

American Federation of Teachers

http://www.aft.org/

The AFT is a union organization representing a million teachers and related education professionals. Its roots began in 1916, and it flourishes today as a national organization committed to workers' professional interests, serving their interests and working to create strong local unions affiliated with the labor movement. The AFT has grown into a trade union representing workers in education, health care, and public service.

Canadian Education Association

http://www.acea.ca/

Since 1891 the Canadian Education Association has been a network for leaders in education. CEA is a national, bilingual organization whose mandate is for the improvement of education in Canada.

National Education Association

http://www.nea.org/

America's oldest and largest organization dedicated to public education; 2.6 million members from preschool to university education. Anyone who works for a public school district, college or university, any other public institution devoted primarily to education is eligible to join.

National Middle School Association

http://www.nmsa.org/

NMSA is the only national education association dedicated exclusively to the growth of middle level education. With over 28,000 members representing principals, teachers, central office personnel, professors, college students, parents, community leaders, and educational consultants across the United States, Canada, and 45 other countries,

Subject Specific

International Association for Technology in Education

http://www.iste.org/

Nonprofit professional organization with worldwide membership. Dedicated to promoting appropriate uses of information technology to support and improve learning, teaching, and administration in K–12 education and teacher education.

International Technology Education Association

http://www.iteawww.org/

Represents 40,000 technology educators through North America. It's the largest professional educational association, principal voice, and information clearinghouse devoted to technology education in K–12 schools.

National Association for Music Education

http://www.menc.org/

To advance music education by encouraging the study and making of music by all. Membership is nearly 90,000 including active music teachers, university faculty and researchers, college students preparing to be teachers, high school honor society members and Music Friends.

National Council of Teachers of English

http://www.ncte.org/

Dedicated to improving the teaching and learning of English and the language arts at all levels of education, offering membership sections for elementary, middle, secondary, and college educators.

National Council of Teachers of Mathematics

http://www.nctm.org/

Founded in 1920, NCTM is the world's largest mathematics education organization, with more than 100,000 members and 250 associate members in U.S. and Canada. NCTM's Principles and Standards for School Mathematics, published in 2000, provides guidelines for excellence in mathematics education and issue a call for all students to engage in more challenging mathematics.

National Catholic Education Association

http://www.ncea.org/

The largest professional association in the world, with 200,000 members serving over 7.6 million students. Serves members in preschools, K–12, parish catechetical/religious education programs, diocesan offices, colleges, universities, and seminaries.

National Science Teachers Association

http://www.nsta.org/

Founded in 1944, this association represents science teachers at all teaching levels. It's the largest organization in the world committed to promoting excellence and innovation in science teaching and learning. NSTA's current membership of more than 53,000 includes science teachers, science supervisors, administrators, scientists, business and industry representatives, and others involved in science education.

National Council for the Social Studies

http://www.ncss.org/

Largest association in the country devoted solely to social studies—provides leadership, service, and support for all social studies educators.

INSPIRATION FOR TEACHERS

Amusing and Touching Stories

http://www.yesiteach.org/funny.htm

Long list of very amusing, touching, and hilarious stories—all are true—sent in by teachers about things students do and say. Site is text only and it's long, so you'll have to scroll down to keep reading. However, it's easy to read or print. Created by the Florida Education Association's Young Educator's Source.

Creative Teaching

http://www.creativeteachingsite.com/

"Resistance is futile. You will be inspired." So begins this light-hearted site targeted to creative teaching and professional enthusiasm. In fact, there are several Star Trek- and Star Wars-inspired ideas for educators here, with more on the way. Dozens of ideas and articles are here, under the categories of teaching style, creative teaching, and teaching ideas. These motivational topics will get you thinking: the ready-fire-aim method of teaching, teacher show-and-tell, creative quote of the day, creative ways to encourage reluctant readers, educational simulations, dogs in the classroom, creative use of video games, text adventure games and reading, and Internet time (an alternative method of keeping time). Created by Robert E. Morgan, Director of the Computer, Space Science, Simulation, and Faculty Technology Training Center, University School (Ohio).

Teaching Humor

http://www.teachersfirst.com/humor.shtml

Posted by teachers, this page is filled with stories of funny things students said or did, as well as the most popular "teacher humor" stories making the e-mail rounds. During morning announcements a first grader said, "please get ready for a moment of silence and medication." A middle school student wrote that the first U.S. settlers were seeking religious freedom in William Penn's colon. A young child, when asked the capital of Pennsylvania, replied "P." Describing her future job, one youngster wrote she wanted to be the princess of whales. Some of the humor is from e-mail jokes being forwarded in e-mail: advice from a Kyoyo (age 9): Never hold a dust buster and a cat at the same time. Page is long so you have to scroll to read.

Inspiration

http://www.thecanadianteacher.com/inspirationindex.htm

Amusing and touching stories, poems, and e-mail "forwards" making the rounds on the Internet, all contributed by teachers. Some of the titles: "Teachers Do Make a Difference" (written by a teacher invited to her former student's wedding), a Shel Silverstein poem about all the excuses kids use on teachers, helpfulness (a collection of quotes from famous writers and philosophers), jokes that students tell, a teacher's survival kit for daily living (assembled, makes a great gift for a new teacher), schools are like jigsaw puzzles, the precious jewel, a teacher is like an elastic band, bridge-builder, several sections of quotations about teachers, and moments that take our breath away. The site's editors welcome contributions from teachers. Created by The Canadian Teacher.com.

Inspirational Stories

http://www.lessonplanspage.com/Inspiration.htm

Readers and visitors to Lesson Plans Page contributed dozens of stories that will inspire and renew your faith in your chosen field. Sample story titles: breakthrough with one special student, a song that impacted an ELS youngster, teaching beyond 3 p.m., teacher's healing words (read by a child at her mother's funeral), empty desk and broken heart, secret Santa and one teacher's generosity, change in career from law to teaching, universal language of music, and many more poems and stories. Created by EdScope LLC.

Top 10 Inspirational Movies

http://7-12educators.about.com/library/products/aatp102901.htm

Educators need to be reminded of the importance of their jobs. Here are ten movies compiled by About.com that inspire teachers and hopefully make them feel proud to be in the field of education where they have an impact on young lives. The movie list features a summary, main actors, and why teachers would enjoy it. Some of the more popular picks are: *Stand and Deliver*, *Dangerous Minds*, *Lean on Me*, *Mr. Holland's Opus*, *Dead Poet's Society*, and *To Sir With Love* (1967). A click on the movie title takes you to a screen where you can compare prices in case you wish to purchase. Created by About.com.

Notes:

Glossary of Internet Terms

Browser—A generic name for software that allows you to view web pages. The two most popular browsers are Internet Explorer and Netscape. Some lesser known ones are Mosaic (the very first one), Mozilla, and Lynx. Web browsers "read" the HTML code (the language in which web pages are written) and convert it into a web page.

Cookie—A tiny piece of information sent by a server to your computer when you visit a particular site, which allows that site to recognize your computer on subsequent visits. Cookies allows you faster log-in, registration, etc. If you prefer, you can choose not to accept cookies from servers by setting that option in your browser.

DOS—Disk Operating System, which is a basic operating system for most computers. Even if your PC has Windows software, it is still being operated by DOS in the background. Most of the time, you will never need to know or understand DOS to use your computer. Prior to the mid-1980s, people had to know DOS to use their computers, but this is not the case anymore. MS-DOS means Microsoft DOS.

Download—The transfer of data (text, graphics, or any other kind of digital file) from a server to an individual PC. Ex: To upgrade your version of *Internet Explorer*, you would have to download the software from the company's Web site.

FTP—File Transfer Protocol. A fast method of transferring digital files from one computer to another. Used by webmasters, universities, and government agencies, because it's faster and more efficient than sending files by e-mail.

Gopher—A computer program that was popular in the 1970s and 80s for sending and receiving digital files among computer users. It has been largely replaced by hypertext browsers (Internet Explorer and Netscape), although Gopher servers are still widely used by universities and government agencies.

HTML—Hypertext Markup Language. The software language in which all pages on the web are written. The language is kind of like a simple code. A majority of the coding has letters or numbers inside of brackets to tell the software what to do with pieces of text. Ex: <b>Internet</b> would make the word "Internet" appear in bold. The first <b> turns bold on, and the second </b> with the slash in front turns bold off.

Hardware—Computers and all their parts: Monitor, central processor, keyboard, mouse, printer, scanner, digital camera, hub, cables, etc. are all considered hardware.

http://—Hypertext Transfer Protocol. It's the beginning of all addresses on the World Wide Web. It means the document is a hypertext document.

Hits—Also known as visits. The number of times people visited a particular website. Ex: Many organizations keep track of hits to their site as a way to show its value or popularity.

Hypertext—Also called a link. Any document on a Web site that has links (connections) to other Web pages. When you click the link with your mouse, it automatically takes you to the new page or new site.

Intranet—A computer network within a company that is only for use by its employees.

ISP—Internet Service Provider. The company you usually pay to receive Internet access. Ex: AOL is a popular ISP for millions of users.

Link—see Hypertext.

PC—Personal computer. The term has come to mean any individual computer that is compatible with IBM computers, which operates using DOS. Technically, a Macintosh computer is not a PC, because it doesn't use DOS.

Server—A specified computer within a network that has software and storage space for other computer users to access. Usually, when a server has problems, everyone on that network has problems. Ex: "Our server is down so I can't send or receive my e-mail."

Software—Any program that is used by a computer. Typical software programs are word processing, database, spreadsheets, e-mail, browsers, chat, games, music players, etc. Computers, scanners, printers, and other hardware also need software to operate.

Upload—The transfer of data (text, graphics, or any other kind of digital file) from an individual PC to a server. Ex: To add a new picture to your personal Web site, you would have to upload the graphic file from your PC to your ISP's server.

URL—Uniform Resource Locator. Also known as a link, a site name, or web address. It is the unique address of a specific web page beginning with "http://"

WWW—World Wide Web. Also known as the Web. It is the entire world's collection of hypertext servers you can view with a browser that combines text, pictures, video, and sound. The WWW also includes the less popular but widely used resources such as Gopher, FTP, and telnet.

Webmaster—The individual who is assigned to oversee a Web site on behalf of an organization. Webmaster duties typically include design or technical coordination of a website, uploading text and graphic files, keeping the information up to date, and answering e-mail from visitors to the site.

